DATE DUE

D1297621

SAGE SOURCEBOOKS FOR THE HUMAN SERVICES SERIES

Series Editors: ARMAND LAUFFER and CHARLES GARVIN

Recent Volumes in This Series

What About America's Homeless Children?

Hide and Seek

Sage Sourcebooks for
the Human Services
32

Paul G. Shane

SAGE Publications
International Educational and Professional Publisher
Thousand Oaks   London   New Delhi

"The Found Boy is from *Somebody Else's Nut Tree and Other Tales From Children* © 1983 by Ruth Krauss. Reprinted by permission of Linnet Books, North Haven, CT.

For information address:

SAGE Publications, Inc.
2455 Teller Road
Thousand Oaks, California 91320
E-mail: order@sagepub.com

SAGE Publications Ltd.
6 Bonhill Street
London EC2A 4PU
United Kingdom

SAGE Publications India Pvt. Ltd.
M-32 Market
Greater Kailash I
New Delhi 110 048 India

Printed in the United States of America

HV
4505
.S53
1996

Library of Congress Cataloging-in-Publication Data

Shane, Paul G., 1935-
    What about America's homeless children? Hide and seek / author,
Paul G. Shane.
       p.   cm.—(Sage sourcebooks for the human services series; v. 32)
    Includes bibliographical references and index.
    ISBN 0-8039-4982-0 (cloth: acid-free paper).—ISBN
0-8039-4983-9 (pbk.: acid-free paper)
    1. Homeless children—United States. 2. Homeless youth—United
States. 3. Homelessness—United States—Prevention. I. Title.
II. Series.
HV4505.S53   1996
362.7'08'6942—dc20

96-10042

This book is printed on acid-free paper.

96 97 98 99 00 01 10 9 8 7 6 5 4 3 2 1

Sage Production Editor: Sherrise Purdum
Sage Typesetter: Andrea D. Swanson

CONTENTS

In memory of my parents, Sam and Belle Shane, who died while the book was in progress: They provided an environment where compassion and concern for others and interest in the world was part of living.

In memory of my maternal grandparents Minnie and Elie Schwartz, barely lettered immigrants: They helped me develop a love of our tradition. They taught me the necessity of concern for other human beings, the imperfect nature of the society in which we live, and the unending struggle, desire, and hope for a world of justice and peace for all—especially children.

In memory of Jean Reynolds, my supervisor and friend, and our few years together at Hull House, where she helped me learn to listen to children and tell them what I really meant.

To my beloved sons Giga and Elie, who have brought to my heart and soul the marvel and strength and fragility of children and life.

And to my beloved wife, Dr. Ana Marjanovic-Shane, without whose love, support, and help this work would never have been completed.

PREFACE

Walking among homeless people in a city is very unsettling. Yet the people one sees are only the tip of an iceberg. Most of the homeless are not so readily found. Among them, the most hidden are the children. Homeless youth are a varied group, among the most vulnerable in the society. As in every congregate of people, some are wonderfully creative, intelligent, and extraordinary people, and many more are very ordinary people. A yearly estimate is that there are a million homeless and runaway youth in the United States.

In addition, there are many homeless families. Many scattered services and people attempt to help the children and their families. Yet homeless children and families have received relatively little attention in the United States. Very little research has been done on the causes, parameters, or efficacy of responses to the homelessness of children.

This book has four goals: to present what is known about homeless children; to let some homeless children and families tell about themselves and their situations, and in this way enter into their worlds; to help develop an understanding of what causes the homelessness of children and how it affects the children and the society; and to examine what is being done, and set out alternative courses of action for the society and its members.

I hope one can begin to understand what appear to be the causal factors. Can homelessness be prevented by changing social policies or mitigated by instituting ameliorative policies and programs? What are the social costs? Could knowledge and social will lead to organized social action that might eradicate homelessness, particularly among youth?

I hope this book will help mobilize interested people to take action and end the neglect and abuse of innocent children. The book is about people and their society as well as the "problem."

OVERVIEW OF THE BOOK

The book is organized in four parts. Part I covers the background and social, educational, and health issues of homeless children, including a discussion of causality. Chapter 1 is a general survey of what is known and not known about homeless youth and families and the estimated parameters of the situation. Chapter 2 focuses on social and educational issues. Chapter 3 focuses on health issues. Chapter 4, based on the Galilean approach—specifically Lewinian and "systems theory"—examines causality.

Part II presents the youth and their families. Two chapters tell the stories of some youth and families from their own perspectives. A third chapter is devoted to examining the situation of babies. A fourth chapter describes some adults who have survived homelessness as youth and what has happened and is happening to them. Chapter 9 discusses how the visual media portray homeless youth through analysis of some contemporary television shows, videos, and films.

Part III is a description of programs and more general societal responses. One chapter describes the ameliorative systems that have been created for and about these youth as well as some of the laws designed to provide relief and/or other help. At the end of the chapter, some alternative responses of other societies are described briefly. The other chapter looks at the organization of types of help.

Part IV, Chapter 12, provides analysis and conclusions. Preventive and ameliorative action on the primary, secondary, and tertiary levels and macro- and microplanes are developed as alternative approaches.

The scientific approach underlying the book is Galilean (Lewin, 1935, pp. 1-42), which means examining a phenomenon dynamically and holistically, from its genesis and in its environment. Thus the homelessness of children with and without families, of runaways, and of those abandoned and rejected, is examined in its milieu as a dynamic situation as well as for underlying causality.

PERSONAL CONNECTIONS

In the early 1980s, I started research on the issue with the Garden State Coalition on Youth and Family Concerns, the network of runaway and homeless youth shelters in New Jersey, as well as the National Network of Runaway and Youth Services, where I met the dynamic June Bucy. We did a study of children in shelters.

Researching and writing this book have been great learning experiences for me—not only in regard to the extent and breadth of the problem of homelessness among children and youth but also in terms of the subject I teach, social policy and programs. What had previously been mostly academic took on greater meaning and life.

It has helped me more clearly conceptualize the application of several theoretical systems for analysis of social problems—Galilean, Lewinian, and systems theory—as well as ways of organizing societal responses using public health concepts of prevention.

I discovered a world of compassionate, concerned people, often hamstrung by lack of resources and overwhelmed by numbers and crises. There are many useful, successful programs and deeply concerned individuals. All gave very helpful information that contributed to filling in the picture and opened my vision to other possibilities. Most indicated that they had to divert attention away from helping to keep enough money coming in. Salaries and prestige are low and yet people persist and do wonders.

As I put it all together, my ideas of what was needed as well as what was possible also developed and matured. As I go through the final stages of the process, I can truly say I have enjoyed it and learned a great deal.

ACKNOWLEDGMENTS

I have an army of people to thank for their help and support. First of all is my wife, Dr. Ana Marjanovic-Shane. Without her help and support in all the little and big ways, her editing and sensible comments, it all would have been much more difficult and taken longer. The idiosyncracies of our computer were negotiated only with the help of her friendship with the beast. I would like to thank Ann Davidon, who spent hours correcting mistakes and giving suggestions for improving the writing and presentation, and Dr. Dada Maglajlic, who did a final read-through. Professor Charles Garvin, the editor of the series, has been most generous and helpful.

I owe thanks to the people in the Children & Youth system of Southeast Pennsylvania as well as in the various agencies who lent this project their time and various documents. Thanks to those who permitted their agencies to be named and described, however inadequately. Thanks, of course, to Dr. Garvin and Sage Publications for seeing value in this project.

Special appreciation goes to colleagues in the former Yugoslavia who, during my Fulbright year there, were so cordial and helpful to a colleague from America. I discovered there an extremely well-conceived, integrated, and well-developed system of social services, particularly for children and the elderly. Although they could not see that they did anything special, they had developed one of the most complete and logical approaches to child welfare in the world.

My biggest thanks are to those who permitted a stranger into their difficult lives, often treating him as a friend. They shared their pains, sorrows, hopes, and dreams with him and thus with you, the reader. I found human beings much like you and me, many of them courageous and persevering. They truly represent all of us. They made the book possible.

To them go my and my family's best wishes and sincere thanks. Our hopes for their lives are the same as our hopes for our own lives. May they live in peace and love, comfort and sufficiency, respect, dignity, and stability in their own homes. May the pain and chaos they experienced be mitigated and fade into remembrances of times in the past. May homelessness evaporate into the mists of vague memory and the very idea become unthinkable.

Part I

FACTUAL AND
THEORETICAL BACKGROUND

Chapter 1

HOMELESS YOUTH
Who Are They?

The Found Boy

Once there was a little lost boy.
He was so lost nobody could even see him
And he was cold too. He was in rags.
Now the more nobody saw him,
the more lost he got, the more cold he got,
the more in rags he got.
(From "The Found Boy" in *Somebody Else's Nut Tree* by Ruth Krauss)

Imagine what it would be like to play "hide-and-seek" and be left unfound. You get lost and can't find your way home. You are left to wander, to make your own way, in a strange and hostile world with no one caring. This bleak scenario is lived by many children and youth in America today. They are homeless children, who in the United States *are* hidden. They are "playing," usually involuntarily, with unclear rules and often without seeker(s). They want very much to be sought and found, to be cared for, to be valued.

This book is about homeless children of all kinds and ages, with and without families. Homeless youth have been among the most "hidden" people in American society. They have been so invisible that their numbers, demographic characteristics, and hiding places are largely unknown. Statistical reports do not count unaccompanied children among the "homeless." American society has been playing "hide-and-don't-seek" with its homeless children.

This chapter addresses the definitional problems, background, and facts of the issue.

DEFINITIONS

One would suppose defining homelessness to be simple. In fact, "homelessness is not and can not be a precisely defined condition" (Wright, 1991a, p. 19). "Getting a handle on what we are talking about, let alone how many, is no simple matter when it comes to homelessness" (Hopper, 1995, p. 341). Conditions of being housed form a continuum rather than distinct categories, similar to many life conditions. The range is from being luxuriously housed with several dwellings, through being comfortably housed, marginally housed, unstably housed, squatting (living illegally, often in abandoned houses), to living without any shelter. People move between one and another of these.

Abuse, neglect, and unstable living conditions are closely related to the homelessness of children. U.S. Representative George Miller (chair of the U.S. House Select Committee on Children, Youth and Families during the late 1980s) offered a very broad definition of homelessness. He considered children without health care and other essential services to be homeless (Kryder-Coe, Salamon, & Molnar, 1991, p. xvii).

We will use a more restricted concept of homelessness: *Homelessness is the lack of a fixed and consistent residence.* Thus a child who moves from one family constellation to another on an irregular basis, or who sometimes stays with parent(s), other relatives, and friends, and sometimes on the street, would be considered homeless. Children left in hospitals or in custody, shelters, cellars, abandoned housing, living with or moving between various friends, foster situations, relatives, or others are homeless. There are essentially four groups of homeless children: familial, unaccompanied, street youth, and babies. (Excepted are children in joint custody who have regular places in both parental homes.)

The *familial* homeless, or homeless families with children, are of all kinds: one adult (mother, father, grandparent, other); two adults (with biological, step-, adopted, or common-law parents, unrelated partner, or other relationship); three generations (grandparent, parent, and child[ren]). They stay in every conceivable place—tents, cars, trucks, abandoned buildings, handmade shacks, shelters, and so on. The children, although predominantly younger, are of all ages—neonates through teenagers. There can be one child or many children in the family.

Some homeless families divide children between parents, relatives, friends, foster care, and so on, keeping only some of the children with them. Most homeless families, however, are female-headed, one-parent, biological families. Generally, the mothers are relatively young, poorly educated, and had their first child as teenagers (Battle, 1990, p. 120; Mills & Ota, 1989). Sometimes the mother is an unaccompanied child herself.

For children with their parent(s), homelessness is somewhat mitigated. They are part of families that, although under severe stress, still are relatively functional. At the least, the parent(s) and children have not rejected each other. In fact, they often have strong allegiance and ties that provide support. In many studies of children in war and other stress situations, the loss of parents is the most feared and distressing part of the experience (Davis, 1993).

Unaccompanied youth are homeless minors without a parent figure. Some left home voluntarily (runaways); others have been ejected (throwaways); others' families have dissolved for various reasons—substance abuse, incarceration, illness, or death. The AIDS epidemic increased the last two categories dramatically in the early 1990s (Lee, 1994). At times, it is difficult to discern into which category youth fit due to complex life situations.

The National Network of Runaway and Youth Services (1991, p. 3) categorizes unaccompanied homeless youth (under age 18) as follows: *Runaway* children are away from home at least overnight without parental consent or knowledge. Actual situations vary from those in which the child is forced to leave to those in which the child has chosen to leave what would generally be considered a decent, caring family. Runaways cannot always be considered victims of unloving and abusive parents. There may well be serious problems in the parent-child interaction but these do not necessarily represent bad parenting. It may represent problems that get out of control and seriously damage the parent-child bond and interactions at a specific point in time.

According to police reports, most runaways return home within a short period of time, usually within a week. Many police departments refuse to take missing children reports until after three days. (This becomes a major source of another problem, namely, that the trail may be cold, which increases the difficulty of finding the child.)

Throwaway children have been ejected from their families and homes.

System youth have been taken into the custody of the state due to abuse, neglect, or other serious family problems. They may be in foster care or an institution. An NASW (National Association of Social Workers) study found "20% of children . . . in runaway shelters come directly from foster care" (Azar, 1995b).

Street youth spend most of their time unsupervised on the street. They may or may not have connections with parents or family. Many touch base with "home" but aren't consistently supervised by it. They may get some financial support from family. However, they essentially depend on their own devices for survival.

Other related terms indicate the overlap between neglect and homelessness. " 'Out-of-home' and 'unsupervised' youth . . . describe [those] who do not easily fit into any of the above" (National Network, 1991, p. 3). These are related to *inadequate guardianship* and *lack of supervision,* relatively new terms being used in cases of child abuse and neglect and two of the top three categories of child abuse and neglect reported in the late 1980s and early 1990s. They were "disproportionately associated with fatalities." Many street kids may not be "truly" homeless; others are, either short or long term, temporarily or permanently. The proportions of each group vary from place to place and time to time (Jones & Botsko, 1987).

Abandoned children are those whose families have either dissolved or disappeared due to illness, incarceration, death, relocation, or other factors.

Runaways, throwaways, and abandoned youth find themselves alone in a difficult, dangerous, and uncaring world. As any parent or person who has worked with children and families knows, separation from family is traumatic in and of itself, even for teenagers. Combined with being homeless, it becomes a doubly stressful experience. (For further discussion of these issues, see Chapter 5.)

Studies done of unaccompanied youth have generally been of the emergency shelter population or of street youth. In these populations, most are over 12. A slight majority are female, about the same proportion or a bit more than in society as a whole. Many of the women are pregnant or have babies of their own.

Babies are probably the least discussed part of the homeless child population. Homeless babies, obviously, represent a distinct population with their own characteristics and problems as well as potential for distortion and exaggeration. Babies become homeless essentially in four ways. A major route is by being the child of a homeless parent. The others are by surviving, being left by, or taken from parent(s).

Because babies cannot survive without intensive care, they are the most helpless and vulnerable group of homeless children. Infancy is the most crucial time in human development. Survival and development are not possible without consistent contact with and care from adults. Babies need more than basic physical care. This will be discussed at much greater length in Chapter 9.

Time

Duration and frequency of occurrence are relevant factors. The seriousness of sequelae of running away or homelessness is generally a function of how often it happens and how long it lasts. Short-term, first-time "runners" are *not* the same as the sporadically homeless or those at the other end of the continuum—the veteran, long-term homeless. Resultant problems and negative effects increase with the number of incidents and the length of time away from home. Homeless youth therefore should be subdivided into short term, midterm, and long term, sporadic and chronic. Rivlin (1990) talks about *chronic, periodic, temporary,* and *total* homelessness. Battle (1990) talks about *chronic, episodic,* and *situational* homelessness. Available data, unfortunately, do not include this information.

BACKGROUND

The homelessness of children is recognized today as deplorable. It has existed, however, since the beginning of "civilization" and probably before that. Poverty, war, conquest, and social dislocations have resulted in the homelessness and/or destruction of family units, which often leave orphaned and abandoned children.

At the end of the twentieth century, much of the world's population hovers between being very inadequately housed to marginally homeless. In the industrialized world, the same was true until the development of welfare states between and after the two world wars.

The housing conditions of the poor of New York City in the late years of the nineteenth century were explored by the photojournalist Jacob Riis (1889), who described and photographed families and youth living in coal bins, handmade shacks, barely converted attics, and extremely inadequate and deteriorated housing of all kinds. The places often were without heat, toilet facilities, or indoor plumbing. Such conditions were almost universal in large cities and small towns throughout the industrialized world and had been so since the beginning of the industrial revolution.

Charles Dickens and Émile Zola wrote about such conditions in England and France during the nineteenth century. The Victorian Era was noted for its complex architecture, fabulous wealth, industrialization, and terrible poverty. For children, poverty and inadequate housing often added up to disaster.

The crowding, filth, standing fetid water, lack of waste disposal, and so on were far from unique conditions of the period and certainly not restricted to one city or country. They were common throughout the industrializing, urban world. They existed as well in rural areas. Many children lived and died in these unsanitary, very inadequate conditions, often orphaned, abandoned, or otherwise on their own.

ABANDONMENT OF CHILDREN

Abandonment of children and babies also is not a new phenomenon. Only recently in industrial, democratic societies have children stopped being considered the property of their fathers (Mason, 1994). In most of the world, they remain without rights or legal position other than as their fathers' chattel. In ancient times, families often abandoned babies. It was a culturally accepted method of population and/or eugenic control. Because girls were considered inferior and a burden, fathers often chose not to keep them.

In ancient Greece, Rome, and other civilizations, abandonment of babies was done by all classes. Babies with handicaps, excess girls, and even boys were drowned, abandoned, or set out either for adoption or for the wolves. Often, designated sites were established for such babies. Children were exposed for varied reasons: that is, as a "political statement," for revenge, because their health or paternity was in doubt, or as a form of family planning (Aries & Duby, 1987, pp. 9-12).

In many societies, the children of the poor were, and in some still are, sold to help the rest of the family survive and/or in hopes that the children themselves would survive. Until recently, this was considered a personal family issue. Pearl Buck wrote novels including such situations in late nineteenth- and early twentieth-century China for which she won a Nobel prize.

Reports continue about such conditions for children in the "Third World." In 1995, a widely publicized instance of such slavery was noted. A boy was sold, at age 4, for $16 to carpet manufacturers in Pakistan. He was killed in 1995 at age 13 while crusading against such practices.

The homelessness of youth also has been given a romantic twist. Huck Finn, Mark Twain's barefoot hero, is a prime example. Many have dreamt of being a Huck Finn. A captivating, free soul having wonderful adventures, he refuses to be captured and "sivilized." He belongs to the folk tradition of the open frontier and "freedom." Many North American folk heroes—Daniel Boone and others like him—started out as runaway youth. Indeed, the great movement of populations over the past few centuries often has been fueled by youth searching for peace and a chance at life. North America was settled or "conquered" in part by runaway European youth. Western North America was repopulated primarily by young people, often those who today would be considered children.

The conditions for children during the migrations that repopulated North America were not ideal (Rivlin, 1990, p. 6). Millions of youth left their families in Europe and traveled to America alone. They fled Europe to escape poverty, war, and oppression. In America, they found a difficult life, often in crowded slums. Poverty, racism and ethnic intolerance, industrial accidents, exploitation, and culture shock destroyed many.

Many children were abandoned and orphaned. Children were often exploited. They worked for low wages, under difficult conditions, in unregulated factories, mines, slaughterhouses, and brothels for many hours a day, six days a week, if they could find regular work. Otherwise, they lived by their wits, and many died.

In 1854, an estimated 10,000 orphans or homeless children lived on the streets, in back alleys, and abandoned buildings of New York City. The Children's Aid Society (CAS), a major social service agency, was inaugurated largely in response to the suffering of these children. Between 1854 and 1900, CAS transported 100,000 "orphaned" children to the West by train. Of these, some found caring families, others were exploited. A fictionalized account of this movement is presented in a film (*Orphan Train,* 1988).

Obviously, not all young people were destroyed in the running away immigration process. Many eventually brought over other members of their families, built productive lives and families, and survived. Among them were organizers, members, and founders of labor unions and businesses. Others fell through the cracks and were destroyed by the adversity and shocks of life in the "New World," or barely hung on to existence in the slums and skid rows of this world. Most Americans are descendants of all of these people. (My maternal grandparents came from Eastern Europe as 15-year-olds, alone, in 1905. They survived many hardships, were exploited and helped found unions, had their own family, and survived to old age.)

In the "developed" "First World" at the end of the twentieth century, conditions such as these are considered history. Homelessness among children in particular is usually thought of as a contemporary problem only of "developing" countries and their metropolises. People "normally" live in the streets of Bombay and Calcutta, the cemeteries, shacks, and culverts of Bogotá, Cairo, Johannesburg, Manila, and Mexico City. The *favelas,* barrios, and similar shack communities of Latin America, Asia, and Africa represent the poverty and urbanization of these societies (Connolly, 1990). Homeless children are the *abandonados* and waifs of these societies. They are the *meninos da rua* of Brazil being shot and killed as they struggle to survive in the shadows (Michaels, 1993). They belong to war, oppression, exploitation, and societies with large poverty-stricken masses, but not to "our" modern, enlightened world. Unfortunately, homeless children exist also in modern America.

CAUSALITY

Obviously, all children are homeless because of family problems. On another level, however, homelessness is a societal dysfunction. Probably two categories of causality—economic and psychosocial—cover all homeless. The issues are discussed and described in Chapters 2 and 4. In general, families are homeless primarily for economic reasons, and unaccompanied youth for psychosocial reasons. This does not deny that many homeless families have psychosocial problems, and unaccompanied youth certainly have economic problems.

In studies of homeless families, high rates of family violence or abuse of the women and/or children have been found. Many homeless mothers are escaping domestic abuse. In addition, some studies report that the adult(s) were abused when they were children. Other studies of homeless families have found that some mothers had been in foster care and/or homeless themselves as teenagers (Mihaly, 1991b, p. 24). Still others have reported that a weak or absent family support system for parents may be a significant factor in becoming homeless (p. 23).

How homeless families compare on these issues with housed families of similar backgrounds and conditions is unknown. There is violence, abuse, and alienation in many American families. Dysfunction is not solely a characteristic of many homeless families.

Although it is difficult to separate economic and psychosocial homelessness, they will be discussed separately.

Modern North America

Economic causality. During the Depression of the 1930s, in the United States and Canada, many people, particularly men and boys, left home for economic reasons, looking for work. They often became prototypical "hoboes" or "bums." Families also became dispossessed, often joining the ranks of migrant workers like those in *Grapes of Wrath* (Steinbeck, 1936). Urban families were often reduced to living in shack communities called "Hoovervilles." In the 40 years from then until the 1980s, economic homelessness was believed to have become history. However, homelessness returned to the public eye in the 1980s. The primary cause of homelessness at the end of the twentieth century has remained poverty (Battle, 1990, p. 117).

Psychosocial causality. In the mid-twentieth century, psychosocial homelessness was discovered. There was a seemingly sudden epidemic of "affluent" youth running away during the "hippie" era of the 1960s and early 1970s. Many young people ran away to centers of new lifestyles. They left affluent homes, ostensibly for greater freedom. For the first time, to the amazement of many people, it seemed that some young people left home, apparently voluntarily, for other than economic reasons. Even more amazing, they often were very angry at their parents and the "materialism" that they left.

At the time, it seemed "hippie" centers like the East Village in New York City and Haight-Ashbury in San Francisco were bizarre occurrences resulting from some teenage fad. Aside from handing flowers out on corners, the young people seemed to be Huck Finns embarked on a rebellious journey to adventure on a river of "alternative lifestyles." The "hull" of the adventure was the search for love. A song of the "flower child" generation said, "All we need is love, sweet love." Unfortunately, the voyage led some to destruction. Some sank into an abyss of drugs, victimization, and self-destruction within a relatively short time, as did the "movement" in general.

As we look back, the running away was probably much more complex than it seemed. The anger at parents is a clue that the families left might not have been as exemplary as was generally thought. The parental search for affluence and material abundance may have been conducted at the expense of nurturing and emotional connections with children. Many of these youth may actually have come from homes where there was abuse and neglect when society had not yet recognized these as problems. In later pages, you will meet some who came from such backgrounds (see Chapter 8, Mona, Veronica, and Joseph).

Change in nuclear families has been accelerating during the post-World War II period. The stereotypical middle-class, two-parent, biological family with wage-earning father, homemaker mother, and two or three children never was consistent with a majority of families. (Prior to the 1940s, most families were poor or near poor, and poor women and children worked.) From 1970 through 1995, this stereotypical family has become almost extinct. Aside from the entrance of middle-class women into the workplace, many families have been riven by divorce and formed single-parent families and stepfamilies.

In 1970, out of 28.7 million families, about 3.8 million or 13+% were single parent and 90% of those female headed. In 1993, out of 33.3 million families, about 10.9 million or almost 33% were single parent. About 86% of these were female headed. About two thirds, or 7.2 million, of the single-parent families in 1990 were white. Many households were composed of adults only. Households with children had become a minority by 1990 (Schmid, 1994). Meanwhile, the stresses on families increased.

The percentages of women working, including mothers, increased consistently during the same time span so that in the 1990s a large majority of mothers, particularly single mothers, worked outside the home. Thus the strains of single and working parenthood have become very common.

THE 1980s AND 1990s

In the 1980s and 1990s, economic and psychosocial homelessness were both recognized. During the 1980s, economic homelessness became widespread. At the same time, psychosocial homelessness continued, as reflected in the growing numbers of young people reported abused and/or neglected.

In the 1990s, people sleeping and "living" in railway and/or subway stations, alleys, doorways, and airports, on street vents, almost anywhere, is a common sight in most urban environments. Newspapers and magazines periodically report on aspects of homelessness (Hernandez, 1992).

Most urbanites have become inured to and annoyed with the barrage of "panhandlers." Stepping over and around dirty and ragged people—young, old, male, or female—has become commonplace in cities. Funding of shelters and other programs for the homeless is a normal part of local and state budgets. Soup kitchens and food pantries spread across the country, in both rural and urban areas, to provide some relief.

Europe and Canada also began to experience increases in visible homelessness. As in the United States, in the late 1980s other industrial societies loosened their commitment to economic equity and social welfare. Similar problems of homelessness and hunger started to be noticed (Schmidt, 1992).

Who Are the Homeless?

The common image of homeless people has been of alcoholics, possibly mentally ill, usually males, of indeterminate age. They are seen pushing shopping carts or carrying plastic bags full of dubious belongings. They seem to be filthy, pathetic, frightening, and unappetizing. Children are rarely pictured but are there. In the early 1990s, a large proportion of the American homeless were children. Formerly chronic runaway and long-term homeless youth, similar to chronically abused youth, also may be disproportionately found among single homeless adults. There are also suggestions that they may be the most difficult to help among this group because they have been victimized so often (Simons & Whitbeck, 1991). Some, however, are able to move beyond this experience (see Chapter 8).

EXTENT AND NATURE
OF HOMELESSNESS OF CHILDREN

The extent of homelessness among children is essentially unknown. Not much is known about where they go and stay or what they do. What happens to them, their health status, mortality and morbidity rates, and subsequent lives as adults are not clear. Few data have been collected in general or on specific subgroups. Available figures on the extent of the situation do not easily lead to analysis and understanding. Short- or long-term, serious or relatively adventurous and benign situations, are together in estimates.

Collection of definitive data in this area is extremely difficult. Definitional problems, as suggested above, and the amorphous, hidden, and dynamic nature of the population produce the difficulty. There are serious methodological, definitional, political, philosophical, and other issues and problems that interfere with accurate enumeration of the homeless in general and homeless children specifically (Burt, 1995; Hopper, 1995; Straw, 1995; Wright & Devine, 1995).

An early attempt to assess the national magnitude of the problem of homeless families was made by the National Academy of Sciences in 1985. One conclusion was that an accurate accounting was difficult to achieve (Jennings, 1988).

WHAT IS KNOWN

The immediate causes of homelessness are not hard to intuit. Homeless children are out of their family homes for two basic, obvious reasons.

Either the family has lost its home or the child has left, or been left by, the family and home.

Indications of the extent of the situation are available. Homelessness among children appears epidemic in the United States. Through 1993, most agencies helping homeless children had reported increases in demands for their services in the 1980s and early 1990s. In the late 1970s, 1980s, and early 1990s, the number of homeless and runaway children, and of homeless families, apparently grew at a greater rate than the general youth population (Children's Defense Fund [CDF], 1992; National Network, 1991; Woestendiek, 1993; Wright, 1991a). According to the chair of the U.S. House Select Committee on Children, Youth and Families, in the late 1980s families with children were "more than half" of the homeless in many cities and the fastest growing group of homeless in America (Kryder-Coe et al., 1991, p. xvii).

In the mid-1980s, homeless families with children became one of the largest groups of recognized homeless in the United States. The Children's Defense Fund reported that "in many [places] most of the homeless people are children and their parents" (Edelman, 1987). A study group of the National Academy of Sciences reported the fastest growing group among America's homeless were children, many with parent(s) (Jennings, 1988).

Families with children, nationally, constituted about 43% of the homeless in the period November 1, 1992, to October 31, 1993, according to data from 25 cities released by the U.S. Conference of Mayors (Burrell, 1993). In 27 surveyed big cities, "requests for shelter by homeless families with children grew by . . . almost 30%" in 1988 and again by 17% in 1989 (CDF, 1992, p. 110). Other national organizations dealing with children and the homeless gave similar reports, as did congressional hearings.

In Philadelphia, Pennsylvania, from 1988 to 1993 a 25% increase was reported (from 30% to 37%) in the proportion of children in the homeless system (as represented by the population in family shelters of the total shelter population). In 1992, approximately 5,000 children sought shelter in Philadelphia, while on any one day "about 1,000 children [were housed] in the 16 family shelters in the city" (Woestendiek, 1993). At the same time, about 30% of all children in Philadelphia were living in poverty. The situation was similar in 1993 (Rosenberg, 1993).

The numbers seem to have continued to increase in 1993. Reports from adult shelters in New York state indicate that larger numbers of teenagers were seeking refuge in them. "Some shelters that are open to all homeless people 'are now almost 100 percent kids' " (Henneberger, 1993, p. A1). A survey done by the U.S. Conference of Mayors found that "between 1989 and 1990 requests for family shelter increased by an average of 17 percent in 30 cities" (Mihaly, 1991b, p. 2). Reports increased of children of AIDS victims, substance abusers, and incarcerated parents needing care, and the growth in relatives, particularly grandparents, taking care of orphaned or otherwise "deparented" children (Lee, 1994).

Demographic Characteristics

Estimates of children homeless with their families range from 70,000 on any night to 500,000 children a year (CDF, 1992, p. 109). Other late 1980s estimates for the number of children homeless on any night ranged from 61,500 to 500,000 (Mihaly, 1991b, p. 2).

The ranks of homeless youth are swelled by unaccompanied youth. In 1992, the National Network estimated 1 million runaways and 300,000 homeless youth. A survey of member agencies of the National Network in 1989 found about 46,000 youth were provided shelter and so on for at least one night in programs funded by RHYA (Runaway and Homeless Youth Act). Other guesstimates suggest there could be up to 2 million runaways each year and 500,000 throwaway and abandoned youth; most are teenagers but a significant number are preteens.

Studies have found that between 2% and 5% of unaccompanied homeless young women have children (Shane, 1991b). The numbers, as promised, are vague. They do not include youth over 17 in similar circumstances and in similar need. An intensive phone survey found the numbers of people who had been homeless in their lifetimes to be extremely high, and that high estimates may be correct (Link et al., 1995).

Unaccompanied youth served generally by National Network (1991) affiliates had the following demographic characteristics in 1989: 57% were female and 43% male. However, 65% of the runaways in their shelters were female and 35% male; 55% of others were male and 45% female. Of those served, 54% were between 15 and 17 years of age, 38% were 14 or younger, 6% were 18 or 19, and 3% were 20 or older. (Few agencies serve youths 18 or older because funding sources are few for those over 17.)

Approximately 6% of the youth served were identified, or identified themselves, as homosexual. Due to discrimination and hostility, it is probable that some predominantly homosexual youth are not willing to declare themselves. Some homosexual groups claim that a high percentage of homeless youth are homosexual.

All information points to the fact that homeless children in the United States are of every ethnic and socioeconomic group, with poor and disadvantaged minorities disproportionately represented. Their origins are European, Asian, African, Native American, and every combination thereof. Homeless children are of every hue: white, brown, red, yellow, and all the combinations. They are of Catholic, Protestant, Jewish, Muslim, and all other religious and nonreligious backgrounds and mixtures. However, the majority of homeless families and youth across the country are Caucasian of Christian heritage.

EFFECTS ON
MINORITY POPULATIONS

Unfortunately, there is an ethnic and racial as well as an economic and emotional aspect to homelessness. African American youth seem to be hardest hit. In all available data, whether national or local, black families and black youth are overrepresented among the homeless. The National Research Council (NRC) (1993) stated that

> the strong influence of racial and ethnic discrimination on employment, housing and the criminal justice system limits the options of minorities and hence, their ability to rear their children. Limited opportunities and the many and painful indignities [they] endure in their daily lives place [their] children [and families] at risk.

The disproportion of African Americans can be seen in a few representative statistics. In Boston's Bridge Over Troubled Waters program, of over 3,000 youth served in 1990, 60% were non-Hispanic Caucasian, 30% black, and 10% Hispanic (Able-Peterson & Bucy, 1993, p. 22). The black proportion of the population of the Greater Boston area was significantly lower than 30%. In the period 1987-1988 in New York City, a program working with street youth had a client population with an ethnic breakdown of 38% Hispanic, 35% black, and 25% non-Hispanic Caucasian (Able-Peterson & Bucy, 1993, p. 22). The non-Hispanic Caucasian percentage of the population of New York City was about double that in this sample. The proportion of Caucasians in the metropolitan area is much higher.

In the National Network (1991) survey, black youth are somewhat overrepresented. About 20% of those surveyed were black (while 14% of the youth population in the country is black). Black youth are therefore about 50% overrepresented. Over 60% of the youth served were non-Hispanic Caucasian. The ethnic breakdown of this subgroup is not given but can be assumed to represent in various degrees every ethnic group in the non-Hispanic Caucasian population. Less than 10% (as in the general population) were Hispanic and about 5% were from another "racial" classification—Native American, Asian, and so on.

Babies

There were reports in the media during the late 1980s of a significant number of babies homeless with and without parent(s) ("Happy Re-birthday," 1993; "Mother Leaves Baby," 1993; Patterson, 1993; "When a Baby Is," 1992). The situation of homeless babies (see Chapter 7) is the least well documented of all.

The traditional melodramatic situation of babies abandoned on church or other doorsteps is periodically reported. Some babies have been found in trash cans. There are reports from all parts of the country. Although of great concern and media interest, indications are that abandonment of babies remains rare. There have been reports of a growing number of babies abandoned in hospitals but this also seems to be quite rare (see the section on "boarder babies" in Chapter 7).

The major issue of homeless babies concerns those with homeless mothers. Many homeless women have babies. In addition, the pregnancy rate for homeless women is rather high, in some samples up to 35%. It has also been found that pregnant women or women with newborns on AFDC "have a substantially greater chance of losing their home" than other AFDC recipients (Weinreb et al., 1995, p. 492).

SOCIOECONOMIC STATUS

Homeless children come from all segments of the population but there is a disproportionate representation from the lower socioeconomic strata. This is particularly evident in data about homeless families. Unaccompanied youth, on the other hand, represent a wider range. The socioeconomic status of the families of youth served in National Network shelters was spread over the entire range although it was skewed toward the lower end (National Network, 1991).

Family constellations of homeless children consistently show higher percentages of one-parent or reconstituted families than in the general population. (Similar figures are found in Dutch research; Angenent & Beke, 1984, p. 67.)

ATTITUDES TOWARD HOMELESS CHILDREN

A common feeling about homeless youth, particularly those without families, is that they are bad, or at least "not good." This goes with a prevalent notion that people bring their problems on themselves (i.e., "blaming the victim"). Society's stereotypical notion of a "normal" family supports the negative ideas; those who do not fit are thought of as deviant and imperfect.

It is also difficult for most of us to imagine how children care for themselves without a family. This makes it easy to fantasize. Images range from *Peter Pan* to *Lord of the Flies*. They either will be irresponsible and playful or become monsters. Because homeless children don't live at home and often don't go to school or have curfews, they don't behave as "good" kids do. Because it is unclear how these youth support themselves financially, it is assumed that they do so through "dishonest" means. (There is evidence that homeless youth are not found disproportionately among shoplifters; Angenent, 1981.)

Homeless youth are envisioned either as victims of unscrupulous exploiters who turn them into prostitutes, panhandlers, thieves, and petty drug dealers (dating back to *Oliver Twist*), or as willing participants. It is assumed that they also drink, smoke, use drugs, stay up most of the night, and live "immoral" lives.

Another claim is that the problem is artificial. A book purporting to tell "the truth about homelessness" suggests this (Baum & Burnes, 1993). The authors indicate that most homeless people are mentally ill or substance-abusing single adults. They propose that the problems are within the homeless individual. Further, they claim that providers of service to the homeless have foisted a canard upon the public for their own benefit because they are more comfortable feeding and housing people than curing them of their illnesses. They also suggest that it gives "do-gooders" something to do.

Apparently, to many, the most titillating aspect of the problem is sexual. The specter of child prostitution and sexual exploitation was part of Reverend Ritter's (1988) very successful pitch for funds for Covenant House. The image helped raise millions of dollars a year. A similar picture, although possibly less sensationalized, was still portrayed in post-Ritter Covenant House publicity (McGeady, 1991).

Indications from many workers in the field, however, suggest that most homeless youth survive on the fringes of society without the sensational happening to them. As a group, they are very much like other youth in society. Most of their dreams and aspirations resemble those of other youth. They try to protect themselves from exploitation. Few are found to be prostitutes

(Shane & Marjanovic-Shane, 1987). The ways they manage and survive vary greatly.

The biggest issue is that homeless youth are in essence nonpeople in American society. This separation from society increases their vulnerability. Homeless minors with or without parents and family have faced myriad problems with practically no support or help in this society. Their lives are irregular and access to social help, health care, and education is limited or nonexistent. The protection, nurturance, and guidance that are supposed to be the birthright of children are either severely limited or totally absent.

WHERE DO THEY GO?

Where they go varies. Some simply disappear. Homeless families are found in special shelters, "visiting" relatives or friends, in government offices, tents, cars, and vans, and hidden away in many unknown places (Hernandez, 1992). Unaccompanied youth are in similar places. For a minority, there are a limited number of spaces in federally, state, locally, and privately financed programs specifically designed for such youth, as discussed in Chapter 10.

Federal monies for homeless and runaway youth are only available for short-term shelter and care. Shelters receiving federal money cannot house anyone over 17. For youth between 18 and 21, only private funds are available, except in New York (1978) and some other states, which provide some state funds. Covenant House has been one of the few programs offering shelter and service to 18- to 21-year-olds.

UNIQUE NATIONAL PROBLEM

The problems of homeless children in the United States have been largely unknown in other "developed" societies since their societies rebuilt after World War II. In Britain, Germany, and elsewhere, however, the 1980s and 1990s have seen increases in both homeless families and children, although to a smaller extent than found in the United States.

HOMELESSNESS AS A SOCIAL PROBLEM

The homelessness of children is a social problem on several levels and reciprocally. In Lewinian and systems theory terms, it is a reflection of societal factors (see Chapters 2 and 4). On another level, homeless children themselves have major social problems individually and as a group (see Chapter 2).

They are, in addition, a social problem within the society with a high residual cost to society. They are candidates for difficult lives and continuing social dislocation. If not simply because of the individual suffering, the personal and social costs stemming from the general waste and destruction of these young lives should be of major concern to American society.

Educational Issues

In modern society, education has become central to living a "normal" life and being employed. Homeless children experience disruption and often termination of education. Institutional rigidities and other factors negatively influence the ability of schools to respond to the needs of homeless children (see Chapter 2). Educational programs, facilities, and opportunities are predicated on stability in children's lives. For homeless children, education is often interrupted and disrupted, if not ended.

Health Issues

The homelessness of children is a public health issue. There are risks to the children and to society.

Risks to the children. Homeless youth are at higher than normal risk for acute and chronic physical and mental illness. Deficient nutrition is a health risk. Further, untreated health disorders occurring during development increase risk of chronicity, severity, and damaging sequelae. Homelessness is a risk factor for mortality. In particular, the first six months of homelessness have been found to have high mortality rates (Benner, Benner, Okeke, & Spencer, 1991).

Sex is another risk area for homeless youth. The likelihood is high for an unsafe sex life, which puts them at high risk for sexually transmitted diseases, including AIDS. They are also subject to sexual assault.

Mental ill health is fostered by the particular conditions of homelessness, which are major mental stressors. In addition, rejection or a failure of nurturance induces emotional trauma. Add to this the scorn of society and one has a cauldron of causes of mental ill health. Many homeless mothers and children exhibit symptoms of post-traumatic stress disorder (Weinreb et al., 1995).

Alcohol and/or substance abuse are dangers. All the factors that are associated with such abuse and addiction are present when children are homeless. Intravenous drug users have a risk factor for AIDS and hepatitis, among other diseases. Substance abuse also is associated with nutritional deficiencies.

Added to all the above problems and risks, the health care system closes out homeless people, particularly youth without families. They are unable to use even most health clinics or other facilities available to the poor.

Risks to society. Homeless children can become a reservoir of illness for the general population. Preventive measures, primary and secondary, are limited in scope and existence. Social and financial costs due to health and social issues are paid by society.

SUMMARY

A factual and historical background for child homelessness and an overview of the situation of homeless youth and children in the United States in the last decade of the twentieth century was the goal of this chapter.

Homelessness is part of a continuum rather than a distinct condition. The four major categories of homeless children are as follows: with family, unaccompanied, street youth, and babies. Most children homeless with families are under 12. Most unaccompanied youth—runaways and "throwaways" (r)ejected by their families—are over 12. System youth have been taken into the custody by the state due to abuse, neglect, or other serious family problems. Short-term, first-time homeless youth are *not* the same as veteran, long-term homeless. Resultant problems and negative effects increase with the number of incidents and the length of time away from home.

In America in the 1980s and 1990s, the primary causes of homelessness for children are economic and psychosocial. The number of homeless children and families grew at a greater rate than the general youth population and the homeless population itself. It is guesstimated that up to 2 million youth run away each year, 500,000 are throwaways or abandoned, and another 500,000 are homeless with family.

Homeless children in the United States are of every ethnic and socioeconomic group, although children from female-headed, single-parent families and the poor and disadvantaged minorities, particularly African Americans, are overrepresented.

The homelessness of children is a social problem on several levels. It is a reflection of societal factors, a symptom of societal problems. Homeless children have major social problems individually and as a population. They are, in addition, a social problem within the society.

The homelessness of children presents a high residual cost to society by producing candidates for the child welfare system, for public assistance rolls, and for the courts and jails. Homeless children experience disruption and often termination of education. Major health problems are related to homelessness. Homeless youth are at higher than normal risk for acute and chronic physical and mental illness.

CONCLUSIONS

Attitudes toward the homeless in society are generally negative, although there are reservoirs of sympathy. The American spirit of individualism and self-reliance coupled with a Calvinist tradition of predestination lead us to devalue those who are unable to "make it." In addition, the puritanical approach to life assumes that when the "girdle is off," people will let go of moral strictures. So homeless children are often perceived as doing the forbidden, sexually and otherwise.

The obverse is a lack of societal recognition of homeless children. Historically, adults received their position in society from their jobs, possessions, and homes; children received their position in society from their parents. In essence, homeless families are positionless, and unaccompanied children are "nonpeople."

Society has averted its eyes from the realities of many homeless youth. Unaccompanied youth are assumed to be an aberration: Surely they have families that want and can take care of them. Often, however, this is not true. Homeless families are often simply thought to be cases needing low-income housing and jobs. Alternately, they are thought to be incompetent. Homeless babies are not generally considered at all.

Homeless youth and families present the society with many dilemmas and issues. The next three chapters will look at some of the issues and dilemmas. Later in the book, ethnographic material is presented, and what has been and might be done is discussed.

Chapter 2

SOCIAL AND EDUCATIONAL ISSUES

Social and educational issues, dilemmas, and consequences arise from the existence of homeless children and families. Some are specific to the homeless. Others relate to the social milieu, from the personal or microlevel to the societal or macrolevel. There has been little research on social and educational consequences, effects, and issues of homeless children. Extrapolation from more general knowledge therefore is necessary.

To put the discussion in context, concepts of reciprocal causality and effects of social phenomena will be discussed. To help the reader better understand how such interrelationships function, a short theoretical discussion precedes the main discussion.

INTERRELATIONSHIPS
OF SOCIAL PHENOMENA

Individual phenomena and the larger environment within which they exist interact and interrelate. A holistic approach springs from the Galilean concept of science (Lewin, 1935, pp. 1-42). In simplified form, Galileo posited that objects behave according to the forces acting upon them, and change as the forces change (Back, 1992, p. 4).

In Galilean science, one approaches phenomena using four specific criteria for examination. *Value-free analysis* of physical or social phenomena is primary. *Universality and gradations* are assumed rather than separate classes. Thus homeless children are not a separate class but part of the range of experience of humanity, in terms of quality and time. The *etiology* of phenomena are important rather than appearances. What is significant is causality, the context, and genesis of a phenomenon. Homelessness therefore needs to be examined through contextual causality. *Dynamic processes* and individual *differences of degree* characterize social and physical phenomena rather than static conditions.

Homelessness is one of the changing possibilities of what happens to people. Homeless youth are not an abstract mass but separate individuals with some common experiences and many individual variations that are ever changing. Their situations need to be approached from a variety of directions and disciplines including ethnographic studies such as single-subject research.

Ethnography has been used in psychological and social psychological studies at least since the beginning of the century. Freud's work was based on ethnography. Stafseng (1994) wrote about the many significant social scientists who based a good deal of their work on ethnography or (auto)biography. These scientists worked primarily in central, northern, and eastern Europe and later in the United States. The most famous of them in the United States were Lewin and Lazarsfeld. Both played important roles in the development of social psychology.

A major theoretician in the development of social psychology, Kurt Lewin used ethnography and the Galilean approach. He developed field theory in an attempt to scientifically examine social and psychological phenomena. In sociology and social work, a similar approach to systems theory has been developed. Both will briefly be discussed.

Field Theory

Field theory (Lewin, 1976) posits that particular social and psychological phenomena are not isolated occurrences. Rather, they are related to and influenced and produced by interaction with other, surrounding phenomena. (Although this might seem obvious to some, it remains a minority approach among social scientists, politicians, and legislators.) Lewin called this the "field"—what surrounds a phenomenon and of which it is a part. His equation $B = f(P \times E)$ means that behavior is a function of the interaction between person and environment. Psychological or social events are a result of the interaction of people and environment (Toro, Trickett, Wall, & Salem, 1991).

Nothing stands completely unique and alone in life. Each is related to the "field" and current occurrences in the "field" in which it is found.

Behavior must be understood within the "larger unit of activity within which [it] occurs" (Toro et al., 1991, p. 159). To fully understand what social and psychological phenomena mean and how to respond, one must look for causal and related factors, personal and environmental. In essence, Lewin's social psychological theory parallels epidemiological and ecological approaches to biological phenomena.

Lewin participated in laying the framework for the acceptance of the ecological and systems approach in the social sciences. "Field theory . . . provides a map . . . to investigate the social environment seriously. . . . The interactions of the elements of culture and the social structure contribute to the creation and maintenance of unique social problems affecting individuals [and families]" (Wheelan, Pepitone, & Abt, 1990, p. 63).

Lewin used the analogy of highways linking geographic areas and interconnecting them while each place retains unique attributes. Each unit or system has properties of its own that are neither the sum of its parts nor identical to the larger system(s) of which it is a part. Lewin also used the simile from physics of ions, atoms, molecules, and the objects that they compose (Wheelan et al., 1990, p. 161). Influences go in all directions: up, down, obliquely, and crosswise.

Systems Theory

Similar theoretical developments in other social sciences, particularly in sociology and social work, produced "systems theory." This approach is based upon the understanding that causality is often not primarily or solely within the individual system but is produced by its interaction with outside factors or vectors in the larger systems of which the individual is a part.

Individual people and families are systems within themselves and are part of, interactive with, and affected by other systems—for example, the individual, other members of the family, dyads and triads within the family, the nuclear and extended family system(s), and so on ad infinitum. All exist within and interact reciprocally with the micro-, mezzo-, and macroenvironment (respectively, the family, the community, and the society expanding to the world). All are, dialectically, constantly developing, growing, changing, and affecting themselves and the others.

Systems, either biological or social, maintain a dynamic homeostasis or equilibrium. Time is part of the equation. Within each system, as life goes on, there are continual changes. In examining one's own life, one can see it change and become different from day to day as one grows and develops.

Relationships with significant others are also continuously evolving and reciprocal. All living things constantly change and yet are trying to maintain balance. Change in one area of a system affects other elements of the system. If change in one part is too rapid or radical, the balance may take some time to stabilize. These are usually times of crisis. Some systems break down under these conditions. The same homeostasis exists between interdependent systems, which are in effect subsystems of a larger system.

Relationship to Social and Educational Issues

The social and educational effects and costs of homelessness of children are myriad. These are among the most value-laden aspects of any discussion of homelessness and of homeless children in particular. One's social philosophy has a major influence upon the approach taken and conclusions reached.

Homelessness does not exist isolated and alone. Each situation is complicated by reciprocal interrelationships on all levels. The child's or family's homelessness is part of a total social construct with effects and causes going in all directions. The homelessness of children is a multifaceted social phenomenon. It has both functional/relational and time dimensions.

Interacting with and affecting each other, neither structures of relationships nor structures of time are independent. In time there are short-, mid-, and long-term effects of homelessness. The functional/relational microlevel, the personal, is the effect of and on the homeless individual or family. The mezzolevel is the effect of and on the social units with which the person has immediate interaction. The macrolevel is the effects of and on society.

Questions Raised

The importance of the issues can be illustrated by looking at some of the questions to which answers are needed, questions about the effects and causes of homelessness on the microlevel. How much of what a person becomes is due to early experiences? To what extent do early childhood disturbances lead to adult problems? To what extent can a person overcome early disabling circumstances? What does the disruption of children's lives by homelessness mean for their future development? Is development of social malfunction inevitable as a result of having been homeless? How does the experience of homelessness affect the social development and later social experiences of children? What are some of the personal sequelae? These are problems that can be answered by scientific study and examination.

On the wider levels: What are the specific effects upon society now and in the future? What are the costs both current and residual to society? Are there ways of overcoming the disabilities caused by the disruption resulting from homelessness? How do the homeless fit into institutions they need for help? At this point in the society's development and in the social sciences, the answers are not clear. I hope they can be answered by scientific study. Some answers can be inferred from what is known of factors affecting children's development.

SOCIAL ISSUES

Social policy as a major cause of homelessness may be the most important social issue. Chapter 4 is devoted to a discussion of this issue. Suffice it to say here that societal policies promote social conditions that are either beneficial or harmful to members of the society (children). Society plays a dominant role in encouraging or preventing homelessness and other risk conditions for children and youth.

The various interactions can be seen from the following. Homelessness affects interactions with the immediate environment—family, community, and peers. It can create stresses and tensions that fray and damage social relationships, solidarity, and protective mechanisms on a reciprocal basis. This in turn can interfere with relationships with society in general and important local representatives of societal institutions: educational, social, religious, and so on.

Macroeffects

A macroeffect of homelessness on children is that in essence they are cast out and lost from society. They don't belong anywhere. They then become potentially damaged members of society that may become dependent upon and/or prey upon society. Representative George Miller pointed out that homeless youth are potential "candidates for our child welfare system, for our public assistance rolls and for our courts and jails" (Kryder-Coe et al., 1991, p. xvi). They are candidates for difficult or tragic personal lives and further social dislocation.

The legal, psychosocial, economic, and occupational effects of homelessness will be discussed here. Educational issues will be discussed in the second half of this chapter, and health and medical issues will be discussed in the next chapter.

Legal issues. Among the social issues relating to homeless children is their position under the law. The legal position of children as chattel is historical and almost universal. Children are considered an extension of the family in American society. In essence, they "belong" to their parents. Minors are eligible for many necessities of life only through the offices of adults, generally parents. Examples are the requirements for health insurance and general health care, access to housing, and other issues. They are disenfranchised from the health care system (discussed in Chapter 3).

Minors cannot sign contracts. Therefore, they cannot rent apartments. They cannot sign for loans. They are not eligible for financial assistance on their own. There are restrictions on minors' ability to work (primarily as an important protection against exploitation and injury).

With the immense changes in modern society, the lack of independent legal standing is particularly deleterious. When parents are capable, concerned, and caring, there is no problem. When parents are in some major way unable to fulfill the child's developmental needs, it can be a major problem. Their legal position may prevent children from receiving the kind of services, protection, and help they need. In general, the condition of being homeless and the children's legal status inhibit their ability to remove themselves from homelessness. When isolated families disintegrate or are under stress, children have few options.

Some European societies have begun to address the issue. Sweden, for example, has written into national law a host of children's rights, including the right not to be abused and the right to adequate education and opportunity. As noted in Chapter 1, the Netherlands has emancipated minors who have most adult rights and can function independently. For example, they *can* receive welfare benefits on their own.

Social conditions. Social conditions can produce risk situations for children. The National Research Council (NRC) (1993) relates specific social conditions as impediments to children's and young people's development, such as "the increase of intensely deprived neighborhoods . . . characterized by racial stratification, homelessness or very degraded housing, inadequate schools, a lack of recreational and employment opportunities and, in metropolitan areas, a high level of crime and violence." Building a "family life that can guide children and adolescents into healthy, constructive behaviors is a challenge of heroic dimensions in [such] settings" (NRC, 1993, p. 237).

Among other social conditions deleterious to children's development are unemployment, or the "downsizing" of corporations widely seen during the early and middle 1990s; disinvestment in school systems, also a widespread phenomenon of the 1990s; racism; sexism; and various forms of pollution.

Relationship to society and authority. The National Network (1991) suggested that young people who have been failed by their parents, families, and the system tend to become angry and lack trust. They develop a negative reaction to authority figures and authority including police, school and school personnel, social services, and so forth. A reciprocal negative relationship is likely to develop.

The workers in these systems see these damaged youth as defiant, uncooperative, and negative, and then react negatively to them. "Since these large institutions are often ill equipped to interact effectively with these youth and to attend to the hurt behind their anger, these youth become further isolated and alienated" (National Network, 1991, p. 7).

The negative cycle leads to further deterioration in the lives and ability of the youth to prepare themselves positively for the future. It also leads to their negative responses to limits, which are at times necessary for adults to place on behavior and activity.

Poverty. Poverty is highly correlated with every condition negatively affecting the well-being of children and is closely related to homelessness.

> Family income is perhaps the single most important factor in determining the settings in which children and adolescents spend their lives. Housing, neighborhoods, [health care], schools and the social opportunities . . . linked to them, are largely controlled by income; . . . on a more fundamental level, income is a powerful influence in shaping that most important of settings, the family. (NRC, 1993, p. 16)

Conversely, the society as a whole suffers from losing large numbers of children from creative and positive futures. Potential contributions to society are blocked. The children may become social liabilities. If not actively playing negative, destructive roles in society, they may often need to be supported and add to future generations of dependency.

Mezzoissues

The midlevel aspects of children's homelessness are varied. They include familial, peer relationship, community, local institutional, occupational, and other issues. Again, they are reciprocal and multifaceted.

Homelessness induces family and relational breakdowns. Support systems fray under the attendant stresses. Homelessness is an extreme crisis when the individual and family needs the most support. Obviously, it is a time when the support has withdrawn, when the network of social contacts tends to diminish. Social contacts become homogeneous, which restricts the breadth of social relationships and influences. The chances to meet varied kinds of people and peers diminish. This restricts the view of how to change the life situation. The perception of options diminishes.

Disruption or termination of education can have negative social sequelae, as discussed later in the chapter. Moves to a "postindustrial" economy have made educational achievement a social necessity.

Personal

On the microlevel, the effect of homelessness on the child is personally damaging. It leads the child to develop negative social psychological responses. The child then carries these and acts on them in his or her social contacts and interactions. A circle of reciprocal negative developments spreads. The social psychological effects then cause other social effects, and so on, for a possibly continuing deterioration in social position and relations. In essence, the circle combines ricochet and direct causality.

Children whose parent figures have neglected them, have failed to provide for or protect them, have abused them, and/or are separated from them are creating a life situation that impedes the children's development. These youth are particularly unprepared for independent living and decision making and yet they are prematurely forced into it.

In examining the interviews in Chapter 8, the four mature survivors have had major difficulties in proceeding with their lives. They have taken much longer to begin to realize their potential contributions to society than those who have not experienced homelessness and abuse. All have been beset by personal, familial, and other difficulties. They remain in therapeutic relationships.

Homeless youth need immediate help such as housing, food, clothing, and counseling. They also need long-term help. Unfortunately, many have to forage for the first three and never receive the last two. The need to overcome the psychosocial impact and destructive sequelae of homelessness is extremely important. The children need to deal with their feelings of betrayal and abandonment. They need help in preparing for adult life, responsibility, and a productive role in society and life.

Longer-term programs reach only a few children who need to stabilize their living situations and prepare for independent life and adulthood. A move toward developing transitional living programs has started and has been recognized in federal law. System youth (those who have spent much of their lives under the care of the child protective system), especially those who have moved around and/or have been neglected and abused, need special help to prepare them for adulthood, independence, and responsibility.

A number of psychosocial issues prevalent among homeless youth were identified in the Pennsylvania Homeless Student Initiative (Commonwealth of Pennsylvania, Department of Education, 1989). The "initiative" was concerned with how homelessness affected children and their relationship to school but the findings can be applied more broadly.

Some homeless children feel different than and inferior to others. They believe they can't fit in with those who are not in their position. *Shame* and/or *embarrassment* develop as a result of homelessness. They fear being "look[ed] down on," which inhibits relationships with nonhomeless children and adults. Estrangement from and hesitance in making friends among schoolmates and other nonhomeless youth may result. Isolation and alienation from general society may develop, which can lead to a further erosion in the ability to recover from the experience.

Feelings of self-confidence and self-esteem are necessary for people to attack obstacles in life and plan for the future. They are also necessary ingredients for motivation to achieve in life. Their deterioration damages future life development. Deterioration in positive feelings about self and one's life situation leads to a generally negative attitude about oneself, others, and life in general.

Homeless youth are found to have *short attention spans*. They often are unable to concentrate and are tired and irritable. The effects of irregular living and irregular sleeping leave them with few reserves to respond to frustration and irritation. They are often aggressive and touchy. Simultaneously, feelings of inadequacy lead them to be defensive. This produces decreased inhibitions on displays of anger and aggression.

Homeless children tend to be *frightened*. The security of stable and secure family and residence needed for positive development has been either taken away or never experienced. Fright is also an emotionally and developmentally inhibiting element. A frightened person is unwilling to tackle new experiences and trust unknown people and places. A frightened person tends to view life and other people with distrust and hostility. Thus a frightened person is inhibited from playing a positive, creative role in society. Fright also adds to a general feeling of paranoia and distrust. All these have interactional implications for society.

EDUCATIONAL ISSUES

Educational issues are in essence a subset of, and interrelated with, the social issues of homelessness. Relationships are also reciprocal. Effects can be examined on the micro-, mezzo-, and macrolevels, short and long term; on the individual child and upon the individual schools, neighborhoods, and families; upon homeless children in general in the community and upon the educational experience and the school system.

Macroissues

In postindustrial society, education and training are essential for stable employment and more than minimal survival. The educational deficits that homeless youth develop are serious economic, social, and health handicaps for their reintegration into society as they become adults. The costs to society of marginally productive or even dependent people are high both socially and economically. If calculating a multigenerational cost, it can be seen that the costs to society last long after the specific homelessness and/or runaway situation has ended.

The passage of the Stewart B. McKinney Homeless Assistance Act, Public Law 100-77, brought federal monies and mandates to states to deal with the issues of education and homeless children. The policy of Congress, under this act, is that access to free, appropriate, public education be given to homeless children on an equal basis with all other children. Part of the mandate was for states to identify problems that prevent homeless children from receiving education and to make plans that overcome them. Like many states, the Commonwealth of Pennsylvania developed such plans and programs to implement the mandate.

The Pennsylvania plan is based on three perceived needs. One is that school districts should know their responsibilities under the act. Another is that state policies should be brought into compliance with the federal act. The third is that specific steps should be taken to assure homeless students equal access to a quality education. The underlying assumption is that homeless children are not receiving appropriate and quality educational experiences due to their own condition and the organization of the various school districts of the state.

The plan described six educational barriers for homeless students. Some barriers are institutional, within school systems. Many school districts have residency and guardianship requirements that prevent homeless students from attending their schools. There is often poor coordination between

educational and social services. Inadequate communication and cooperation between social services and educational services within a system were
seen to result "in delays, an inability to track homeless students, overlapping services and ultimately, underserved and unserved students" (Commonwealth of Pennsylvania, Department of Education, 1989, p. 6).
Transportation is another institutional barrier. For many homeless students who find shelter outside of their home district or neighborhood,
transportation to their home school is problematic where services are
limited, unaffordable, or unavailable. A fourth institutional barrier is that
of missing records. Problems with transferring previous school records or
health and immunization records, or with unpaid bills may impede school
enrollment.

Systemic educational problems. For the schools, homeless children are
often an added burden to an already difficult task. In Philadelphia, as in
many public systems, the accepted *minimum* class size is 33 children. In
many parochial school systems, the norm is the same or even higher. In a
"normal" situation, this is a large number of children for a teacher to work
with creatively. With children who are under stress and feeling bad about
themselves, such as homeless children, it may well be impossible. For
urban school systems, add to the homeless the high proportion of children
living in poverty and distress and you find an untenable situation.

In addition, schools systems in many communities, especially the urban
ones, are facing severe financial constraints. In Philadelphia, New York,
Los Angeles, Chicago, Houston (and many others), the amount of money
needed to run the schools has been much greater than the taxes raised. In
many of these communities, school budgets have outstripped the available
money, and public school systems have had to look for ways to cut
expenditures.

Roman Catholic parochial school systems have been faced with similar
economic crises and falling urban enrollments. Homeless children and their
special needs become overwhelmed in the unmet needs of the schools in
general.

Mezzoissues

Under optimal conditions, most school systems are organized to provide
a standardized education. They operate in a rather industrial manner.
Children proceed through them in relatively large groups and receive
graded evaluations. Children who disrupt the mold are generally considered problems.

Taking into account individual needs and abilities, although often discussed, is unusual in such a system. Thus the system has trouble accommodating children who need special attention, as many homeless children do. At the same time, these children often are disruptive to the system and interfere with the smooth functioning of the classroom and other components.

From the school establishment's position, mobility interferes the most with children's function within the educational establishment. Homeless children often move from one school to another and from one district to another. School attendance often is sporadic, due to their life problems. They move into and out of the schools and school system much more than the average. Sporadic school attendance has a negative effect upon learning and educational development. The state initiative said that, "without the stability of a permanent home, meaningful education is extremely difficult" (Commonwealth of Pennsylvania, Department of Education, 1989, p. 3).

Outside of the school systems and problematic lives of the children are social barriers to successful educational programs for homeless children. Foremost among these, probably, are lack of information about homelessness, the special needs of the children, and all other aspects. Stereotypes and prejudices abound among the general public about homeless people, which reduces concern and sympathy for them. This allows the public to reject either passively or actively specific measures that would seem to cost money and raise taxes. Concepts of homeless people as mentally ill and drug- and alcohol-addicted adults interfere with sympathy for homeless children. It translates into resistance to providing for the special needs of these children.

In Pennsylvania, public and professional ignorance about the needs of individual children and the extent of the problem within a school or school system were found to be an impediment to provision of appropriate educational services. The need for "educators [to have] more information about the numbers of homeless children on their rolls and how conditions of homelessness impact upon those students' ability to learn" were identified as crucial to development of effective programs (Commonwealth of Pennsylvania, Department of Education, 1989, p. 7).

Microissues

Rafferty (1991) found both developmental and educational problems among children and youth homeless with their families. She found homelessness linked with "developmental delays, emotional problems, poorer school attendance and lower academic performance among school-aged children" (p. 130). Half of homeless and runaway youth in another study were found to be dropouts, severely truant, or expelled. This study also indicated these youth to be at high risk for school failure (Kurtz, Jarvis, & Kurtz, 1991). In achievement tests, homeless youth scored far below citywide averages in both reading and mathematics (Rafferty, 1991, p. 124).

School attendance was inversely related to age; therefore, the older the child, the greater the disparity between average attendance rate in the general population and his or her attendance rate. Homeless elementary school students had an average attendance rate of 74% compared with the citywide average of 89%, while homeless high school students had an average attendance rate of about 50% with the citywide average of 84% (Rafferty, 1991, p. 129).

Developmental delays. A number of studies have reported developmental delays to be prevalent among homeless preschoolers in shelters with their families. These include delays in language development, gross and/or fine motor coordination, and personal and social development (Rafferty, 1991, p. 106). Both associated symptoms and behavior "are reversible with a change in domicile" (Whitman et al., 1992, p. 118). Delays in language and cognitive development are reportedly correlated with "deprivational environments" (p. 119).

Failure to thrive (FTT) syndrome and "psychosocial dwarfism" are related to these. The latter is associated with poor growth and development and various behavioral and biological abnormalities, primarily in eating and drinking.

Ziesemer and Marcoux (1992) found that about two thirds of elementary school students residing in shelters indicated some degree of social and educational difficulty. The students were found to be quite diverse in their needs. Some seemed to adjust relatively well to being homeless; some exhibited primarily behavioral problems; others, primarily educational problems; and a significant minority, both behavioral and educational problems. About two thirds scored below the percentile considered to be in the clinically affected range, "indicating need of further evaluation" (Whitman et al., 1992, p. 82). Academic performance fell behind grade level in both reading and math in increasing proportions at higher grades. The gap between actual and expected performance included almost 100% of the older children in the sample.

Other barriers pinpointed in the Pennsylvania plan are inherent in the homeless situation with its associated problems. Some result from the instability of the life of homeless children as well as the familial problems that surround child and family homelessness. The conditions surrounding homelessness create difficulties for students in concentrating and studying. Frequent absenteeism is common among homeless students. With the need to assure basic survival needs, schooling often is low on the priority list of family and/or child. "Irregular school attendance may interrupt important assessment procedures necessary to a student's placement in special or supportive educational programs" (Commonwealth of Pennsylvania, Department of Education, 1989, p. 6). Interruption of the continuity of the educational process leaves students behind and frustrated. It is also difficult for educators who are well meaning to respond to the children's special needs when they don't show up regularly or don't stay very long.

Problems of homeless children that inhibit the educational process have been identified: Support and self-support are often disrupted. Homework is difficult to do in chaotic and nonprivate situations. Studying is similarly disrupted. Sleep may be disrupted, which leads to tiredness in school. In addition, children may be hungry. Many homeless children come to school without breakfast and possibly no snack or lunch. These further interfere with school-related activities, concentration, ability to learn, and tolerance levels.

Another educationally disturbing effect of homelessness is the emotional stress of the experience (Gewirtzman & Fodor, 1987). The stresses of survival keep one from concentrating and paying attention. This is compounded when the youth (usually older) needs to be concerned about subsistence. If homelessness continues over an extended period of time, these factors often preclude remediation and catching up, at least until much later in life and at great personal, social, and financial cost.

Inadequate apparel and supplies are further problems. At-risk and homeless children often are unable to get new clothing. In many social and educational settings, clothing styles become important peer-valuation indicators. Without peer-acceptable clothing, the social environment in a school may be untenable, especially for insecure and already frightened children. Needed supplies may be inaccessible for financial reasons. Both lead to further deterioration in the relationship of the children with their peers and with the school setting.

Parents of homeless school children often compound educational problems. They often may be unable to help being under terrible stress themselves or being physically or emotionally unavailable. Abusive, neglectful, or absent parent(s) detract further from the ability of children to learn. The parent(s) may add to the stresses on the children and thus negatively affect school situations. Problems with attendance, concentration, and outside support lead to further educational deficits and impediments to educational attainment. These can be gaps in academic skills, delay in development of academic skills, and delay in forward movement both in grade and in subject matter.

A pilot preschool (Head Start) program was started for children who had been expelled from other preschool programs for homeless kids for being uncontrollable. Their "mothers are crack addicts, mentally ill or abusive or all those things. The children suffer and can be insufferable" (Winerip, 1993a). The children's feelings of anger, disappointment, and frustration erupt in various social and psychological manifestations including blind rage, which totally disrupt their ability to cope with school situations and learning as well as dealing with practically anything else in their lives.

The parent(s) in a disproportionately large percentage of homeless families left school before high school graduation (Mills & Ota, 1989; Ziesemer & Marcoux, 1992). Similar low educational status characterizes those living in poverty and large numbers of homeless people in general. Although frequently there are other immediately precipitating factors in the homelessness of families, low income and low education are parallel to many of them.

Educational systems and institutions are often incompatible with and nonresponsive to the needs and lives of large numbers of their students, particularly minorities, the poor, and those with difficulties. But those who have not been able to navigate through the educational system are also most vulnerable to not being able to navigate through the economic and social systems of life.

There are many things educational programs, institutions, and systems could do to engage and otherwise more positively serve at-risk children (to be discussed in Chapters 11 and 12). Homelessness exacerbates whatever else interferes with a child's learning.

SUMMARY

The personal, social, and educational effects and costs of the homelessness of children are myriad. A child's or family's homelessness is part of a total social construct with multidirectional effects and causes. Homelessness is caused by and exacerbates a dysfunctional situation, with reciprocal interrelationships on many levels.

The homelessness of children is a multifaceted social phenomenon with functional/relational and time dimensions. Field theory and systems theory help establish that social phenomena are part of social interaction, interrelationships, and interchanging causality and effect between many different aspects of society and life. Interacting with and affecting each other, neither structures of relationships nor of time are independent. In time, there are short-, mid- and long-term effects of homelessness. In the functional/relational dimension, homelessness has consequences on all levels—micro, mezzo, and macro. The society's social policy is a major cause of homelessness. A macroeffect of homelessness on children is that they are cast out and lost from society. Among the most deleterious social issues relating to homeless children is their position under the law. The law puts children in particular jeopardy when they are homeless, especially without families. The children's legal position may prevent them from receiving the kind of services, protection, and help they need. Medical institutions are often closed to these children. There are many issues related to school and education. Future possibilities in terms of occupation and jobs are also affected.

Social conditions are related to high-risk situations for children. These include poverty, racial and ethnic problems, inadequate low-income housing, inadequate schools, a lack of recreational and employment opportunities, family instability, and crime and violence. Poverty negatively affects children and is closely related to the homelessness of families. As a consequence of negative experiences, homeless children may develop a negative reaction to authority figures and authority.

The midlevel aspects of children's homelessness are varied. They include familial, peer relationship, community, local institutional, occupational, and other issues.

Homelessness is personally damaging to children. It leads a child to develop responses that include anger, distrust, shame, low self-esteem, and fright.

Educational issues are also reciprocal as well as multileveled and multifaceted. On the macrolevel, educational barriers for homeless students have been identified. Institutional barriers are residency and guardianship requirements, poor coordination between educational and social services, transportation, and problems with records. For the schools, homeless children are often a burden added to an already difficult task.

Mezzoissues are schools' trouble accommodating children who need special attention. The children often are disruptive to the system and interfere with the smooth functioning of the classroom and other school components.

Microissues found were developmental and educational problems associated with homelessness among children and youth such as developmental delays, emotional problems, poorer school attendance, and lower academic performance among school-aged children. Homeless youth are at high risk for school failure. Parent(s) may add to the stresses on the children and thus negatively affect school situations.

CONCLUSIONS

Homelessness is clearly detrimental to children's social and educational development. It is also harmful to society and to educational systems. The social development and relationships of homeless children and the society itself suffer on the micro-, mezzo-, and macrolevels, in the short and long term.

The educational development of children and educational systems suffer on all levels and in all time frames from homelessness. Learning is greatly impeded and made difficult for the child. Teaching is impeded and made more difficult for the educational institution and the teacher.

Health issues related to homelessness of children will be discussed in the next chapter.

Chapter 3

HEALTH ISSUES

Homelessness is not healthy for children and other living things.

—Wright (1989b)

Shelter, food, and clothing are usually paramount when we think about homelessness. Health is a major issue usually relegated to lesser importance if thought about at all. In this chapter, mental and physical health aspects of homelessness for children and youth will be explored. All are public health concerns (Shane, 1988).

Health hazards and damage have multiple effects on homeless children. Homelessness also affects the health of the total population. Homelessness puts children's health at high risk. The conditions of life of homeless children are deleterious to their health. In turn, health affects the condition of their lives and their ability to deal with life demands. Health problems, particularly individual or family mental health, contribute to homelessness.

Homelessness also has general public health connections. The issue has been noted by major medical organizations. The American Medical Association (AMA, 1989) and the American Academy of Pediatrics (AAP, 1988) expressed concern about the health problems of homeless youth. Both said these issues need to be further examined and addressed by the health community.

Health hazards, acute and chronic physical health issues, mental health issues, family health, public health issues, results of research and related work, and probable relationships between homelessness, health hazards, family health, and public health will be discussed in this chapter. The reciprocal effects of these factors will also be discussed.

HEALTH HAZARDS

Homeless children are among the most vulnerable populations in the society. The reasons are poverty; poor nutrition; unstable and unhygienic living and eating conditions; lack of protection from nature and antisocial elements; alienation from family and other adult institutions of support; unsafe sexual practices; abuse of alcohol, drugs, and cigarettes; histories of neglect, abuse, and associated factors; and educational deprivation and disruption. The lack of health care and the subsequent neglect of illness increase vulnerability.

The health sequelae of poverty and of homelessness are similar. While children are homeless, they are also in poverty. In addition, specific health risks are peculiar to the homeless, some among all and some particular to subsets of the homeless population. In particular, three well-studied health hazards have been malnutrition, substance abuse, and smoking.

The health of their parent(s) affects homeless children. Many parents of homeless children have mental health problems and/or are substance abusers; others are ill with complications of poverty (Shane & Marjanovic-Shane, 1987). Parents who are ill have added difficulty dealing with the complications of homelessness and their children. A relatively new phenomenon has been the problem of children of HIV-positive mothers.

GENERAL RISKS

Living Conditions

Probably most hazardous for homeless youth, and the homeless in general, are unstable and often unsanitary living conditions. By definition, homelessness means living in inadequate shelter with a high rate of instability and mobility. Shelter often means cellars, abandoned buildings, parks and the street, as a "guest" in crowded quarters, in self-made shelters, boxes, and so on, without adequate hygienic facilities and probably unsafe water sources. It often means unclean surroundings, perhaps with vermin. From these follow most of the remaining health hazards.

Lack of Health Care

Another major hazard for unaccompanied youth is the lack or unavailability of health care. Being ill affects one's functioning. Wright (1989a, p. 73) noted that homeless people are often simply too ill to address their problems. On top of this, being homeless, particularly as an unaccompanied child, means one is essentially outside the health care system. In the United States, people under 17 cannot receive private or public health insurance. They can only be covered as members of a family or as wards of the state. Minors without families thus are in increased jeopardy, unless they find the rare program that provides free health care. Most, if not all such programs are short term by design.

Lack of health insurance restricts access to hospital emergency room care. Most hospital emergency rooms demand proof of insurance or ability to pay prior to admission, except for the most dire circumstances. Therefore, in addition to the problem of unavailability, the care that is available for homeless children is short-term, acute care. Preventive and consistent long-range health care is impossible for them.

A medical and educational truism is that early treatment is most effective. Neglect of health problems invariably leads to more damage through greater severity and length of illnesses, increased susceptibility, and the attendant consequences.

Babies

The health issues of homeless babies are physical and developmental problems for the babies and associated problems for the parent(s). Pregnancy or having a baby while homeless puts parent and child at particularly high risk. The effects of malnutrition, substance abuse, smoking, and so on are transmitted directly to the fetus/embryo. The developmental and health dangers, to baby and mother, are heightened by unattended pregnancy.

In general, "prenatal care rates are particularly low for [minority], poorly educated and teenage women" (CDF, 1992, p. 62; Weinreb et al., 1995). Mental health risks are probably heightened as well given that pre- and postpartum psychological problems are common even among the housed population.

Adequate prenatal care is generally unavailable for homeless women. They also often lack adequate professional help when giving birth and within the crucial days thereafter (Weinreb et al., 1995). Poor nutrition and inadequate prenatal care correlate with high infant mortality, prematurity, and/or low birth weight. High "perinatal and infant mortality rates and . . . low birthweight babies" are reported for homeless women (Whitman et al., 1992). These are predictors of birth defects, slow development, developmental difficulties, and disabilities as well as mortality. "Infants born too soon or too small are 40 times more likely to die in the first month of life than other newborns" (CDF, 1992, p. 61).

These babies are also unlikely to get the kind of extra help they need. Further, the high incidence of drug and/or alcohol abuse, STDs, and pregnancy-induced diabetes or hypertension put fetus, baby, and mothers at additional high risk. Some of the results of these risks are described in Whitman et al. (1992, p. 115).

Among homeless mothers and their babies, high risk for the babies exists whether the baby remains with the mother, is left with the mother's family, or some other arrangement is made for the baby. Failure to thrive (FTT) syndrome is exacerbated by conditions of deprivation. FTT can result from chronic disease or from psychosocial problems in bonding with parent(s) or primary caregiver(s). FTT and problems of psychosocial dwarfism are described briefly in Whitman et al. (1992, p. 117). Both are also further discussed under mental health issues, later in this chapter.

The problems of depression, endemic among the homeless, interfere with the mother-baby relationship. This may cause deprivation for the babies, who have special needs for emotional and physical bonding. It is well recognized that the embryo, fetus, neonate, and infant have special needs for adequate nutrition and a hygienic environment. Neonates and infants also, obviously, have special needs for physical and emotional care, nurturance, and protection. During these stages, the baby experiences crucial growth and development, both physical and mental. Malnutrition and lack of nurturance and love are destructive for healthy development.

Underweight children and babies, particularly, have problems with "thermoregulation," which puts them at high risk of illness in inadequately heated and insulated shelter (Whitman et al., 1992, p. 116). Immunization is apt to be almost impossible under homeless situations. Thus babies born or propelled into homelessness are almost certain to experience deleterious physical and psychosocial conditions.

The remainder of this chapter will set out what is known, through the limited research findings, and extrapolated, from general knowledge, about health issues and needs of homeless youth.

DISCUSSION OF RESEARCH DATA

Not much research has been reported about children's homelessness and their health status and prognoses. Little more research has been done on the health of homeless adults. No research known to me has been done on public health effects. Most data on health and homeless children are general; that is, they do not separate street youth from nonstreet youth, or children with and those without their parents.

The American Academy of Pediatrics (AAP, 1988) summarized a number of studies of homeless populations. The John-Pew Health Care for the Homeless (HCH) program of the mid-1980s (Wright, 1991b) included research. A comparative study, including health issues, was done of homeless women with and without children and homeless men (Burt & Cohen, 1989). Weinreb et al. (1995) did a study of homeless pregnant women.

Mortality

There is a lack of direct data available about death rates of homeless youth. From related data it can be extrapolated that, particularly among unaccompanied homeless youth, the death rate is much higher than for the corresponding age level in the general population. Data in Philadelphia for single homeless adults found mortality rates are significantly higher during the first six months of homelessness (Benner et al., 1991). Swedish data (Jahiel, 1992) show the homeless mortality rate almost ten times higher than average.

Among homeless Swedish young men between 1969 and 1971, the death rate was nine times higher than among other men aged 20-29 and more than twice that of older homeless men. A study in the United States showed similar high rates (Jahiel, 1992, p. 49). This shows a very high rate given that young men, in general, in the United States, have high mortality from violence. The deficient diet of homeless youth increases mortality risk through malnutrition, starvation, and reduced resistance to disease.

Poverty

Homeless youth suffer all the deprivation, health hazards, and health problems of the poor with additional risks. Most of the following conditions are found in general among the poor. Others, such as ineligibility for personal health coverage, are peculiar to unaccompanied homeless youth and adults.

Nutrition

The effects of improper and/or inadequate diet have been well studied. General malnutrition or deficiencies in diet correlate with disease and developmental problems. The effects of malnutrition upon physical and mental development are well researched. Embryos, fetuses, babies, and growing children are most vulnerable. Many diseases of poor children are directly caused by malnutrition and/or nutritional deficiencies (Karp, 1993, intro.; Physician Task Force, 1985).

Data released by the U.S. government in 1993 indicated the danger of lack of calcium and too much phosphorus (from soda, tea, and so on) in the diets of teenagers, especially females. It is directly connected to both age of onset and severity of osteoporosis in later years. Children who are homeless and/or born to homeless women are at high risk from the effects of their mother's and their own inadequate diets. However, the nutrition of the homeless is virtually unresearched (Wright, 1989a, p. 26). Wright (1989a, p. 21) did find a significantly higher rate of nutritional disorders among homeless youth than among the control group. However, the differences were not as strong as had been imagined. An overlap between poverty and homelessness might be responsible. (The control group were youth in health services for the poor.)

To understand the food preferences of homeless children, one need only look at children in general. Many children and youth prefer foods and drinks high in fat, salt, sugar, and empty calories, such as pizza, hamburgers, french fries, soda pop, and sweets, rather than those that provide essential growth elements. Children's avoidance of vegetables has been a subject of humor.

Combine these tendencies with the unsupervised lives of homeless youth, their poverty, the poor choices available to them, and the overpowering desire to satisfy hunger with whatever is closest at hand. Then contrast this with the special nutritional needs of young children and youth in their final growth periods, their bones, brains, and bodies developing and in need of special nutritional input. They need fortification for the future as well as daily sustenance. Nutritional deficiencies set the stage for future if not immediate trouble.

Alcohol, Drugs, and Cigarettes

Wright (1989b, p. 95) found alcohol and drug abuse rates among teenage homeless youth to be significantly higher than in the control group. So much data substantiate the damage caused to users and embryos/fetuses by alcohol, drug use, and smoking that it is not necessary here to spell it out. Fetal alcohol syndrome (FAS) is relatively easily diagnosed, even from photographs and years after birth. FAS, substance abuse, and smoking sequelae are a particular danger to homeless children. Other health hazards more specific to homeless youth follow.

Exposure

Homeless youth are vulnerable to exposure to the elements and illness. Often with inadequate shelter and clothing, hypothermia is a risk, and when ill and/or wet they have inadequate conditions in which to recover. They are very apt to be exposed to disease-causing vectors and more likely to be affected by them.

The inadequate shelter of homeless children and families exposes them to rodent bites and insect- and rodent-borne disease; lead ingestion from lead-based paints; falls from broken stairs, stoops, and unprotected windows; poor and unprotected wires; and so on (Whitman et al., 1992, p. 119). Extreme variations of temperature present risk, particularly for underweight infants (Whitman et al., 1992, p. 116).

Victimization and Injury

"Evidence from a variety of sources indicates that victimization and traumatic injuries are a major cause of death and disability among the homeless" (Padgett & Struening, 1992). Traumatic injuries have been the major cause of hospital visits for homeless adults. "Broken bones were the most common, followed by cuts, falls and burns" (Padgett & Struening, 1992). Wright (1989b, p. 22) found sprains, bruises, wounds, abrasions, and burns to be significantly higher among homeless men in their mid- and upper teens. Males, 16 to 18, had the highest rates of traumatic injuries (p. 78).

A high rate of injury among the homeless, particularly young men, from accidents and carelessness, abetted by tiredness, poor nutrition, use of psychoactive substances, and interpersonal violence, is not surprising. Interpersonal violence is probably engendered by the associated lack of supervision, frustration, instability, and mental stress. There are also indications that the unsafe living conditions of homeless families "contribute to physical injuries" for active children (Whitman et al., 1992, p. 119).

Homeless youth are victimized. They are robbed, assaulted, raped, and the like at high rates, often by other homeless people. In fact, much of the crime and violence to which the homeless are subject is reported to be perpetrated by young homeless men (Fischer, 1992, p. 93). However, as with other vulnerable populations, one would suppose they also are victims of nonhomeless people looking for victims.

Victimization is also a cause of homelessness. Homelessness as adults was correlated with abuse as children for a large proportion of women with children. Mate abuse is also a factor precipitating homelessness (Fischer, 1992, p. 98). Studies point to abuse as a major factor in the homelessness of unaccompanied children. Runaways were found to have been physically and sexually abused at rates from four to eight times higher than other youth using the same outpatient medical clinics. Fischer (1992, p. 99) concludes that available studies "clearly establish abuse in the home as a significant contributing factor" to the homelessness of children and youth.

Sexual Abuse and Abuse of Sex

Sexual assault and exploitation, as well as consensual unregulated and unprotected sexual encounters, are major health hazards for homeless youth. These are forms of victimization and causes of injury and illness. For women, particularly young women and young men, the lack of protection, supervision, and support afforded by a family, economic stability, and a secure shelter leaves them open to sexual abuse, assault, adventures, and exploitation. In addition, lack of available preventive and curative services leaves them vulnerable to chronic sexually transmitted diseases (STDs) including HIV infection. A high percentage are infected (Rotheram-Borus, Koopman, & Ehrhardt, 1991, p. 1191).

Nonconsensual sex or rape is a particular danger. "The incidence of sexual assault on homeless women is about 20 times higher than among women in general" (Wright, 1991b, p. 110). The problem of male rape is ignored, and there is only inferential information such as that "three-quarters of homeless victims of sexual assault were women" at San Francisco General Hospital's Sexual Trauma Service (Fischer, 1992, p. 96). Obviously, the other quarter were men. Just from the circumstances of vulnerability and exposure, one might imagine it probable that rape of males is not rare.

Acute Physical Health Risks

Wright (1989b, p. 23) found high rates of respiratory infections, genitourinary infections of various kinds, skin disorders, and problems specific to either males or females. Wright (1989b, p. 78) found males to be less healthy than females. "Rates of nearly all acute disorders and traumas are higher among [homeless] youth than among [control] youth, frequently by large margins" (Wright, 1989b, p. 89). He found infectious and parasitic diseases, tuberculosis, other respiratory infections, lice and scabies infections, sexually transmitted diseases, and skin diseases among the homeless youth (p. 22).

Chronic Physical Health Risks

Chronicity results from untreated illness, poor living conditions, and low rates of health care. The chronic disease rate among homeless youth was "nearly twice the rate of chronic disease observed among [control] youth." Most common were problems of the eyes, ears, teeth, gastrointestinal and respiratory tracts, infestation, and neurological impairments (Wright, 1989b, p. 89).

Among adult homeless (Wright, 1991b, p. 110), chronic lung disease was six times more prevalent and tuberculosis endemic—from 25 to hundreds of times higher than among the general population. Problems of the "extremities—chronic infected skin ulcers, cellulite, edema and other disorders associated with peripheral vascular insufficiency—are some 15 times more common . . . than among the rest of the population." Neurological problems such as seizures, nutrition disorders, disease of teeth and mouth, skin, liver, lice, and scabies were three to six times more prevalent.

Chronic sexually transmitted diseases (STDs). Adolescents in general are the most vulnerable segment of the population to STDs other than AIDS. "Each year (nationally) about 85% of STDs occur among teenagers and young adults. By age 21 about one in five young people has had treatment for" an STD (CDF, 1992, p. 66). Even without specific data, one might conjecture that homeless youth are more vulnerable for STD chronicity.

HIV+

It has been estimated that homeless youth, particularly older teen males, have a relatively high HIV infection rate. New York City and Los Angeles have the highest seropositive rates. Homeless young women may also be particularly vulnerable. In general, "women and children are the fastest growing population infected with HIV" (CDF, 1992, p. 65). "The living situations and specific HIV risk acts, such as unprotected sexual intercourse and sharing needles and paraphernalia when using intravenous drugs," as well as a high number of sexual partners, often bisexual, and early sexual activity are implicated in the high prevalence of HIV among homeless and particularly street youth (Rotheram-Borus et al., 1991, p. 1191).

A conference was convened in Washington, D.C., in the early 1990s to explore issues related to AIDS (HIV infection) among homeless and street youth. A major problem found, aside from vulnerability, was that preventive measures may be more difficult to disseminate, to control for consistency of practice, and to promote among a population of alienated, disorganized, and beset youth.

Mental Health

Issues related to developmental delays are discussed in Chapter 2. Other acute and chronic mental health problems are common among homeless youth. According to Wright (1991b, p. 113), the mental health of the homeless is the most written about and researched aspect of homelessness; he provides an extensive bibliography. However, the mental health of homeless youth has not been *well* researched or written about.

It often is difficult to determine which comes first, homelessness or mental health problems. Homelessness exposes one to mental health risks. The lack of a stable place to sleep, take care of hygiene, and keep belongings is a psychic assault and destroys self-esteem. Abuse, exploitation, fear, insecurity, and rejection augment the assault.

However, there are indications that for portions of the homeless population, mental health problems antedate homelessness. Mental health problems may have been precipitating factors in their homelessness. Many homeless youth come from situations with high mental health risks.

In our New Jersey study, two thirds of the sample reported conflict in their families and poor parent-child relationships. About the same proportion (which is not necessarily coincidental) had previously been homeless and/or run away. More than a quarter of the sample suffered from depression, and an equal, overlapping fraction from other emotional problems. Almost 15% were reported to have attempted suicide. About 20% were reported to be substance abusers (Shane, 1989, p. 78, 1991b).

Other researchers have found high correlations for mental health problems among homeless youth. Bassuk, Rubin, and Lauriat (1986) and other researchers have found anxiety, behavioral problems, and high levels of depression (Rafferty, 1991, p. 109). Gewirtzman and Fodor (1987) found reports of high stress with aggression, disorientation, family disorganization, grief (over loss of possessions, relatives, and friends), and social withdrawal.

The conditions of homelessness are reported to interfere with the development of perception and spatial-relationship concepts. Most mental health disorders were found to be at least four times "as common among homeless youth as among ambulatory youth in general" (Wright, 1991a). Other studies have found high anxiety, depression, and attempted suicide as well as alcohol and/or drug use or dependence among homeless youth. A Hollywood study found a "life-time and 12 month" major depression rate about 25% higher than in the general population. High anxiety and about a 30% rate of suicide attempts (highest among females) were also found (Robertson, 1992, p. 74). The effects of victimization and assault leave damaged mental health. Although true for all kinds of victimization and assault, it may be particularly true among those experiencing sexual assault. It is judged that victims of sexual assault experience "some degree of psychological trauma in addition" (Fischer, 1992, p. 96). One can assume that the vulnerability experienced through victimization of all kinds, added to the insecurity and instability of being homeless, would produce emotional and mental trauma and repercussions similar to post traumatic stress disorder.

Family Health Issues

The health of the family, its members, and particularly the parents has rarely been examined in regard to causes of homelessness of children. Mental health issues would probably be dominant and significant. In some families, "multiple personal problems often interacted with poverty to produce homelessness" (Fox & Roth, 1989, p. 146). Homeless families and families of unaccompanied youth tend to exhibit one or more of the following characteristics: substance abuse; physical, mental, and/or sexual abuse and violence; emotional distress or mental illness. Bassuk et al. (1986) concluded that, added to external factors, "family breakdown, psychological deprivation and impoverished self esteem contribute to the downward cycle of poverty, disruption, stress and violence."

In our New Jersey study, family problems associated with mental health issues were reported by many of the youth as a reason for being homeless. Almost two thirds of the sample reported family conflict and/or conflictual parent-child relationships. Almost half reported physical or emotional abuse, while over 10% reported sexual abuse (which is usually very underreported, so the rate could be higher in reality). Over a quarter reported drug/alcohol problems in the family. More than 20% reported physical/mental health problems, while just under 20% reported conflict between parents and/or violence in the family (Shane, 1991b). Family mental health issues are associated with the homelessness of children. The relationship of mental health and physical health issues needs to be further explored.

PUBLIC HEALTH

The public health issues of homelessness among youth can be approached essentially from three angles. Discussed previously were the general health status of the youth involved, incidence and prevalence rates, morbidity and mortality, risk conditions, causes of disease, and necessary preventive and curative actions. Next are the costs to society of having a sizable population with impaired health. Third is the effect upon the health of the general population. To recognize the public health dimension is actually to recognize the risks to society of ignoring homelessness. In this section, we will discuss the last two.

Costs

Some of the costs of homelessness of children and youth to society and to themselves can be measured by direct expenditures, ancillary expenditures for health care, and loss of productivity and positive contribution. All three elements are involved in our discussion. We will look at them separately.

Direct expenditures. Direct expenditures are the costs of providing health care. For the homeless, it is provided primarily through emergency and/or special services. Being out of the mainstream, living somewhat "chaotic lives" (Fox & Roth, 1989), homeless children have no direct, regular access to general health care, preventive action, and early treatment. The society is thus faced with costs of treating acute and chronic disease, both mental and physical, often at their worst—usually through the least cost-effective means, such as emergency rooms. Late treatment for illness, as for almost everything else, is more expensive and less effective than prevention and early treatment. Because the homeless can't pay, society pays when they do get treated.

Ancillary expenditures. Other expenditures are incurred secondarily. The homeless do not live in isolation from the rest of society. There are many areas of contact, often intimate, across which physical illness can travel in both directions. Homeless youth are often exploited for sex by nonhomeless people receiving and giving STDs. Homeless youth may sell drugs to or buy drugs from the nonhomeless, thus participating in the drug epidemic. They cough into the air that the nonhomeless share with them. There are thus the additional costs of taking care of people infected by the homeless with TB, other respiratory infections, STDs, and a large variety of other possibilities.

There are also ancillary costs of having mentally and emotionally injured or ill people wandering around without care or treatment, and continually vulnerable to more damage. These costs might be sudden and random violence, disturbing behavior such as ranting or cursing in public, foul odors from urine or other excretions, and other distressing and assaultive behavior such as aggressive panhandling.

Losses. The society loses when potentially productive and creative people don't contribute to the society. The impaired physical and mental health of youth who experience homelessness often leaves them less able or unable to contribute their talents to the society. Many of them remain dependent on the society rather than contributors to its development. Possibly worse are the dangers of passing homelessness and its sequelae on to further generations.

As has been documented previously, homeless young women are very liable to have children both while homeless and afterward. These children then may suffer the various liabilities mentioned earlier. If they survive without the problems associated with prematurity and the like, they face the further difficulties of being raised by possibly emotionally and physically damaged parent(s). This introduces the costs of homelessness to a second generation. In addition, the homeless are a reservoir of illness, both chronic and acute, for the rest of society.

SUMMARY

In this chapter, mental and physical health aspects of homelessness for children and youth were explored. The conditions under which homeless children live negatively affect their health. Poor health interferes with their ability to positively respond to life challenges. Poor health may also have been a contributing factor in their homelessness. The health problems and conditions of homeless children are also a general public health issue.

Six areas were discussed: health hazards, acute and chronic physical health issues, mental health issues, family health, and the effects of homelessness on public health. Homeless youth have multiple mental and physical health problems. Their exposure to various health hazards makes them one of the most highly vulnerable populations in the society.

The health of the families of homeless children, family members and particularly the parents, is a major issue. Homeless families and families of homeless youth tend to be families with one or more health-related problems.

Public health issues are the general health status of the youth involved, incidence and prevalence rates, morbidity and mortality, their risk condition, causes of disease, and necessary preventive and curative actions, as well as the effect of the homelessness of youth upon the health of the general population. The long-term costs of a sizable population with impaired health are high for society.

The costs of homelessness of children and youth to society and to themselves can be measured by direct expenditures, ancillary expenditures for health care, and loss of productivity and positive contribution.

CONCLUSIONS

A homeless child health syndrome has been identified. It consists of

poverty-related health problems, immunization delays, untreated or under-treated acute and chronic illnesses, unrecognized disorders, school, behavioral and psychological problems [depression, lack of self-esteem], child abuse and neglect. . . . To be a poor child is one thing, but to be poor and homeless is a thing apart. It is hard to imagine a social environment less conducive to health or normal maturation and development. There is virtually no aspect of a homeless existence that does not aid in the destruction of a person's well being, whatever age, race or gender. (Wright, 1989a, pp. 95-96)

Many homeless children suffer greatly in all areas relating to physical and mental health with possible continuing repercussions for much of their lives as well as for future generations. Society must address these issues for its own health as well as for reasons of compassion. It must ensure that if children are to be homeless, they at least have preventive and curative health services.

Chapter 4

SOCIAL CONTEXT
OF HOMELESSNESS

. . . and God heard the cry of the child.
—Genesis 21:17

Every child's life is shaped not only by its parents, but by neighbors, classmates, by the schools and ultimately by the whole civilization. And we need to face it: We are guilty, all of us, of neglecting the children.
—New Year's message from the Jewish
Theological Seminary (1993, p. E8)

Homelessness is a social phenomenon whose causality cannot be separated from its social context. In the light of the Galilean scientific approach, as typified in Lewinian theory and systems theory, homelessness is a product of the society and its social policies. Similarly, social responses to the phenomenon are also products of the society and its social policies. In this chapter, the social causality of homelessness among children and the societal response will be discussed in the context of societal issues, policies, and relationships.

A brief outline of the interrelationships of natural phenomena provides a foundation for the discussion. Learning about biological realities helped me better understand the parallel social realities. The parallels are maintained in this chapter with the discussion of contemporary changes in social policy and conditions in the society and their relationship to homelessness. Both historical and current social issues related to family problems also will be addressed and related to homelessness of children and families. At the end of the chapter, some implications for further research will be presented. The conclusion suggests social policy development and social responses needed to ameliorate or eliminate homelessness among children in American society.

Lewinian and systems theoretical concepts set out the interrelationships between social phenomena. Epidemiology and ecology examine the interplay and interrelationship between environment and biological happenings.

Epidemiology began in the nineteenth century with the introduction of scientific principles in the search to understand causes of and to cure or prevent disease based on the discovery that disease is a product of environmental factors, or vectors, plus local or personal factors. In significant ways, epidemiology has paralleled the development of the concepts of ecology.

Ecological concepts, also based on biological, scientific principles, have developed over the past several decades. The earth, life itself, consists of a series of interdependent and interlocking, larger and smaller, ecosystems all within more inclusive systems. Each system is not a unitary, isolated thing but is composed of many smaller ecosystems and ecosubsystems, interacting with the neighboring ecosystems and part of a larger ecosystem. These interact with other neighboring systems and are part of even larger systems, including the earth, with its life-sustaining envelope, and ultimately the universe. As scientists have become more aware of this, the way we view and understand ourselves and our small ecosystems has changed in relationship to life on earth.

HOMELESS CHILDREN
AND SOCIAL CAUSALITY

Homelessness is a social epidemic within the society. Social vectors are causal or contributory. Personal factors are also part of the causality. There may be something within the specific individual or family system that makes it more or less susceptible to particular social factors.

A biological example: High winds in a storm cause a tree to fall. Obviously, the high winds put stress on all the trees, but not necessarily evenly. Those that succumb may be strong, healthy trees hit by particularly strong gusts of wind or those with some internal weakness from former events that made them weak. But, if not for the storm, the particular tree might have survived for years.

To relate this to homelessness of families and children, some are like the strong tree buffeted by unusual wind gusts, and others like the trees that have internal weakness and succumb more easily. For all, external conditions are the factors that provided the final blow in pushing them to homelessness.

To uncover the social vectors relevant to children's homelessness, it is necessary to examine the larger systems of which the children and families are a part and to understand underlying social relationships and possible causality. Social conditions and policies of the larger society, as well as the social history of the family and individual, are part of the story.

RELATED SOCIAL PHENOMENA

At the beginning of a change in national administration and political direction in 1993, the relationship between social policy, economics, and the plight of America's children was acknowledged: "The talk has mainly been about economic recovery, productivity, the deficit, investment and international competition. But churning below the surface . . . is a larger unease . . . in particular an anxiety about the next generation of Americans" (Steinfels, 1992, sec. 4, p. 1).

Business Week, a relatively conservative newsweekly, said, "Growing income inequality in the U.S. is an unfortunate legacy of the tumultuous '80s and '90s" ("Attack the Income Gap," 1994, p. 76). *Business Week* suggested that the continuing division of the society into affluent and poor with widely divergent prospects and life experience was dangerous to the society and even to the affluent.

A number of social phenomena occurred in the 1980s and early 1990s (and were planned to be reinforced by new legislative bodies, both national and state, in 1995) with clear or probable causal relationships with the rising incidence of homelessness, particularly among children. Political, socioeconomic, and social issues and policies were encompassed. Among them were the rapidly increasing disparity between socioeconomic strata within American society; the related rise in poverty especially among children and women; changes in women's status and opportunities; the rapid, much greater than inflation, increase in the cost of housing; the concurrent decrease in low-income housing; and changes in governmental policies relating to support for the poor (Barlett & Steele, 1992; Dugger, 1995; Jones, 1995).

Further, they occurred coincidentally with increases in single-parent families, separation and divorce, and unmarried parenthood, coupled with the continued weakening of extended-family ties in many families. All of this plus other factors have put severe strains on parents and families and are integrally related to the increase in homelessness among children.

HOUSING

A major cause of homelessness among families has been the overall decrease in low-income housing throughout the nation while the costs of housing, rented and owner occupied, soared. Reports abound of the destruction and abandonment of high-rise, low-income public housing projects. In St. Louis, Newark, Philadelphia, and numerous other cities, many public low-income high-rises functionally disappeared during the 1980s and early 1990s. They were not replaced.

The Reagan administration announced early in the 1980s that building of public housing would cease. Simultaneously, administrative procedures to get an apartment in public housing projects became more cumbersome. Other programs for subsidizing low-income housing were similarly reduced during that era. As private housing prices were increasing at much more than the inflation rate, the government was reducing its commitment to provide low-income housing.

In 1993, a group of homeless families attempted to force the Philadelphia Housing Authority (PHA) to expedite procedures. The families believed that a stock of city-owned housing was empty due to "bureaucratic barriers." They were told, "We don't write checks and we don't give away houses on demand. There's no quick fix. I wish it were easy to give away houses and money" (Rosenberg, 1993, p. B1).

The government's housing policies and practices did not go unnoticed. "This [Reagan's and Bush's] government has engaged in a deliberate program of cutting federal housing subsidies for the poor at the same time housing costs have been soaring. As a result, there is a shortage of almost 4 million low-cost housing units" (Kryder-Coe et al., 1991, p. xiv).

The effect of rapidly rising housing costs was illustrated in a 1994 article. It describes the increasing inability of workers to afford housing in tourist and other boom areas. In some areas, workers have been priced out of the housing market and had to resort to camping and other unsatisfactory means of shelter to have access to work (Jaynes, 1994). Similar problems have occurred in major metropolitan areas.

Another observer also saw a continual rise in the cost of housing, coupled with a government policy dictating the decline in low-income housing (and subsidies) (Edelman, 1987, p. 42). In 1991, the director of the Pennsylvania Housing Finance Agency (PHFA) said that "between 1981 and 1989 federal housing subsidies for low-income [people] shrank 73% . . . from $33 to $9 billion" (Hartheimer, 1991, p. 1) while the need has increased.

Socioeconomic Issues

A number of other socioeconomic issues are related to homelessness. Among these are the increasing inequality of distribution of the country's resources and wealth as a result of social policy. From 1973 to 1990, the percentage change in average cash income of the lowest fifth of families with children went from $10,500 to $7,300, a decline of 30%, while the upper fifth average family income increased 13% (Jones, 1995, p. 499). In the mid 1990s downsizing became an issue. Books published in 1996 discuss this (Gordon, 1996; New York Times, 1996) *Business Week* noted:

> Growing income inequality in the U.S. is an unfortunate legacy of the tumultuous '80s and '90s. Thanks to a vast array of economic, social and cultural changes . . . the gap between rich and poor is the widest since the Census Bureau started keeping such statistics in 1947. ("Attack the Income Gap," 1994, p. 76)

"The country got richer and those on the bottom didn't" (Bernstein, 1994, p. 38). The magazine editorially regretted the phenomenon in relation to the economic development of the country:

> The income gap has widened in the face of a boom in American jobs. In Europe, the impact of global competition and technological change has been blunted by heavy taxation, government redistribution, and mandated high minimum wages. The result? Less income inequality but more unemployment. The U.S. has chosen more flexible labor markets, with lower unemployment but greater inequality. . . . The widening income gap has economists worrying that it may be hurting [societal economic] growth. ("Attack the Income Gap," 1994, p. 76)

Correlated changes in social conditions for children were dramatic:

The 1980s was a decade in which youth lost. Youth lost to an overburdened foster care system, to a growing national deficit, to increased violence in the schools and on the streets, to HIV and crack epidemics, to increased physical and sexual abuse, to an increase in poverty, an increase in juvenile incarceration and in the school drop-out rates. (National Network, 1991, p. 1)

How can this be related to the changing distribution of wealth? *Business Week* discussed the effects on education:

The kids are hurt not so much by poverty itself as by despair bred by economic disparities. Indeed Korean and Taiwanese students outperform American in math and science even though their incomes are much lower. But experts say children whose families are losing ground—while the affluent gain—often don't see the point of school. . . . Poor kids score 30 points lower than affluent ones on standardized math tests . . . [which] weighs down the average score of U.S. 12th-graders. (Bernstein, 1994, p. 36)

A UNICEF (United Nations International Children's Emergency Fund) report, released in 1993, stated the situation quite starkly: The United States ranked lowest among 27 industrialized nations on social indices related to the well-being of children. The nations included all of Europe except the former Yugoslavia, the countries of the former Soviet Union, and Albania ("The Health," 1993).

This report indicated that the United States was among the worst places in the world for children to live. The United States ranked "well behind other industrialized countries in providing a social safety net for children, while countries in the Third World have made enormous strides in child welfare over the last decade." In that report, the United States was found to have more than twice the rate of children living below the poverty line than any other industrialized nation (Robinson, 1993).

The U.S. rate of 20+% was more than four times higher than most European countries, all with rates under 5%. In Britain, the one European exception (with similar social policies), in the same period, the rate of children in poverty had risen to 10%. In many poor, developing countries, the rates of poverty and other negative well-being indices for children had been falling significantly during that time ("The Health," 1993).

Another indication of the poor condition of many American youth (from the same report) was that "ninety percent of youth homicides in the industrial world occur in the United States." The deputy executive director for UNICEF suggested that the "national commitment to child welfare needs 'review, action and change' " (Howell, 1993, p. A3). The reports did not include the extremely high suicide rate of American youth, which was second to homicide as a cause of death.

Other sources have noted the poor conditions for youth in the United States. The National Research Council (NRC, 1993) pinpointed the following four conditions that, they asserted, created and sustained high-risk situations for children and youth in the 1980s and early 1990s:

> 1) the large and increasing number of families [in the 1980s and 1990s] living in or near poverty and experiencing the emotional stress it brings; 2) the concentration of poor families in some urban and rural neighborhoods and the increase in the numbers of intensely deprived neighborhoods; 3) the nation's major service institutions and systems—health, academic and vocational education and employment and training—are not meeting the needs of many young people; and 4) the strong influence of racial and ethnic discrimination on employment, housing and the criminal justice system limits the options of minorities and, hence, their ability to rear their children. (NRC, 1993, pp. 236-237)

Federal government social policy changes during the 1980s and early 1990s were clearly causal factors that had deleterious effects upon large segments of youth in the society. Barlett and Steele (1992) detail a few factors that influenced or were part of the decline in living standards and conditions for large numbers of Americans in the 1980s and early 1990s. They also relate them to changes of social policy and priorities of the federal government and the elite in the society. "The wage and salary structure of American business, encouraged by federal tax policies, is pushing the nation toward a two class society. In 1990 the top 4% made as much as the bottom half of U.S. workers" (Barlett & Steele, 1992, p. ix).

The change was accompanied by, and related to, changes in the job structure of American industry and business. These include an enormous loss of relatively well-paying, unionized, industrial jobs with secure pensions and health benefits, and an increase in low-paying, low-benefit "service" jobs.

Barlett and Steele (1992) specifically separate these changes from the effects of economic recession. They contend that when and if the recession ends, the restructuring would remain. "That is because the plight . . . is rooted in serious structural problems within both the economy and society that go beyond the recession" (p. xiv). The Clinton administration made some suggestions for policy changes in an attempt to move the society toward less uneven income and resource distribution. However, the 1994 elections made most of these moot.

According to Barlett and Steele, the previous administrations' economic and social policies had the effect of "dismantling the middle class" and impoverishing larger proportions of the population. "For those people in Washington who write the complex tangle of rules by which the economy operates have, over the last twenty years, rigged the game—by design and default—to favor the privileged, the powerful and the influential." Apologists for these policies said that high pay and benefits had made American business noncompetitive. Barlett and Steele suggest, on the other hand, that skimming of excess profits and lack of reinvestment and modernization were the causes of the deindustrialization of America.

For the Reagan and Bush administrations' (and, after 1994, Gingrich et al.'s) policy to redress the high cost of labor, it was necessary to "reform" the tax system, enable "companies to trim or cancel health-care and pension benefits," subsidize businesses "to create low-wage jobs," deregulate business (which undermined established and stable businesses and communities through hostile takeovers and leveraged buyouts), reward businesses that "eliminate positions in the United States and transfer work abroad," and effect policies that have led to steep increases in the costs of housing and education, and remove the "unfair advantages unions afford to labor" (Barlett & Steele, 1992, p. 3). The Republican majority elected in 1994 in many state legislatures and the national legislatures set out a "Contract With America" that had similar goals and plans as the previous Republican administrations'.

The deliberate policy of societal disinvestment relates directly to homelessness. The families and individuals who are most vulnerable to homelessness were the object of specific decisions to disinvest societal resources in them. Social disinvestment results directly from changing priorities for governmental investment. Disinvestment in certain groups and places usually is accompanied by increased investment in other groups and places.

To exemplify the shifts in national social priorities, at the same time as the society was decreasing its stake in low-cost housing, the value of mortgage interest deductions subsidizing home ownership went from "about $8 to $23 billion" (Edelman, 1987, p. 43). This represents an increase of almost 300% in housing subsidies for the middle and upper classes.

[The policies] reflect conflicts of interest and differential power among societal groups. The rise of homelessness in the 1980s is explained by the growing power of affluent individuals and corporations and their increasing

demands on the government, . . . along with the disinvestment of people who
had been dependent on the government for support or who had to be sacrificed
to allow investment in other people. (Jahiel, 1992, p. 15)

Another study sponsored by the Center for the Study of Social Policy
found deterioration in the social and economic condition of children during
the 1980s. "Nationally, there were substantial increases in the percentages
of children in poverty, juveniles who are incarcerated, out-of-wedlock
births and teen violent deaths." The coordinator of the study was quoted
as saying that "in Washington, it was considered a victory for child-advo-
cates if they stopped program cuts" ("Study: For Children," 1991, p. 4A).
These cuts were not evenly distributed across the population. The Hispanic
and black minorities were disproportionately affected.

Further effects of these policies, in tandem with economic conditions,
are found in analyses of the 1990 census. Over 25% of the children in
American cities of 100,000 or more were impoverished in 1989; 85% of
those cities saw an increase in poverty over the year before, and of them
all over the decade. The highest levels were 46+% in Detroit, Laredo,
Texas, and New Orleans. Twenty cities, among them some of the larger
ones, had child poverty levels of over 36% ("Far-Reaching Human," 1992).

The U.S. Census Bureau reported in August 1992 and again in October
1993 that the trends of familial impoverishment were continuing. The
proportion of the "officially" poor in the society continued to rise about
0.7% a year, from 12.8% in 1989 to a high of 14.5% in 1992—1.2 million
more people than the previous year (Scanlan, 1993).

Unevenly distributed through the population, the burden disproportionately affected children because families were hit the hardest. Of those
officially poor, 40% were children under 18 (and about 12% were elderly);
this means that 22% of all children under 18 are counted as poor. Unmarried
women were the hardest hit. "About 35% of female-headed, single-parent
households were in poverty, compared with 6% of married-couple families.
. . . Most poor people were white—66.5%. But 33% of blacks (and 29% of
Hispanics) were in poverty" ("Far-Reaching Human," 1992, p. F2). (At the
time, about 12% of the U.S. population was black and 6%-8% Hispanic.)

These figures were based on a deliberately low estimate of the problem.
The definition of poverty had not kept up to financial reality partly due to
changes in the way it was computed. In 1990, the Department of Labor set
the poverty level for a family of four at $13,000+ per year (Knox, 1992).
In reality, in the early 1990s $13,000-$14,000 per year was far below the
poverty threshold for families of four in much of the United States. In many

urban and suburban areas in the United States, where the large majority of the population as well as the poor live, it was almost impossible for a family to exist adequately on an income even 20% above the official poverty limit. Also due to other causes, the problems of the poverty and suffering of children were graver than official figures indicated. The census does not include children who are not part of a family, and the segments of the population most subject to these negative trends are undercounted. Many municipalities challenged the results of the census for undercounting their total population, particularly the poor, minorities, and the homeless, and understating the severity of the problems these populations encounter.

The three most important weapons in the socioeconomic restructuring of America were deregulation, debt, and taxes. (A fourth was reintroduced in 1995 with an open, stepped-up, concerted attack on the "safety net.") Stewart (1992) describes how deregulation of banks and securities exchanges allowed for corrupt and insecure loans, "insider trading," junk bonds, and hostile takeovers.

In financial scandals of the 1980s and early 1990s involving the savings and loans, BCCI, and the financial dealings of those like Boesky, Trump, and the firm of Drexel, Burnham, a small group of people made enormous fortunes out of shaky empires built on enormous debt with little collateral. When caught, they received little more than a slap on the wrist if not outright sympathy. The nation survived the S&Ls' collapse, the fall of once proud department store chains, the centralization, restructuring, decline (and rise in indebtedness) of American industry and business; but Americans will be paying for them for a very long time—and some are paying through the extreme of homelessness. These are among the by-products of the above social policies.

The important element is that policies that greatly increased poverty and the economic instability of large numbers of American families also increased homelessness (see Barlett & Steele, 1992; Edelman, 1987; Wright, 1991b). For many families, socioeconomic factors brought them to homelessness. As the Children's Defense Fund (CDF, 1992) report concludes, "Family incomes are declining and the supply of low-cost housing is down. These two trends are the greatest causes of [family] homelessness today" (p. 111).

The same changes also limited the resources available for responding to the social effects on vulnerable populations. The CWLA characterized the result to be "years of neglect . . . of neighborhoods, of poor families, of poor kids" (Woodall, 1993, p. B6). The refurbished attack on "welfare" in 1995 (Dugger, 1995) in many states and nationally would only accelerate these trends.

With the advent in 1993 of a new federal administration espousing a somewhat different philosophy of government, it was hoped that there would be significant changes in these factors during the mid-1990s. Attention in the society at large to the plight of its children, it was hoped, would result in governmental policy and action. In 1993, however, there was little consensus on how to proceed beyond the basics (Steinfels, 1992). The 1994 elections dampened such hopes.

FAMILY ISSUES

Major family issues also relate to children's homelessness. Among these are weak extended families, changing nuclear families, children as property, and changing social support of families. None of which insure family trouble but for some lead to it.

Weak extended families. Traditionally, American society has encouraged weak extended-family ties. This permitted and indeed encouraged the mobility needed for people to settle and build a new country. Historically, America was a young people's society built by youth able to leave their families—culturally as well as physically—for opportunities elsewhere.

The social history and structure of the society depended and depends on weak extended-family links. Migrants and pioneers needed to be able to leave their families of origin. The arduousness of migration ensured that many of the immigrants to and migrants within the country were young people, single and married, with and without children. Pioneering life was difficult and resulted in short life spans with further family fragmentation and a concomitant increase in focus on the nuclear family.

It also led to the development of the nuclear family as the central cultural institution. The lifelong nuclear family as a social and economic cultural core, with a working father, homemaking mother, and two or more children, became the cultural stereotype of families during the 19th and early 20th centuries. It probably "reached its apogee in the middle of the 20th century" shortly after World War II, when women returned to domestic life from working in the war industries (Popenoe, 1990, p. 40).

Changing family structure. Since then, the nuclear family has been subjected to various onslaughts. There is talk of the "decline of the family" resulting in, or the result of, women moving into the workforce, increasing childbearing outside of matrimony, rising divorce and recombining families, and other phenomena (Popenoe, 1990, p. 40). Clearly, the function and perhaps even notion of family has been in the process of changing.

Although, in and of itself, it may not be negative, combined with the social policies and trends of the 1980s, it had major negative effects upon large numbers of families and their children.

Children as property. Historically, children have been seen as property of the family. By law they belonged to the father. As in ancient times, he essentially had the right of life and death over his children. This was part of an authoritarian approach to children. In the past, and in some families still, this means that children were to obey and not question, to "be seen and not heard."

Current social trends are for children to be considered people in their own right. A modern notion of family is a unit with everyone having rights. (Often there is some confusion about obligations.) In families where parents maintain some of the patriarchal ideas of the past and children have developed more individualistic notions, the potential for strife between children and parents increases.

Changing social policies. Social policies developed during and after the New Deal of the 1930s were designed to provide public support to families. With a major change in governing philosophy, these policies were altered and weakened radically in the 1980s and early 1990s. The intent and reality was for government to withdraw from these activities. This became a social "underinvestment in children" (Fuchs, 1990).

The contradictory impulses in society produced social and familial conflict. Individualism, independence, mobility, and weakness in extended families conflict with ideas of children as property, totally dependent upon and subject to family authority.

Factors related to change. In recent years, the changes in families as they traditionally have been known and generally thought of have been compounded by several factors. As has been noted, one factor has been the increasing movement of women into the workforce. This has occurred for both economic and social reasons.

Economically, there has been the necessity of multiple incomes in nuclear families for survival. "For the first time in history, a generation of Americans may see their standard of living fall below their parents', although most families today have two wage earners" (Burkins, 1992, p. F1). Socially, women have begun to see work outside the house as a life prerogative. Female-headed, one-parent families have also become increasingly common. These changes have meant that fewer families have in-home child care, that is, a parent at home.

Organized, affordable, alternate child care is scarce. This has led to a variety of mechanisms being developed to provide for children—having neighbors, friends, or relatives provide after-school supervision—as well as an increase in "latchkey" children, those who carry keys home and care for themselves while their parents work. The need for and propriety of day care has become a major social issue. At the same time, there has continued to be a major disparity between the incomes of men and women. Women in the 1990s still make, in general, about two thirds of men's incomes. Female-headed households are about six times more likely to be in poverty than male-headed households.

Governmental social policy in the United States not only led to a socioeconomic restructuring of the society but, by purposely withdrawing from the social welfare sphere, effectively took on a decidedly antifamily bias under a screen of "profamily" rhetoric. Social policy of the 1980s and early 1990s minimized involvement in provision for and support of families in general. The rationale given, based upon the concepts of the "Poor Laws" (see Chapter 10), was that the government cannot and should not interfere in families' rights and obligations to provide for themselves.

An interesting social phenomenon that has developed to enable families to deal with the decrease in affordable housing has been, in some ways, a profamily shift. It was a movement toward doubling and tripling up with extended families, or two or more families living together (CDF, 1992, p. 110). This is a reversal of the trend of the past 100 years toward nuclear households. There have been articles in various media describing the situation and discussing its pros and cons (e.g., "Family: Cheaper," 1992).

The establishment of multinuclear or multigenerational family households is not necessarily a regressive social trend. For some, perhaps the majority, this might be a generally positive experience. There can be strength and mutual support in such arrangements. Children often have an enriched emotional and cognitive environment in such households.

Unfortunately, for many other families, doubling or tripling up is often a step on the road to homelessness. Some people have called the "hidden homeless" those families in involuntary multifamily households (and families in which parents and children involuntarily live separately) (Mihaly, 1991a, p. 16). In many cases, the house is crowded, privacy is limited, conflicts arise, economic and other problems come up, and the "guests" have to leave. Sometimes it provides opportunities for relatives to abuse and exploit children, which may also lead to breakdown in the arrangement.

Extended-Family and Family Support

A factor found to lead to children's and family homelessness is the lack of family support systems, extended family, and/or friends. When one doesn't have family or friends upon whom to depend for help, both practical and emotional, families in crisis are more apt to become homeless. A study of homeless families in Los Angeles found that there was a "striking lack of friends or family to whom they could turn. One-third did not have a living mother, one-third did not have a living father and about one-sixth were orphans. Many had family members far away or were estranged from their relatives" (Mihaly, 1991a, p. 23).

Similar factors may well play an important role in those families from which children become independently homeless. One can expect that children from problematic nuclear families are less likely to end up homeless if they have supportive and caring extended-family units that help and care for them.

Family Conflict

Unaccompanied homeless children primarily come from difficult family situations, although economic pressures may be among precipitating factors. "Dysfunctional families may be more vulnerable to breaking down during economic crises due to problems with the welfare system, housing aid, child welfare or employment" (Kryder-Coe et al., 1991, p. 44).

Sometimes the effects may be reversed. There has been a noticeable increase in family stress and conflict seen by therapists and other professionals directly related to financial stresses. " 'The American marriage and family already is under assault from all directions. . . . The economic situation puts it under additional strain, from a financial perspective as well as a psychological perspective' " (Burkins, 1992, p. F1).

Independently homeless youth are somewhat different than families in terms of causality, as well as socioeconomically. They come from all socioeconomic strata, all kinds of families, and every ethnic group. Even though one cannot take what is reported as verifiable reality, youth overwhelmingly report family and parent-child conflict, violence, and abuse as causes for their homelessness. A significant minority report alcohol/drug problems in their families of origin (see Chapter 3). Many independently homeless youth have been either abandoned or rejected, some because of parent(s)' death, incarceration, illness, institutionalization, and so on. Some parents find contending with adolescents impossible. Others are going through crises of their own and can't manage the adolescent or child.

One cannot deny that, for parents in late twentieth-century America, child rearing involves many difficulties as well as pleasures. For the middle class, it often includes tremendous financial demands as well as time and emotional demands. Often the difficulties and pleasures end in conflict. It is very hard for parents working two and three jobs or overtime to have much time or emotional and physical energy left for their children. With the growth of two-working-parent and single-parent families, this may become a major deficit for the children. The attendant stresses may lead to destructive family or parent-child conflict and violence.

The difficulty of raising children is at least doubled by single parenthood. The fact that the vast majority of single parents, fathers as well as mothers, manage somewhat successfully to raise their children is very good. However, a minority break under the strain and the child(ren) become part of the statistics of homeless and/or street children. Difficulties are both financial and emotional in nature. They are particularly pressing when there is a weak social support system.

The widespread failure of separated, noncustodial parents (primarily fathers) to provide support for their children has been the subject of much discussion in the media in the 1980s and 1990s. There have been special laws enacted to remedy this. In many places, the courts place liens on the nonsupporting parent's wages to ensure support. Lack of financial support is probably accompanied by lack of emotional support, or is reciprocal, which compounds the problem for both the custodial parent and child(ren).

On the other hand, giving children time and emotional support may lead to financial stress. There are reports of parents having to choose between promotions or even their jobs and family responsibilities. Family involvement may endanger upward mobility in the workforce. The lawyer who leaves work to attend his or her child's educational, sports, or cultural event may lose in the promotion track. This has obvious financial repercussions. The movement toward family-leave legislation indicates societal acknowledgment of these problems. Unfortunately, legislation does not solve the financial problems or the resistance of employers to promote employees with family responsibilities.

Stepfamilies. Other family situations of the late twentieth century have a strong correlation with homelessness of children. Problems of remarriage, increasingly common in the society, at times prove overwhelming. Reconstituting or forming stepfamilies has many emotional and often economic difficulties. Emotionally, they intrude on already settled relationships between parent and child. They involve elements of loyalty to the "other" parent. They may involve accepting a new authority figure and probably new rules in the family, at the very time that the adolescent is moving toward self-rule. The wicked stepparent so common in fairy tales is based on very real issues and situations. Most reconstituted families succeed to some extent, although there is a higher failure rate for second and third marriages than for first marriages. Obviously, the tensions often lead to "deconstituting" the reconstituted family. This often in itself leads to problems for children. What exactly is one's relationship with an ex-stepparent?

Economic problems are created by financial responsibilities to a previous or subsequent family, thus removing resources from the current family. Some reconstituted families, for a variety of reasons, resolve these problems by removal or ejection of the child who presents the most obvious irritant. Some children are sent to boarding schools, others to grandparents, aunts and uncles, and so on. Some end up homeless.

Adoption. The effects of adoption on family stability seem to have been a neglected area of research. Adoptive families have not been separated for analysis in homeless youth data, as far as I have been able to discern. One would imagine that there are some special issues related to adoptions and homelessness of children though these have not been pinpointed.

Reports have been seen of a growing, though small, phenomenon, the disolution of adoptions. Some are terminated by parents, returning the child to teh child-wellfare system within one or two years. Some end after 10 or 12 years. Faulty adoption proceedings have been suggested or facts of health or mental status of which the adoptive parents were not informed. A very few adoptive parents act as though they went to a store, bought an appliance and returned it as defective.

Some adoptees, particularly from very developmentally distructive situations, and older teenagers, have suffered so much abuse and instability that they can not accept the adoptive family regardless of how hard the parents try. It may be that up to 1/4 of adoptions of teenagers fail. Some end up as unaccompanied children.

Distribution. In our study, homeless and runaway children originated from all family situations. The greater difficulties of single-parent families, however, are reflected in the distribution of the families of origin: 34% of the homeless children came from one-parent families; 22% of the children came from a nonnuclear family arrangement; almost 20% from reconstituted families; about 18% from two-parent "intact," including adoptive families; and 7% did not come from a family (Shane, 1989, p. 211).

Running away. In reviewing literature explaining the cause of runaway behavior, Angenent and de Man (1989) found in the Netherlands that this phenomenon can also be explained as an interaction of individual characteristics, family environment, and weakness of social supports that leads the youth or child to perceive the environment as being stressful and triggers runaway behavior. Through being homeless and young, however, the children themselves become part of the lowest socioeconomic stratum, at least while they are separated from their families. So economic factors are added to the familial and emotional elements of homelessness.

It is not difficult to demonstrate the lack of societal support for families. It is expressed in regressive social policies and programs as well as in social and legal traditions. The problems of finding adequate care for children while parents work has been discussed and written about extensively.

The lack of family-leave policies, unique in the industrialized world, can strand parents with having to choose between economic security (their jobs) or caring for sick or disabled family members, usually their children. The paucity and/or lack of other supportive programs for families belies the society's concern about "family values." As Marian Wright Edelman (1987) has written, "Both public and private sector neglect and anti-family policy have contributed to a downward spiral for families and children" (p. 23).

Our legal traditions have led to the treatment of marital problems as legal and adversarial rather than as mediative and repairable. This has the effect of removing the best interests of children from the center of consideration. One of the chief results of all the above has been the increase in homelessness, helplessness, and despair of children.

SUMMARY

The homelessness of children and families cannot be separated from its social context. Homelessness is a social epidemic—a product of the society and its social policies—and is not autonomous. The social responses to the phenomenon are also products of the society and its social policies. Social policy, economics, and the plight of America's children are related.

The major cause of homelessness among families has been economic. As private housing prices increased at much more than the inflation rate, the federal government reduced its commitment to provide low-income housing. Simultaneously, the nation moved toward greater disparity between classes with an increasingly unequal distribution of economic resources. This was accompanied by a clear deterioration in the social and economic condition of children during the 1980s.

Changes in family have also contributed to homelessness of children. Social policy of the 1980s and early 1990s minimized involvement in provision and support for weakened families. Increasing single parenthood brought financial and emotional difficulties in a society with weak social support. The economic and social policies during the 1980s and early 1990s led directly to the concurrent increases in homeless children and families.

CONCLUSIONS

In this chapter, the "field" or ecological system that has created the homelessness of children and families has been examined. The field has been seen to consist partially of social policies that have led to a restructuring of society and an increase in poverty and economic stress among the lower socioeconomic strata of the population. All this is added to a general economic crisis of relatively long standing in the United States.

Further, the historical cultural deemphasis of extended family and the emphasis on individual responsibility compound and support the negative effects of the economic stresses being felt by large numbers of American families. The recent changes in family structure and roles are further stresses that have affected the homelessness of children and youth. The homelessness of children is a systemic rather than an individual phenomenon, although personally felt.

Generally, the social structures that have been built to deal with homeless children, as with homelessness in general, function on assumptions that consider the phenomenon to be separate and unique. They operate on the ideas that children and families are homeless due to emergencies and/or personal issues, that unaccompanied children have functional families that want them and can provide for them. Thus simple palliatives such as providing temporary shelter, finding the family a place to live and a job, or returning the child to his or her parent(s) with short-term counseling and other short-term programs are thought able to remedy the situation.

But homelessness in this era, particularly for children and families, is a symptom of larger social dysfunction. To solve the problem, or even to address it effectively, changes are needed in underlying and often seemingly unrelated social policy and practice. As Lewin taught, to understand social phenomena, one must understand the total field of which they are a part. Then to resolve a social condition, one must seek to resolve the underlying, causal social conditions.

To stem and reverse the epidemic of homeless children, change is needed in policies that, on the one hand, increase poverty and lower the socioeconomic status of large numbers of families and, on the other, reduce the social and economic supports society provides to families, particularly as the needs increase.

Consistent policies are necessary that support and strengthen families and lead to the improvement of the social and economic status and stability of the lower and middle segments of the population, if for no other reason than to strengthen the health and well-being of its children.

At the beginning, there are two possible directions for changes in social policy, or some combination of the two (Steinfels, 1992). One is support for the "traditional" family as well as governmental help to maintain and reinforce that norm. Another is recognition of and support for the changing and evolving forms of family. Some believe that economic reforms are most important in helping families. Others would join this to reinforcing family structure.

There seems to be some agreement that

neither the traditional liberal emphasis on government programs nor the traditional conservative emphasis on family stability and moral discipline will do the job alone. Health, education and antipoverty programs would have to go hand in hand with frank endorsement of sexual and parental responsibility. (Steinfels, 1992)

The consensus seems to be to combine economic supports and measures with "cultural initiatives."

As Lester Salamon, director of the Johns Hopkins University Institute for Social Policy, said in 1989:

Homelessness among children and youth is too serious a problem to be ignored in our national social policy. Both for its immediate effects on those who are homeless and for the inadequacies it reveals in our social support systems, homelessness among children and youth has truly been a national tragedy. (Kryder-Coe et al., 1991, p. ix)

In an era of changing family structures and ties, the society needs to help families strengthen their abilities to raise their children positively. There is also a need for positive and adequate alternatives when the family becomes unable or unsuited to do that. It is a truism to say that children are the future of society. However, American society's practices do not yet appear to recognize that the way children develop and are cherished determines what happens to the society as a whole.

Part II

THE PERSONAL DIMENSION

The Found Boy (continued)

Then, one day, somebody did see him
First, she felt his shiver in the air.
Then she heard his rags whipping him
in the wind of the shiver.
And then, at last, she saw the boy.
(From "The Found Boy" in *Somebody Else's Nut Tree* by Ruth Krauss)

Homelessness is a human problem. It has many dimensions and facets, as has been discussed in Part I. A major facet is the experience of the person. The second part of the book encompasses stories of homeless children and families as well as stories of adults who were homeless as youth, "survivors." What happened to them? How do they feel about it? What are they doing about it? What are their plans for the future? What are their responses to the help they have received, if any?

Statistical analysis cannot give us this dimension, only ethnography can do this. This section of the book is thus largely devoted to the people themselves.

In Part II, there are five chapters. Chapter 5 includes stories of unaccompanied homeless children as told by the children themselves. Chapter 6 contains stories of homeless families as told by the parents and some of the children. Chapter 7 consists of information about babies unable to talk for themselves. Chapter 8 presents stories of people who have survived homelessness as children and as adults have eventually succeeded in building constructive and productive lives. Chapter 9 is a look at some films dealing with homeless children. It also includes discussion of some of the difficulties of presenting the situations and problems of homeless children in film and video.

Interviews were carried out at various shelters that try to help homeless children and families as well as with individuals who had been homeless as youth. All places and identities are disguised to protect confidentiality and privacy. As part of learning about homeless children, we will also discuss some information about homeless babies, who, obviously, are impossible to interview. Depictions of homeless children in film and video are intended to round out knowledge about the general situation of homelessness. I hope that, as one personalizes knowledge about those who are or were homeless, it will lead to a deeper understanding of how one becomes homeless, what it means to be homeless, and the effects it has on people's lives.

Chapter 5

UNACCOMPANIED CHILDREN

"Unaccompanied" children, either "runaways" or "throwaways," have many stories to tell. These stories represent how the child has seen and understands his or her life situation. It is imperative that adults listen to understand them better: "There is consensus [among psychologists] that children's observations and statements must be taken seriously for the sake of these children's development, as well as for our own understanding" (Garbarino, Stott, et al., 1992, p. xi).

The stories in this chapter were related by children in federally funded Runaway and Homeless Youth Act (RHYA) shelters. Their stories are largely in their own words, but partly from shelter records. Record material and my summary of parts of their stories are in brackets. The stories come from children in two different shelters—one urban and one in a small town. All places have been disguised and names changed to protect the identity of the children.

The children were of diverse backgrounds, from 10 to 17 in age, male and female. They were from various kinds of families—one- and two-parent, intact, recombined, and adoptive. The families are of various backgrounds and economic levels.

These ethnographic data, although not statistically representative, provide the opportunity to take a journey into the world of homeless children. Because of the stories' similarities, however, they could well represent the stories of a large proportion of such youth. In their specifics, they are the lives of individual children.

SEVEN CHILDREN
FROM AN URBAN SHELTER

The shelter is in a very urban, deteriorating section of a medium-sized city. The two-story stone building is unlike any other in the vicinity. Of the seven children and youth at the shelter on the day the interviews were conducted, five were female, two male.

The children were not ambivalent about telling their stories to the interviewer, although some were more interested in doing so than others. Some of the stories are thus rather brief.

The children had just come back from school and were involved in a recreational program in the basement. They came one by one to talk to the interviewer. All interviews were voluntary.

The girls were sisters, 12 and 13; a 14-year-old; a pregnant 16-year-old; and a 17-year-old. The boys were 16-year-olds.

Some of the young people chose pseudonyms for themselves. Others could not think of another name by which they would like to have their stories told, so names were suggested by the author until they found one they liked. The first story is of a biracial young woman who, along with her siblings, had been sexually abused by her father. She reported him to the police and he was sentenced to jail. Her mother and sisters then left her, accusing her of breaking up the family.

"I'm Only Trouble"

[Faith is 17 years old. She was under the legal guardianship of the state child protective agency. Her father is Caucasian, her mother black. She identifies as Catholic. She was very uncomfortable talking about her situation.]

I like school but I don't do very well there. Before coming to the shelter I lived with a friend's mother. My mom and sisters moved away and don't want to have anything to do with me. They blame me for all the trouble.

My father was convicted of sexually abusing me. I reported him to the authorities. He is an alcoholic and drug addict. My mom left town and moved to [a distant state] with my younger sister and brother, when my father was jailed. She abandoned me and my twin brother. I don't know why she's so angry at me for telling the truth. She drinks sometimes.

There are six of us kids. I have two older sisters, one younger sister and two brothers, my twin and the youngest. My twin brother is in [a public institution for children in trouble], where he tried to kill himself. He has used a lot of alcohol and drugs. One of my older sisters smokes "sess" [a narcotic].

My dad had sex with me and the others for years. But my mother and older sisters accuse me of lying and breaking up the family. They all knew about it. I ran away overnight once the year before I came here. I really couldn't stand it anymore.

My mother told me I was only trouble and that I lied about what my dad did. My mother said I seduced him, it was all my fault. So, she didn't say it didn't happen just that it was my fault and that I broke up the family. She doesn't want to have anything to do with me anymore. My sisters didn't say it was my fault but they said I shouldn't have reported him. I don't understand why. I haven't seen or heard from my parents since this happened. I'm very unhappy and don't know what to do or what I should do.

[Faith wrote a paper about her feelings, which was in the agency file. In it she said she had suicidal feelings and felt guilty for breaking up the family. She wrote that she couldn't stand it any more and didn't understand how her siblings could not back her up. She felt used by her father sexually. She wrote that she was unhappy and scared.]

* * *

The next two children are from a single-parent family. Their mother had been a drug abuser. They have had several family constellations with different men in the house. They were taken from their mother when she was placed in a detox and rehabilitation program.

Two Sisters

[Eva, 13 years old, and Sylva, 12, are black, and relatively small and slight. They had been living in a large city in another part of the state with their mother and siblings before being placed at the shelter by the child protective agency. They are Protestant.

Family. There is no clear information about the mother or father or anything about their families. The girls themselves knew nothing about them. According to the record, their mother had her first child when she was 13 years old, so she may be between 26 and 31 years old. (The records are inconsistent and confusing in terms of family information.) Eva and Sylva's father is supposed to be four years younger than their mother. Eva was born when her mother was either 15 or 18 or 19 according to her recorded age, or there is another older child. The family lived a rather unstable life. They moved frequently within the same city. Both girls attributed their school failures to the frequent changes in school. The family has had a longtime connection with the state child protective agency.

According to the records, the mother drank and used drugs. She used to be very pretty and wanted to be a model. She left home at 13 when she had her first child. The family has been homeless from time to time. The mother became debilitated due to fights, alcohol and drug use, and other destructive factors. She had entered a drug rehabilitation program a few days before the girls came to the shelter.

Siblings. According to the records, there is a half sister two years older than Eva, a brother one year older (in foster care at the time), and a half brother one year younger than Sylva. Sylva's records indicate that she is Eva's half sister but Eva's do not corroborate this. They have contact with their jailed father. They and their mother also have lived for a long time with a man who is called their stepfather in the records. He is about 20 years older than their mother. There is an indication that the mother used physical punishment (belt or hand) at least with Sylva. The record states that Sylva was sometimes sore for days after being hit. Both girls had been left back in school, Eva twice and Sylva five times (she is in second grade).

The girls were interviewed separately. Their descriptions of their life situation and hopes for the future follow.]

Eva. I like school. I don't mind being here 'cause it's good to get away from the family. I talk on the phone to my brother and sister almost every day. My mom needed time to herself so she can get off drugs. I can't wait until Dad gets out of jail this year. He went to jail for snatching someone's pocketbook. I'm sure Mom will get off drugs and things will get better, like it used to be. We used to live like rich people. We had a nice apartment and everything when we lived with Mom's friend.

My dad writes a lot of letters to me. I love both my dad and mom. I'll always love my mom no matter what. Things have been bad and good in my life. I'll be glad when my mother will be off that stuff and we'll be living together in our own home.

I want to be a nurse. I'll treat kids nice. I won't take drugs, drink beer or smoke pot.

Sylva. We got locked out of the place where we were living. Then we had to go someplace to get food to eat and to the "Welfare," which sent us to a hotel. We spent a day in a shelter. After that our mom thought she should go into the drug [rehabilitation] program and [the state child protective agency] brought us here, where we been five days now. I know Mom will stop using drugs. Then things will be better. [She was asked what she thought of the agencies and programs that were helping her.] School didn't help us. I think it's wrong that I been left back five times and [am] still in the second grade. It wasn't my fault that we moved so much. Those school people didn't even try to help me. The Welfare don't give people enough money to pay rent. They don't help. It's all their fault that this happened, except for the drug program. [The child protective agency] don't help people the way they should. The only place that really helped us was this place. The people here are nice and really tried to help me and my sister.

[I asked Sylva what she thought should be done to help people. She smiled and said] All the homeless people should be given a few bucks and have a house bought. [Who should do this?] I don't know, maybe the president.

I wish things were the way they were when I was younger, when I was seven. We lived in a three apartment house on the second floor. We lived nice, had furniture and everything we needed. It's sad how we have to live now. All the rich people don't care about anyone but themselves. If I was rich I would buy everyone a house.

* * *

The next young woman was born in Africa of an American man and African woman. She was left with her maternal grandparents and then brought to the States. She shifted between her parents until she was thrown out. She then married and was divorced when she became pregnant. She apparently has been rejected by both her parents. Her right to be in the States is not secure.

A Soon-to-Be Mother

[A. J. Saye is a 16-year-old African American. She is Adrienne in the records but calls herself Jasmina. She changed her name and became Muslim when she married about a year before the interview. She was four or five months pregnant when her husband divorced her by Muslim law and threw her out. She had been homeless and run away several times previously and had lived with one or another parent. She was referred to the shelter by a large shelter in a city in an adjoining state.]

When I had to leave my husband I came here 'cause I had been here before and they helped me and were nice then.

My father is about 40. He is an American. He's worked regular at the same job for a long time. My mother is about 35. She is West African. My parents met and got married in Africa, but it wasn't legal in America. Me and my brother were born in Africa but somehow our father didn't register us. We were brought to America when we were young children. My parents separated when I was young and Mom sent me and my brother back to Africa to live with my grandparents.

[AJ's mother left her father reportedly due to physical abuse. Both parents subsequently remarried and each had two more children.] My mother lives in [another state] with her husband and family. My father lives here with his second family. He drinks occasionally but not too much.

Besides my brother I have four brothers and sisters, two from each of my parents. My brother is two years older than me. He lives on his own here. It seems that we both been abandoned by our parents. My dad's two boys, 6- and 8-year-olds, live with him. My mom has twin 3-year-old girls who live with her.

When I was 6 my brother and I were sent to live in Africa with my mom's parents. Both my parents remained here. We stayed in Africa until I was 11. My mom brought us back to the States to live with her. After a while she sent us to live with our father.

I did not get along with my stepmother. She's about 40. We fought a lot. I was in track and for some reason she couldn't stand it. She kept trying to make me get out of track. Finally she threw me out of the house. I was in the 10th grade then and I got so upset I dropped out of school.

I came to the shelter on my own then. The people here then sent me to the police, who sent me back to the shelter. I stayed for a month.

[It is not clear if she returned to her father and stepmother for a while or started moving around right after she left the shelter.] My father hit me a lot and sent me to live with a friend of his. I didn't like it there. It was too crowded, too many children, messy, noisy. So then I went to live with a cousin. My cousin was on Welfare so I couldn't stay there long. My father did not help me. I got pregnant during this time and had an abortion.

After that I met [her ex-husband]. I became Muslim and we got married in a *masjid* [mosque]. I got pregnant. After a while we had a big fight. My husband divorced me by saying, "I divorce you," three times and sent me away a week ago. I came here. Like before, they sent me to [the child protective agency], which then sent me back here.

My brother and I have a big problem. The immigration wants to deport us. Since our father is American we should have American citizenship. However, we've been told by the Immigration and Naturalization Service [INS] that we're illegal and might be deported. Our father won't give us the papers we need to clear this up. My brother asked me for help, but what can I do? I don't have anything I can help him with since I'm in an even worse situation. I don't know why our father won't help us in any way. I don't really know what will happen in the future. I hope I can work and take care of my child. I don't want anything special, just to get a GED [high school equivalency]. I don't want to be near either my father or mother. I want to be near my brother and little half brothers. I don't want to get back at anyone. That just makes things worse. Besides, according to Islam it's not up to people to punish other people. In the next life they'll get what they deserve.

The shelter is a good place. They help you. Separation between parents hurts children and brings lots of problems for them.

* * *

The next young woman was abandoned by her biological mother and adopted by a middle-class family. The adoptive mother apparently resented and abused her from the beginning. The young woman is very intelligent and has ambitions of becoming a doctor. She left her adoptive family.

"I Had Enough"

[Pamela, 14, is a very articulate black woman. Her biological mother committed suicide while in a mental hospital at which time Pamela and her twin brother were placed in foster care. At age 5, she was adopted.

In addition to her twin brother, Pamela also has an older sister and two older brothers. She hasn't seen any of her siblings since adoption and has lost track of them. There is no information about either of her biological parents.

According to the records, Pamela is an only adopted child in a middle-income, two-parent, black family. She has been under the state child protective agency's supervision for years due to physical abuse by her adoptive mother. The mother was characterized in the records as being strict and abusive. Her father was characterized in the records as being "unavailable."]

My dad and mom are about 47 years old. They both have good jobs. My father makes medical tools with machines. My mother makes computer parts. I don't know if either of them went to college.

I went to [private school] until I transferred to public high school. I'm in the ninth grade and I'm a good student. I would like to finish school at a boarding prep school, go to college and eventually become a doctor.

I first ran away when I was 7 because of being beaten. I was abused by her [mother] from the time I became part of the family. [The records say that she was *found* by the police the same day and returned home.] I went to the police to complain about all the abuse. The police were very nice and helpful. They called [the state child protective agency], which then put me with [the adoptive parent's] relatives. I stayed with them for two months and the agency was supposed to be working with my parents. Then they returned me to them.

The abuse started again and I was afraid to do anything. I was beaten real bad. I told Dad but he wouldn't or couldn't do anything. He was good to me. He never hurt me and I love him.

With my mom it was like a man beating a baby. My mother beat me with her hands and whatever she could get her hands on. There were bruises even on my face. Nobody ever asked me about them. Nobody at school seemed to notice. When I transferred to public high school I worked in the guidance office from the beginning of my first semester there. They asked for me to work there. They noticed something recently and asked me what had happened. I didn't tell them.

Then last Monday I decided I had enough. I went to the police again and they told me to go back home to my parents. Then I got in touch with [the protective agency]. They would not listen to me. Finally, I got my father to bring me here. Then they [protective workers] paid attention to me.

If a child is being abused, the protective workers shouldn't just make the family go for counseling. The abuse should be stopped and then the situation should be monitored. They shouldn't just take the parent's word for what is happening; they should ask the child. My mother told the workers that everything was all right. They never asked me. I think children should be listened to. They should not depend only on the parent's story to know what is going on in a family.

I won't go back to my parents after what I've been through. My mom doesn't want me back but my dad does. After this I'll fight back if someone tries to abuse me and someone will get hurt. I never resisted before. In abuse the child should not let it go on; they should report it. Abusive parents should get help to stop abusing your child[ren].

I would like to go to a small college preparatory school and find my real parents. I want to go to college and become a doctor. All I ever wanted was to find my real parents. I'd be happy then. I just want to forget about this family. [The case worker at the shelter arranged a scholarship at a prep school. The shelter then would act as a family for her and she would go there on vacations.]

* * *

The following young man refused to identify with his stepfather. He has dreams of being reunited with his biological father and an older sister.

"I'm a Full German"

[Anthony is 16 years old and in the eighth grade. He is in special education classes but not necessarily due to mental retardation. His mother is reported to be alcoholic.]

I lived most of my life with my mother and stepfather. Both of them are 40-years-olds. My mom drinks and we fight a lot. But the real problem is my stepfather. I hate him.

I think he's a janitor. He dropped out in the 11th grade. My mom's a nurse and works in a doctor's office. She's been married to this guy for 13 years. My real father is on the run in Arizona. He's in trouble with the law.

My dad's parents live in a small town somewhere. My mom's mother is dead and her father, who is 71, lives with us. I don't want to talk about my stepfather's family. They're nothing to me. Our family spends a lot of time with them. I hate it. They're a pain, like my stepfather.

They make me use my stepfather's Italian name but I prefer my dad's name, which is German. I'm a full German. Both my real father and my mother are German. My parents separated when I was less than a year old.

I have an older full sister, I don't know where she is, a 12-year-old half sister and 10-year-old half brother. Both the younger kids live with me and my mother and stepfather.

My mom and me have some hard times. Sometimes I get very angry at her and then I'm afraid I'll hit her. But I love her. This is the second time that they threw me out. I stayed at the shelter for 53 days before [the previous late summer and early fall].

I had trouble with my stepfather since I was 10. He wants his kids to be Italian like his family. I don't want to change being German.

My stepfather used to hit me a lot. About a year ago I hit him back and he hasn't hit me since. I hate him. I think Mom might care about me deep down. But I could care less about this family. I'm angry at Mom and my stepfather.

When they threw me out of their house the last time, the police brought me here to the shelter. This was the third or fourth time I'd been out of my house. All the times were within the past year. The first time my mother sent me to the shelter in order to teach me a lesson. I stayed five days. I went home for two weeks, then they locked me out and I called the shelter. I went home for one day but came right back to the shelter. I've been at the shelter for three days this time. I been at the shelter too much.

I never talked with people at school about my problems. Last year they suspended me a lot. I was hanging out with the wrong crowd. I got in fights, talked back and did other things. If I'm suspended one more time I'll be kicked out. I don't mind. School is boring and a waste of time. I lost a year in school during the fifth grade. It was the first year I had trouble with my stepfather. I like sports, baseball, street hockey, and roller skating.

I don't want to go back home; I want to go to a foster home. It's risky being someplace you don't know but I hope for the best. It must be better than all the problems at home. I want it to be nearby, not too far away, so I can still see my friends and my girlfriend. We've been together for about two months. She's 16 years old in high school.

I want to be a mechanic. I also would like to be a teacher. I don't know about college. Maybe I'll go if I got a scholarship. What I really would like is to go in the Army or Marines. I hope I can finish high school.

I would really like to get together with my real dad and find my older sister. I haven't seen her since I was 2½ years old. The counselor knows where she is. The counselor thinks that my sister should contact me herself so they won't give me her address. Why can't I call her myself? It would be really great.

[What would help people who are in a situation like this?] They need a place to go to get their minds off things. A little time out. Call a place like this and talk out your problems.

* * *

The following young man lived with his father and stepmother. He was abused and given many household chores to do. He felt that he was being used as a maid. He finally said he wouldn't take any more abuse.

A Street Dancer

["Julingus" is a 16-year-old African American male. He dresses somewhat flamboyantly and wears modified dreadlocks. He is very articulate.
He ran away from home, where he had been living with his father and
stepmother. The immediate cause was his father's beating him with a dog
leash. There was no information about the stepmother or about the father's
family. The mother is recorded to be a crack addict. According to the
records, his father drinks and smokes pot. "Julingus" is recorded as being
a male "Cinderella," doing all the chores and taking care of his brother.]

Family. My father is 37 years old, a construction worker. I think he
drinks and smokes too much. He married again. My brother is 2.

My mother is 38 years old, and lives in [another state]. She also has a
daughter a year younger [15] than me. They live together.

I feel like a housekeeper. I ran away two times before. Once I went to
an aunt and the other time to my grandmother.

I'm in the 10th grade of high school. I'm not too good in school and
wouldn't go if I didn't have to. I hate school. It's boring. I don't like the
teachers or the other students. But I haven't missed any school.

I am a dancer, a street or break dancer. I dance at clubs, at parties and
on the street if I have a radio. I dance for money if I can but do it anyway
'cause I love dancing. I'm really good at it. Whenever I get a chance I
dance. It's the only thing I really want to do.

My dad has always beaten me—not often, but whenever things built up.
Then he beat me really badly. I got fed up with having to be a housekeeper
and being abused. I love my younger brother but also don't like him. He's
a pain, spoiled. I first ran away one month ago. I went to my mother's sister.
After a short while my father's mom came and took me to her house. I
stayed there for a week.

Then my father took me back home and put me on restrictions. I wasn't
permitted to go out except to school or to talk on the phone. After one and
a half weeks, when I got caught talking on the phone, my father grabbed
me around the neck. It hurt. I left the next day. First I went to a friend's
house, around the corner. I stayed there three days. Then the friend's
mother sent me to my grandmother's. The police were looking for me.
Grandma was afraid of getting into trouble so she called my father. My
father took me home and beat me something terrible. He said the police
gave him permission to hit me.

I spoke to a friend who told me the shelter was a good place. When I
called the shelter I was told I couldn't come on my own but I had to come

through [the protective agency]. The next day, I went to a teacher who I like. The teacher suggested I talk to the principal, who told me to talk to the social worker at the school. After I explained what had been happening the social worker called [the protective agency]. I already had a worker from earlier. Then I went back to my grandmother's to meet the worker. The worker brought me here to the shelter. I've been here a week now. I'm glad I came here. I think that before everything is finished I'll have to go to another place like this and then to a group home.

The police weren't helpful. They just told me to go back home.

I want to live in a nice place where I can go outside and do the things I like to do. I dream of becoming the best dancer I can possibly be. I want to be known and recognized for my dancing. Or, maybe I will become a doctor.

I don't ever want to see my father again. I love my mom and I want to keep in touch with my sister and younger brother. But I just want to live happily. People should live in peace and harmony. Let's not fight. We should live together with no racism—like brothers.

For other people like me there should always be shelters like this one. There should be a hot line they could call when they are in trouble. Young people who need it should be able to just come to a place like this alone. They should be able to help themselves by coming here.

* * *

We now move to a small, shore town shelter.

COASTAL HOUSE:
CHILDREN IN A SMALL TOWN SHELTER

In a small town near a coast, the RHYA program is in a four-bedroom, ranch style house, similar to surrounding houses. It is on a wooded street with large lots at the edge of the town.

There were eight children in the shelter when the appointment was made. Two days later, when interviewed, only six were in residence, four female and two male. One female and one male did not want to be interviewed.

This is a young mother who has been separated from her child. She dreams of a stable family situation in which she can be reunited with her child. She left her biological parents' house.

A 17-Year-Old Mother: Babbs

[Babbs is a thin, relatively short young woman with hair dyed bright red. She talks almost compulsively about her situation, with occasional dramatic flourishes.]

We're Scottish, English, and Southern or rebel. I'm 17. I finished the 9th grade and signed out in the 10th. I had to take care of my baby son, who's 18 months old. He was born on my 16th birthday. I'm not interested in school. I can't think in terms of going [to] school or work. I'm going to marry my boyfriend and stay home and take care of my family.

I grew up in a small town, not far from here. I am the middle one, the only girl. My family is my parents, two brothers and baby son. We live in a house next to my dad's parent's house. We're Baptist though our mother is Catholic. I don't go to church.

My father beat me all the time. He's in his mid-forties. He's a salesman. He's worked for the same company for 17 years and makes good money. I'm not sure if he went to college, but I know he graduated from high school. His sister lives very far away. They're the only kids. He's very close with his folks.

My mother is in the mid-forties. She has a license to work on heating equipment. She's real sweet, and we get along OK although we argue sometimes. I could never hit my mom. I respect her too much. She sometimes hits me but it doesn't hurt much, not like Dad's beatings.

She works at a military base as a school custodian. Mom had a hell of a life. She was one of fourteen children. They were all beaten by their father. One of my aunts was raped by him and then later by Hell's Angels. She's mental. Mom's mother left them all and they were put in foster care.

I loved my dad's folks. I used to spend most of the time with them. I was Granddaddy's little girl. He died when I was 10. We did everything together. I often slept or ate there. It was a haven. My dad's sister despises me because she's jealous that Granddaddy loved me more than her.

My baby is very big. When he was born he was half as tall as me and almost 10 pounds. He was born a month late. He had a 15' head and was the biggest baby in the nursery. The nurses called him little bubba. He never wore new-born clothes—he was too big.

[He was a birthday present?] I really suffered when he was born. I had a really bad time. Labor took 24 hours. I finally had an emergency C-section. I didn't believe in abortion then. I changed my mind and since then had two abortions. I'm not ready to have another kid now. When we're settled I want some more, but not now.

My parents have custody of my boy until I'm 19 and he is 3. They've cared for him since he was born. They love him and take good care of him. Mom takes him with her to work and leaves him at the base's day care center. They're really good to him. But I want him back. He's mine, you know.

I never got along with my father. He's a jerk. I can't stand him. He thinks everything revolves around him. He's overprotective. I've been under the supervision of [the state child protective agency] since I was 13. When I was pregnant he kept on beating me. But he was careful not to hit me where it might hurt the baby. He hit me on the face. Once he cut my hair, battered my face and gave me a concussion. My grandmom called the police twice about my dad's abuse. He also used to beat Mom a lot—until two years ago when my older brother beat him and warned him not to hit her again. He hasn't since, far as I know.

I was kicked out three times and left home once. This is the second time I've been here. I won't go back home again. My boyfriend has known me for years and takes good care of me. He's one of the few who didn't hit me.

I don't know very much about my boyfriend. He doesn't like to talk too much. His father left him and his mother when he was a little boy. Babbs is his nickname for me. I don't like to ask him too many questions because it upsets him. I think he's also a Baptist but like me he don't go to church. He graduated from high school. We're going to move south for him to get a job. Everything is cheaper down there. But I'll be coming back to visit my son every two weeks so he won't forget me. I hope I can finish high school there. This time I'm gone for good. Dad doesn't want me in the house anymore. He loves my son, though.

The first time I was thrown out of the house I went to the police. They contacted [the child protective agency], which put me here. This time I been in a foster home and program for those in trouble with the law. The police had me transferred to the shelter. My dad and I had a big fight. He accused me of taking one of his guns so I could kill him. He had me arrested. I didn't take the gun. I don't know what happened to it.

I'll miss Mom and Grandma. I get along OK with my brothers but I won't miss them. Grandmom will be moving south near me in a few years. I really want her to do that. She's the one I love the most.

I would like to have three wishes filled. First I would like to have Granddaddy back. Second I would like to get rid of my dad. Third I would like to have a decent life. I hope everybody would change and get along, be nice to each other. I've been through hell.

I'm taking all my boy's clothes that mom doesn't use yet, to be prepared for when he comes. I'd like to have another child in two or three years, but not now.

Not only children but parents should be straightened up too. There should be physical abuse groups for them to help them. Parents are as much or more at fault than children. There should be more places like this one—a decent place—for young people to go to. Kids, if anything is wrong, get counseling, help. I don't want to tell adults anything. If they don't know any better that's their own problem.

The police helped me and so did the home tutor from the school. In ninth grade when I was pregnant I had a tutor and she was good. [The child protective agency] helped me a lot and the counselor at the shelter has been really nice.

* * *

The following young man although he has a very complicated and difficult family background says, "Don't run away."

Shorty

[Shorty, 14 years old, is a dark-skinned, Hispanic male. The family history is very confusing and full of broken relationships. All grandparents are "divorced." His parents separated before he was born. His family lives in or near a small inland resort town.]

My father is 34 and a Protestant. He has one brother and one sister. My mother, 33, is Catholic. My mother uses drugs and drinks a lot. She has two brothers and 'about 15 foster or adopted' [siblings]. Her mother is in her late forties. I don't know how old her father is.

My sister is two years older than me. She is smart, a senior in high school. She skipped a grade and is going to go to college. Each of my parents has a younger son.

I don't like school except that I see my friends there. But I do pretty good in school. I graduated from the eighth grade and will be starting high school in the fall.

I have a 5-month-old son living with his mother, my ex-girlfriend, and her parents. They are half Hispanic and half white. She's 16. I wish we hadn't had the child. I only see him sometimes and it makes me sad I can't do anything for him.

I've been living with my mom's grandfather. Now the court has ordered me to live with my father. I have to go there in a few days. I don't like it and I'll just run away again. I don't like him. My father's a salesman for a large company. He hit me a lot. I only fight with him, not with my mom or grandparents or anyone else.

I've been moving between family since I was 10 years old. I ran away three or four times. I moved from one school to another. I've been in lots of schools. The counselors at the schools helped me see that it wasn't my fault that God made life this way and that it would someday work out in my favor.

[It is not clear if he left home as a runaway or was ejected.] We had a family fight. I called up [the old protective agency worker]. I had been given a new worker so he referred me to the new worker. Meanwhile I stayed with a friend. The new worker sent me to the shelter. I've been at the shelter for nearly a month now. I don't know why they're insisting that I go live with my father. I told them I don't want to be with him. I want to live with my mother or grandmother. They won't let me. The court declared my mother wasn't living in good conditions.

[According to the records, Shorty was removed from his grandmother and uncle's home because of abuse and neglect. Both the shelter and the protective agency are concerned that Shorty is resistant to his father but they don't see another alternative.]

I'd like to become a veterinarian, 'cause I love animals. I'd also like to have a nice family—two or three kids and a nice wife. We would live in a town like where I live. I wouldn't mind working in a place like this one. I'd like to come back as a volunteer.

[How can kids be helped?] More attention should be paid to kids. All kids with these kinds of problems should hold on. They should try to work things out or go to a counselor, police or protective agency for help to work things out. *Don't run away!* But no parent has a right to violate a child's privacy or to beat them.

* * *

The next young woman is from an intercultural marriage that didn't last. She has been torn between her parents and is looking forward to making a new life for herself.

"I Want to Get on With Life": Sonny

[She is an articulate, attractive, dark-haired, mature-looking 17-year-old who is going into the 10th grade in the fall. She's a Baptist. Her parents divorced and remarried.]

My father, 37, is a southern white Baptist, part Indian. He has one brother. He dropped out of school in the 10th grade and joined the service. After he finished the service he worked as a stock clerk at night but he is an artist. He would get a great job if he went back to school. He is with his third wife, youngest son and stepson in [a southern border state]. He lives near his mom. My stepmother is almost thirty. My brother lives with Dad's mom. My father didn't have any children from his first marriage.

My mother, 36, is a Puerto Rican Catholic. She has 10 brothers and sisters. She was born in Brooklyn, New York, but moved [to this state]. My mother graduated from high school but she really has a third-grade education. She doesn't read or write very well. She is in the process of divorcing her second husband. She has been a drinker and drug user for many years. I'm very concerned about my brother who lives with her and I want to help him.

My family is kind of mixed up. My brother is two years younger than I am and each of my parents had another son from their next marriage. I also have a stepbrother from my stepmother.

When my parents first split up we stayed with our mother. About 10 years ago Mom's parents called my dad and told him that there was drug dealing, usage and alcohol abuse in our house. I found a sugar cube with "acid" on it when I was 6. I took it and overdosed. My mother beat me with a belt buckle, which hurt me very bad. My father and grandmother in the South got custody of both of us.

My brother has lived with my grandmother since then. I lived with my father, then my grandmother and then in a state Baptist children's home. I'm not sure why they moved me around so much. Several months ago I decided to leave the home because some young men who worked there were harassing me. I developed ulcers and various things. The staff of the home accused me of faking being sick and lying about the staff.

I arranged with my mother that I would leave the home and take a bus to [the nearest large city]. My mother agreed to pick me up there. Friends at the home helped me. I was scared to be traveling alone, so I attached myself to an adult so that it would seem I was not alone. When I arrived my mother came late to meet me. This frightened me. After I stayed with my mother and stepfather, I saw that they were fighting a lot and mom was drinking and taking drugs. Mom had promised that all that had changed. After three months, I realized that I couldn't live there. I called the police and my father. The police took me from the house and called [the protective agency]. They sent me to the shelter. I'm waiting for my father, stepmother and grandmother to come and pick me up.

I can't wait until I'm 18 and can get on with my life. I want to graduate from high school so I can go into the service. I would like to be either a nurse or a navigator—some field where I can help people. I might go through college and the ROTC so I can become an officer. I would like to work with people. Even though I have lots of problems I like to help people, to make them feel good.

[How can other kids be helped?] There ought to be more places like this and they need to be better known. I didn't know about the shelter before I was put here. There need to be educational programs for kids to help them deal with problem parents. Someone should help parents who are not doing things right—this might be someone from the family. Schools should help kids like me; instead they often go back to the family.

I'm looking forward to my family coming to pick me up so I can start on my grownup life. The counseling I got at the shelter helped me to understand things better.

* * *

The final young woman is from an "intact" family. She was heading for college in the near future and hoped that would enable her parents to acknowledge that she was growing up. She felt that her situation was petty compared with that of the other young people in the shelter with her.

"Parents Have to Let Children Grow Up": Lisa

[Lisa is 17, well dressed, and articulate.] My situation is so boring. It's ridiculous, especially when you compare it to that of the other kids at the shelter. My situation would not interest anyone and I really don't want to discuss it.

I live in [a neighboring small town]. I work at an amusement park in the summer. I just graduated from high school and will be starting college in the fall. I'll live in the dorms.

My family is pretty comfortable. We live in a nice, big house and have everything we need. My father is (Slavic) Catholic about 40 years old. He graduated from college. He works as an accountant for a big company which sells medical products from overseas. He has a big job as comptroller of the company. He has one brother. His parents live about 1-1½ hours away in [another part of the state]. They are retired and live on a big pension. His father worked in business. My mom doesn't get along well with them so we hardly ever see them.

My mother, also about 40, is Greek, Italian, and American Indian. She had one year of college but doesn't work. She volunteers for the Girl Scouts and other organizations. She is very close to us, her children. I've got two younger sisters. We're all about four years apart. Mom also has two sisters. Her parents live nearby. Mom's mother is in her late sixties and came as a young child from Greece. She works for a cosmetics packaging company. Mom's father, in his midsixties. He works as a truck driver. He worked hard for everything he did. Our family is Greek Orthodox, but not too much.

[According to the records, Lisa's mother's sisters are "problematic" and Lisa's mother is afraid Lisa will be like them.]

I'm basically a good kid. I don't drink or smoke. Before this I was very close to my mother. She knows everything about my life. Then I do one thing wrong and it causes a big catastrophe. I want a little independence. This was the second time this year my mother got angry and declared me persona non grata. The family found out about the shelter the first time. Most of my problems are because my parents don't approve of my boyfriend.

What caused this ridiculous problem was I stayed late at work one day and stopped at a friend's on the way home without telling my mother. She expected me home early. The weather looked like it wouldn't be good for work, so Mom told me to come home early. However, the management asked me to work late. Then I stopped on the way home. My mother was very upset that I didn't come home when she expected and that I hadn't called. When I got home she was angry, said she hated me and she had been worried.

The next morning I went to the hardware store with my father. When we returned home, my mother had moved all my things from my room and put them in the attic. She forbade me to use the room and my things. I had to sleep on the couch. I got very angry and said I was leaving. We had a big fight and my mother threw me on the floor and laid on top of me to stop me from leaving the house. I bit her finger and my mother left the house with my two younger sisters. She moved into a motel and refused to return unless I left. My father stayed with me but after two days gave in to her. They called the shelter and my father brought me here. I've been at the shelter for two weeks. I'm returning home tomorrow under strict restrictions.

My parents have given me three choices, all bad. I can live at home like a boarder and not talk to anyone. I can live there with severe restrictions. I can live somewhere else. I didn't have a choice. How could I live at home like a stranger? Where else would I go? I agreed to return home under the conditions. They're about my social activities, phone calls, and personal life. I will have really hard restrictions. The situation is all boring, stupid, blown out of proportions. I feel ridiculous being in the shelter and telling this story.

My mother's anger will blow over. It's all been a waste of time, energy, and emotion. I want to develop a more adult relationship with my family. I'll continue to love them but be independent.

I'm just waiting to leave for college. It's less than two months. There my parents can't restrict me and control my life. In college I'm going to major in psychology and animal behavior. I've wanted to work as an animal trainer and with animals since I've been small.

[What would be helpful to others?] Places like the shelter are good for providing a cooling down place. When you're having trouble with your family you need to be able to get away from them and the trouble. People here really care about us. The important thing is that the counselors try and help the family communicate better with each other. I don't think they did too well with my parents, but they helped me understand things better. The most important thing is that parents have to let children grow up and become independent. They can't keep you a child forever.

DISCUSSION

These youth all felt abused, misused, and mistreated. All had some vision of a better family. Only the two sisters, who were among the youngest, looked forward to reunion with the parent with whom they had been living and to reestablishment of their family. Most of the others stated that they did not want to go back to the parent(s) they had been with. They just wanted to forget it all and get on with their lives. Some had fantasies of reunion with unknown parent(s) or placement in caring foster families and a new happy family life. Older youth were ready to go out on their own and live adult lives. A number of them had very unrealistic notions of their futures. All had dreams of some happy home and loving family.

Of the young women, one had a baby and another was pregnant. Both were planning to have families of their own and raise their children, although they clearly were not well prepared for the task.

For many of the youth, there is almost an unreal, dreamlike quality to their notions of the future. They look at the future with rose-colored glasses. Only one of the older females talked about learning something from the experience and the counseling.

The children's stories of their family relationships portray families in which the children are exploited, abused, and mistreated; parents are jealous of their own children; adults are angry; communication virtually doesn't exist. In a number of the families, parents are substance abusers. Although all the young people have a fantasy of happy families, most come from dysfunctional ones. Even in the seemingly functional family in which the family relationships are thought to be warm and close, there is simmering trouble. The mother violently turns against her daughter at a major sign of independence and disobedience.

The goal of family reunion as set forth in most programs for unaccompanied youth seems unrealistic when one considers these stories. Although many unaccompanied minors do go home, those with situations such as these seem better served by other solutions. They should be moved toward more realistic visions of life and enabled to take care of themselves, particularly teenagers 16 and older. Younger children need solutions that would provide the stability and nurturance that they apparently have missed. This indicates a need for longer-range rehabilitative services, group homes, selected foster homes, or some other transitional living and support programs.

The response expressed by all the youth to the programs at the shelters was positive. They felt that it was good to have a place where people seemed to care and tried to help. It was hard to get them to pinpoint what was helpful. In a few cases, the counseling and help in developing insight were cited as important. In general, most of the youth just seemed to be grateful to be in a safe place where they found respite.

Recommendations for helping unaccompanied children are in another chapter. Included there are descriptions of various programs, the shelters in which these children were, as well as a regional response to the needs of unaccompanied youth.

Chapter 6

FAMILIES

Homeless families are probably not different than many housed families in having various family difficulties. The director, in 1993, of OSHA, the city program for the homeless, believes "housed families are exactly like homeless families except for the important additional factor of homelessness."

In this chapter, five homeless families' stories are related. They are, primarily, the parents' view of their situations and lives because most of the children were too young to tell very much, although, when possible, the children's voices have been included. All have suffered major dislocations and shocks. Some of the parents are goal oriented and rather organized; some self-destructive. Some of the families have good relationships; some not so good.

The five families were partially overlapping "guests" of a small rehabilitative program. The parents are from different economic, religious, and ethnic backgrounds. The goal of the program is for the parents to break any addiction, find a permanent place to live and a regular source of income, and improve life skills. The families have contact with many different volunteers. The average stay is three or four months although one of the families stayed eleven months in the program.

All names, places, and specific details have been altered to ensure confidentiality. The first mother comes from a middle-class background. Her mother and stepfather have had a stable relationship for many years and live comfortably in their own home in the city in which she has been homeless.

JUDY, JONATHAN, AND KARLA

[Judy, 26, is African American and has three children—Audrey (staying elsewhere), Jonathan, and Karla. Judy, Jonathan, and Karla were nearing the end of their stay with the program. Their room was quite disorderly, with partially-made beds, bundles open and lying around, and generally little care shown to amenities. Judy and her family were leaving the program without graduating.]

I never thought I would be in this position. When I saw other people living on the streets I thought that they were different from me. *They* didn't manage well. I was raised in a good, comfortable, Christian home, brought up in church. I learned to turn the other cheek and to follow the Golden Rule. I always tried to help other people but they took advantage of me.

I was born in 1966, in Carmel. My parents divorced when I was 2. I am their only child though I have half siblings from their second marriages. As a child, I lived with my mother in Carmel. When my mother got remarried, we moved to Rehovoth, where I went to high school and graduated. Most of my family are still in Carmel. My life has been spent in these two places.

After Audrey was born I continued living with my parents. But when I was 19, and pregnant [with Jonathan], my mother and stepfather made me leave because they disapproved of my boyfriend and the way I was living. I went to live with my mother's mother in Carmel, where I met Karla's father. We got married after she was born and had a nice apartment in a suburb there. We lived real good but then things went wrong and we lost everything.

I went to school to be a beautician and that's what I've done mostly. I also have done secretarial work. The problem is I can't work a computer. Most of the work I've done has been under the table so I could also get Welfare. I'm working now for minimum wage. The director of the program made me do it. It's a dead-end job and doesn't give me time to do what's needed to get out of this situation.

My mother is in her mid-forties. She's been a registered nurse [RN] for 20 years and works in a hospital emergency room. She's also an only child, born and raised in Carmel. She's been married twice. My 12-year-old brother is my stepfather's son. They live here in Rehovoth and own their own house. They live real nice.

My [maternal] grandmother, in Carmel, has been a widow for 20 years. She graduated from high school and had one year of college. She worked as a seamstress and was really good at it. I've lived with her on and off since they first threw me out. Audrey [the oldest child], is living with her and going to school in Carmel while we're here.

My father is in his late forties and lives in Carmel with my stepmother and their four children. He's a high school graduate and computer technician. He has a nice house and everything. I have a hard time saying anything good about him. I don't like him or his family. [Her father and stepmother have a daughter and three sons.] My half sister is one year younger than me.

My dad's father really broke up their marriage. He blamed my mother for my having asthma as a baby. He thought that my mother didn't take good care of me.

My stepfather is a year younger than my mother. I don't like him at all. He works at the post office and graduated from high school.

My brother is a spoiled brat. I've got sibling rivalry. . . . He has his own room with a phone; an Apple computer; and a large, color TV. I didn't have all this. I had only a small black and white TV and he got everything. [Her friend sitting in on the interview said that Judy spoils him also, with which she agreed. The records indicate that she also was materially well off while with her mother and stepfather. Her mother claimed she was spoiled.]

Until I was 19 everything was fine. Then on Christmas my mother and stepfather threw me out of the house, pregnant and with a 3-month-old. I lived for two years with my grandmother. Then I got an apartment with my fiancé. He's not very educated but he always worked, generally semiskilled jobs. Everything was good until we were burned out of our apartment and had to go to a shelter.

Audrey was sexually molested by a woman in the shelter. Because of that we left the shelter with another family and rented a large house. Then my husband started abusing me and I found he was using drugs. When he lied it made me really angry. Then things got more mixed up. He had an accident and was unable to work so we moved to the city [Carmel] and I went on Welfare. After a while I couldn't stand it any more, him lying, abusing me and using drugs, and I went back to my grandmother for a while. He started threatening to hurt and kill me. To get away from this I came here to my mother. We stayed with her over the winter. I graduated from beauty school and got a beautician's license then.

I started to work and rented a house, which turned out to have structural problems. When I withheld the rent I got evicted so we had to move again. After six months the new house was sold. For eight months we moved from one place to another. Always there were some problems with the houses. One house was condemned. After three months, at the beginning of summer, we ended up in a large shelter. Because Audrey had been molested in the other shelter I sent her to her father in Carmel for the summer. When school started she went to live with my grandmother to go to school.

After a month in the shelter Jonathan got very sick. As a result the three of us were thrown out of the shelter. For a month or so me and the two children stayed with one friend and another, finally in September (four months prior to interview) we came here.

I'm not happy with this situation. It's not good for me and the kids, even though it is better than a public shelter. In the shelters, you're treated as if you're an addict. They make you go to AA and NA meetings even if you don't need it. Here there is more freedom. But 90 days isn't enough time. They can't do what they promised. I get angry when things don't go the way they should.

I don't like the constant changes. Just when you get comfortable you have to move. It would be better if you could stay in one place. Another thing is all the volunteers. It makes me nervous leaving my things alone all day. I'm afraid they'll get stolen. How do you know who all those people are? It's like being in a warehouse.

The director pressured me into taking a minimum wage, low-skilled job with wages that barely cover day care. The director is pushing me to do things that take a long time. I'm on the waiting list for apartments in several projects but I don't know when they'll be available. I can't stand to start moving from one friend to another. I'm ashamed to be in a condition like this and wish I could get better quickly.

The situation hasn't worked out well for the children either. At first things seemed to be all right with the younger children. Audrey hates being away from the family. She made things tough for her father and then my grandmother. She had lots of problems in school. But since Christmas she seems to be doing better. Karla became angry about one month after we came here. She started fighting with kids in school who had homes. She is very unhappy and cries a lot. She says she wants her own place to live. Jonathan doesn't want me to work. He wants me to be around. He hates all the changes and can't understand them. The hardest thing is working and keeping up a happy image for the kids when I feel so bad. I want to go to nursing school and get an apartment so we can all be together again.

Things are really wrong. There should be more jobs available that pay decent wages. What are you supposed to do with your children? Day care costs $110 a week for two children. People either have to make a lot more money or day care has to be less. Housing needs to be cheaper too. It's strange that there're all these abandoned houses around and people have no place to live. There needs to be money to fix up and keep all those houses fixed up.

[*Jonathan,* a very pleasant 5-year-old, played incessantly when the interviewer was around. His speech was quite articulate and certainly at age level, if not above. He played quite harmoniously with the other boys. He had befriended Eddie, the 2½-year-old son of a volunteer. He and Eddie looked forward to their meeting once a week over a period of five weeks. They talked about each other during the week between visits. The other children would announce when they saw the volunteer and his son, "Here's your friend Eddie." Jonathan was very protective of the younger boy. He held his hand when they went from one place to another, such as from the dining room to the play room. He pushed him on various toy vehicles. They would run to greet each other with hugs when meeting.]

[*Karla* seemed to be an unhappy little girl. Her hair was usually only partially kempt. She often had a runny nose and had frequent disputes with the other children. She often kept her finger in her mouth and frequently went crying to her mother. Judy held her and kissed her at times; at other times she would admonish her not to cry.]

Judy seems to have somewhat unrealistic constructs of what has happened and about her life. She is rather dissatisfied with what has been done to help her and blames her situation on other people taking advantage of her. She claims that she never expected to be homeless but has been homeless on and off for a number of years. In the end, she rejects the help in the form in which it is offered and goes off to solve her life's situation on her own. The next family has a much more positive response to the help offered. The mother had a rather disorganized and disrupted early youth. She had a very stable middle-class foster family, however, and seems on the way to reorganizing her life.

YOLANDA AND SANDY

[Yolanda, a 32-year-old African American, was born in 1960 in Rehovoth. She and her son Sandy had been in the program for about one and a half months at the time of the interviews. She has two younger children who are living with their father until she gets an apartment and job. The interview was held in Yolanda and Sandy's room. It was very neatly organized, beds nicely made, luggage neatly stacked and closed, things put away. A table had some personal belongings and photos of the three children and a photo of Yolanda at a holiday party.]

My mother worked in a bar and was involved with a married man who was my father. I was her sixth child. There were two more children born after that, eight in all. I don't know anything about my mother and all my brothers and sisters, and haven't had contact with them. At 2 I was put up for adoption but ended up in foster care. But it's really like I did get adopted. I stayed with my foster family until I was 21. I see and talk to my foster family all the time. They are my family.

My foster father died of cancer when I was 5. My foster mother is my mom. She's a schoolteacher. They didn't have any children of their own so they took in eight children, two girls and six boys. That's who're my brothers and sisters. We lived nicely.

I graduated from vocational high school with a business diploma. At 21 I went into the Job Corps for three months in [another part of the country]. There I got on-the-job training. When I left the Job Corps I married my boyfriend. He was in the service. Within a year Sandy was born. When Sandy was 2, my husband left the service. The three of us returned here and moved in with my husband's mother.

Then the problems between us got bad and we separated. I got me a job and apartment. At first I worked in unskilled industrial jobs. After a few years I got a secretarial job with a branch of the armed forces. I had that job for two and a half years. Then I got a better-paying job in private industry, which I kept for a year until I got pregnant and took maternity leave. I never went back to that job.

A boyfriend is the father of my 3-year-old daughter and son almost 2. We lived together for a while but there were some big problems. Several times we had fights that put me in the hospital. Five months ago he told me to leave and take Sandy. I left the two younger children with him until I found a place to live.

For a while Sandy and I lived with my niece. She's one of my foster sister's daughters. Their place was nice. But they used kerosene for heat. I can't stand the smell of it and am afraid of fires. I had to leave them. I went to the [municipal social services], which sent me to a shelter. From there we came here.

Sandy and I have been with the program for two months. I'm using this as a time to pull myself together. I'm going to school for computer operations and saving money to rent a house. I'll probably graduate from the computer training in six months. However, I think I'll have money for a house in three or four months. Then I'll get the two younger children and we will all be together.

The program has been a good experience, uplifting and fulfilling. It enabled me to take care of things without worrying about keeping a roof over our head. The changes and all the people didn't bother us. Sandy [is] adjusting well to it all.

[*Sandy,* 9, also spoke to me. He was in the third grade at a local school.] I flunked a grade. I like this program. It's fun meeting new people. I like the volunteers helping me with my homework. I don't mind anything but being away from my mom. If I couldn't be with her I would be sad and angry. I like school, especially lunch, lunch recess, recess and gym. My favorite subjects are art, music, reading and geography. I don't like science, because I don't like the teacher.

I miss my younger sister and brother. I love 'em and I want to be with them. I'm really looking forward to having a house so we can be together.

[When asked what he wanted] No fighting, no war, arguing, or cussing, just peace and quiet. The main thing is there should be no rap music—just jazz and *no* guns. I like jazz. I also want my own house, to meet new friends and be with my brother and sister. Also we should all have bikes so we can ride together. Mom needs to buy a bike so she can ride also. I'll teach her to ride. Mom should have a job, so we can live OK. I want to get an education and go to college to be a classroom teacher. [At the end he asked if he could write his name and excused his handwriting. He printed his name, "Sanford Major Jones, Jr."] Thanks for talking to me. It was fun.

ROSALYN, SADIKKAH, CARRIE, AND JEAN

The next mother has had a very disorganized and disrupted youth with abuse and sexual molestation. She states that she has been homeless all her life. She has had a number of relationships with men but all seem to have been negative. She does indicate a strong commitment to making a stable home for her children.

[*Rosalyn,* 28, is an African American woman with three children— daughters Sadikkah Jones, 9, and Carrie Johnson, 7, and son Jean (French pronunciation), a year old. All three children have different fathers. At the time of the interviews, she was in the process of making arrangements to move into an apartment, having been with the program for four months.]

I've been homeless or something like it for almost all of my life. I hope it will stop now. I want to get my life together so I can live with my children. I would rather live without a man. They make things too hard.

My parents separated from each other then married other people. Then my father and stepmother separated. However, my mother and stepfather live with my two sisters and two brothers. A mother's children are your brothers and sisters. A father's children are half brothers and sisters. My mother has nine sisters. She also has another daughter four years older than me who never lived with us.

My father has two younger children, my half brother one year younger than me and my half sister five years younger.

I love my father and stepmother. I love him dearly even though he is far from perfect. He is a womanizer and has always broken his promises. I think of my stepmother as my mom. I lived with her when I was 6 and 7 years old and again in my teens. I hate and always hated my mother and stepfather. My mother always beat me because I looked like my father. My stepfather molested me and my mother did nothing although she knew about it.

I started running away when I was 5 years old. The first time was in the middle of the winter. It was snowing. I went out in shorts, a T-shirt and sneakers to go to my mother's friend who I loved and thought of as an aunt. I walked across streets and far to the projects but couldn't remember the building in which my "aunt" lived. I was standing on the corner not knowing what to do. I thought of calling my [paternal] grandmother. I knew her number. I asked a passing man to help since I couldn't explain where I was except near aunt Jeanne's. The man told Grandma where I was. Grandma called the police, who returned me to my mother. After that I ran away about three or four times a year until I joined the Job Corps when I was 15. This was after I had a miscarriage because my boyfriend beat me when he found out I was pregnant.

I stayed in the Corps for three years and got my GED. I left the Job Corps when I was 18 and became pregnant with Sadikkah. I lived then with a friend and was very sick for four to five months. When I was better I got a job as a cook and then my own apartment. After a while I couldn't keep up the rent so me and the baby went to live with my stepmother for a year. Then I moved and lived with my mother's sister from 19 to 21. I met Carrie's father then. I never lived with him but with his niece while we were going together. I felt there was no future with him and stopped the relationship but we are still friends. We lived in a bad neighborhood but I kept the apartment for a while.

Then I married another man but the marriage was bad from the start. We fought all the time. I prayed I wouldn't get pregnant and have his child. My prayers were answered. I didn't have a child. The marriage lasted for 11 months. We had rented a three-story house, which I kept for a while but it was too expensive to maintain.

Then I moved in with my dad's mother in 1990. While there I went back to high school. I got my diploma and went to the prom.

After, I went to a career center to become a secretary. But just before I was to graduate I found out I was pregnant again by another man. When Jean was a year old I went back to school. I won a lawsuit against [a company where she had worked]. With the money I bought furniture and got an apartment where I stayed for a short time. It became too difficult living on my own and with relatives and I was referred to the program. My children hate me and the instability of their lives and feel I'm not a good mother.

[In the four-plus months Rosalyn had been with the program, she saved up enough money to get an apartment.] I really benefited from the parenting sessions. My relationship with my children has gotten much better. I finished secretarial school and got a job, through an internship, two and a half months after joining the program. The [large nonprofit] agency that hired me as an administrative secretary has about 20 sites. They teach developmentally disabled people life skills. After the probationary four months are up, I'll get a raise. They are also going to start me in a part-time second job. The people at the agency respect me and appreciate my work. I have a lot of responsibility.

When I first got involved here it was very hard. But we have gotten used to it. I appreciate the positive aspects, the help I've received and the ability to catch up on our money situation. We're looking forward to moving into our own apartment and having a stable life for the first time.

[Carrie, who's in the third grade, came over while I was talking to another child and said she wanted to talk to me also. When I was done, she took me to a table in the main room, sat down on one side, and very vivaciously and assertively organized the situation.] Sit on the other side and take a chair. Do you have a clean piece of paper? [She put her name on top. If I stopped writing, she reminded me to keep notes. She was very "official."] What do you call this talk? [She went through several words and settled on "interview" with the help of her sister, who came over as we started. Carrie was clear that it was her interview and she didn't want Sadikkah to interfere.]

What are the questions? [I said that they were about the general situation and how she felt about it.] My mother goes to work and we are getting a very large apartment with lots of rooms on all three sides. The building has a big stair and a lot of floors. There are more rooms on each floor as you go up the staircase. When we went to see the apartment we met my mother's cousin, Peggy, who lives in there. [After checking this with Sadikkah] I have to go do my homework and Sadikkah will finish my interview. [When asked later if she wanted to continue] No, I'm finished.

[*Sadikkah* is in the fifth grade at the local elementary school. She took her sister's place but did her *own* interview. Not liking the place her sister had chosen for the interview, we had to move.] It's too noisy and the other kids are all around. I know where we can have some privacy. [She took me to a corner of the room where the kids have some toys, cleared away the toys, and placed two chairs facing each other.] Sit down. Could you give me some paper? Also could I have that board you're writing on so I can make notes. [As we sat together, the other kids came in to play and see what was going on.] Let's move away from here. I know a good place [a corner of the kitchen]. Let's take our chairs. The children are not permitted in the kitchen but no one will bother us here. [Sadikkah wrote on her piece of paper—Need a house. Very large.]

[Sadikkah was very verbal and talked without much need for prompting.] My mom needs a new apartment. The moving around [in the program] is all right but there are some things wrong. The van is too packed. It's very embarrassed to be living in shelters, most people don't. I was very embarrassed when someone from my class saw us moving with our luggage. The volunteers are nice and stuff, but why do they always serve the food? Sometimes we want to serve ourselves. They also give people who should have a lot too little and the other way. Isn't that dumb? I like spending time with the hosts but sometimes I'm afraid that they are talking about us. In some places the hosts who sleep over don't have their own room and have to sleep in the hallway. If someone came in to rob them they might get hurt.

[What did she like about the program?] I love [the director-counselor] of the program, my school, and the fifth grade. I like science, but not dissecting a frog. I like going to church. We belong to the New Life church. Once I saw Jesus sitting next to the pastor. [Jesus] was talking to me but I couldn't hear him because the pastor was making too much noise.

[What does she want?] I want to have a big house or apartment so we have enough room to live. Sometimes we lived in places where there was no washing machine and dryer. It's embarrassing to be dirty and look bad. We have to have a washing machine and dryer. We also need a couple of bucks in our pocket. I want to go to college and be a medical doctor. I heard they make $100,000 a year. I'll split my money half and half with Mom, so she won't be poor anymore.

[*Jean* was nonverbal and didn't walk yet. He moved around in a walker, usually with a pacifier in his mouth. He interacted normally with the other children, all of whom were older. His sisters kept an eye on him and he kept his eyes on Mommy. When she got out of sight for too long, he would start to cry.]

* * *

The next family started out as a two-parent family but the mother left the program soon and the father and children remained. Their backgrounds are toward the lower end of the socioeconomic scale. He is of Puerto Rican background and she is of Euro-American background.

RANDY AND MARY

[Randy and Mary had entered the program a few weeks before the first interview. Randy, of Puerto Rican background, is very heavy and quite Indian in appearance. He speaks literate, accentless English. Mary is of mixed Western European and American Indian ancestry. With blonde hair, culturally she is essentially working-class Anglo-Protestant. The interview was conducted solely with Randy.]

I met Mary when she was 28 years old and I was 23. My first love, Bonita, threw me over. She's the mother of my oldest daughter, also named Bonita, who's 13. I really loved Bonita and felt awful when she told me she didn't want me anymore. It wasn't even that she had another boyfriend. I even gave her son a name. He's my stepson Jaime, 16, her kid from another guy. I gave him my family name, Gonzalez, and still think of him as my kid.

Mary told me I was her first boyfriend and lover. We've been together for over 11 years. We got married six years ago. We have five children, four of them came here with us: Reggie, 11, Melanie, 5, Linus and Freya, 2-year-old twins. Our other daughter, Diamond, 6, is severely disabled, retarded, epileptic, and with a skin disorder. She eats through a tube in her stomach and is in foster care.

[During the second week in the program, Mary and Randy had an argument, during which Mary became physically abusive and stabbed Randy in the leg with scissors. The other women present came to his aid, called the police, and Mary was committed to a mental hospital. She was discharged from the hospital within two weeks and was staying with her mother. At the time of the interviews, Randy had gotten a restraining order to prevent her coming near him or their children.]

Mary [according to Randy] was born here [in Rehovoth]. She's 40, graduated from high school and worked as a waitress. [Of English, French, German, and American Indian background, she is by appearance a fair Caucasian.] Her parents were cousins. Her father was a skilled construction worker. She has an older brother.

Mary was born in and always lived in this area [where the program is]. Her mother still lives in the same house. The neighborhood changed from mostly Caucasian to mostly black while Mary was in elementary school. She went to school primarily with blacks for the upper grades and high school. She often got into fights and she was bounced around a lot.

Mary was a Daddy's girl. He died 17 years ago. She never got along well with her mother. Mary used to get depressed and went for mental treatment. She gets really nasty, but won't ever apologize. [Reggie said that Mary "often said her father always told her never to say you're sorry and she doesn't."] Mary and her family curse a lot when they talk. I don't like it and don't want my kids to talk like that.

[*Randy,* 35, who is extremely obese, rather short with straight black hair, black eyes, and olive complexion, was born on the West Coast, where the family lived until he was 12. He left school after the tenth grade. Randy speaks English fluently and also Spanish, according to Reggie.]

I've got a sister and a brother. My sister is one year older. She graduated from high school here. She moved back to the West with her husband one year after her son was born, ten years ago. I haven't had contact with her since. My brother who's one year younger left school in the ninth grade. He got involved in petty crime. He left for the Southwest 12 years ago shortly after his son was born deaf. He abandoned his girlfriend and child. They stayed here. He married another woman in the Southwest and had at least one daughter there. I haven't had any contact with him in six years.

My parents married against my mother's family's wishes. She was four years older than my father, Agustino. He came from a large peasant family. He was considered low class by my mother's family. My mother, Dona Miranda, an orphan, lived with her aunt and uncle. They considered themselves high class. They lived in town. An older brother, my uncle, still lives in the same Puerto Rican town. After their marriage they left Puerto Rico for the West Coast.

We were born there and lived there until I was 12. Then we moved East, and after a year moved here. My father brought us to his sister's apartment in a public housing project. We stayed with her for a while. Then one day he went out for cigarettes and never came back. We haven't heard from him in 20 years and don't know where or how he is. This hurt me very much.

Dona Miranda got an apartment in the same project after a few months. That's where we lived and she still lives. She's about 61 years old. She talks about going back to Puerto Rico, but who knows?

She was against both my girlfriends. But she finally accepted Bonita. Not Mary though. It wasn't so bad when we weren't married. When I actually married Mary she disowned me and my children. She didn't like my marrying an American. I haven't seen or heard from her since. [Reggie said that Randy gets very angry if the children say anything joking or bad about Dona Miranda. He'll say, "Don't talk like that about my mother."]

When I left school I became an alcoholic. Most of the time I worked I drank. I finally pulled out of that, but not soon enough. I haven't had a drink for a long time.

For thirteen years, until three years ago, I worked as a shipper and receiver. I became very active in the union. I became a shop steward and eventually a vice president of the local. After a while the union work kept me my job. For a while I also worked part time as a machinist. I made good money with both jobs, but got worn out and had to drop the second job.

I should have saved and invested the money instead of using it for alcohol, pot and cigarettes. I also got problems with my back and leg which interfered with my work. In the past seven years I've gained almost 200 pounds. I was a bit heavy when I was working but weighed almost 375 pounds when we came here.

The problems started when I lost my job. I got laid off when I had to give up the union activity, due to health, three years ago. Then I got unemployment insurance for six months. At the same time Mary had been getting Welfare. After the unemployment ran out I took over the grant and the major problems with Mary started.

Everything was fine between us until the job problems got serious. We had started family counseling about a year before that. Mary then had a recurrence of her problems. We started having arguments and she got violent. She often hit me, sometimes with baseball bats and other implements. She stabbed me in the leg with a kitchen knife, threw bottles at me and cursed a lot. Whenever I would tell someone she would laugh at me and say, "Look at him, how fat he is. Do you believe that I could hurt him?" She also started to psychologically abuse Reggie. She would say to him, "Come here, slave," when she wanted him to do something.

During all this discord and craziness Mary got pregnant again. I was very unprepared for this. I didn't have a job and things were getting more and more chaotic. I had begged her to use birth control since Reggie was born, and even bought it for her but often found them unused, in the drawer. But I would never tell the children that I didn't want them.

After an argument when my unemployment benefits were about to run out Mary took the children and went to stay with her mother. That's when Diamond was put in foster care and the family got a [child protective] worker. The [child protective] agency got involved with the family when

Diamond got hit by a toy hammer Freya threw while they were staying at Mary's mother's house. They made me guardian of the children, and I took over the Welfare grant but we stayed together as a family. Mary started receiving disability payments. [The child protective worker continued working with the family through the time of the interviews.]

When the twins were born we needed more room than we had. We finally found an empty three-story house, that needed a lot of work, nearby. We made an agreement to fix things up and pay a low rent. Mary claimed the kitchen as hers but kept it filthy. I took care of the rest of the apartment.

About a year ago Mary started stealing the house money and spending it on toys for the children and junk. I didn't realize that the rent and water bills weren't getting paid. She was supposed to take care of that. Finally, when we ran up a debt of over $3,000 to the landlord, he talked to me. I told the landlord that we couldn't pay and we were evicted. By then I owed over $5,000 in various debts. The child protective worker told us about the program.

Although we had a month to prepare and I reminded her we needed to pack, she didn't even start packing until a day or two before we had to leave. We left lots of things behind including toys and furniture, although some were put in storage.

I hope that one day Mary will wake up, realize what has happened and come to her senses. She will realize what she should do. I want the Mary I married and a house where all the kids have rooms.

We are very different. I want my kids to grow up with some style and class, to appreciate music and art and know how to dress and talk right. Mary isn't interested in that. I think the kids need discipline; she lets them do anything. I like organization; she doesn't. I don't like cursing; she cursed a lot. We might go back, some time, to marriage counseling.

My goals while here are to save money and pay off all my debts. I also want to finally get my high school equivalency so I can feel that I've accomplished something with my life. I think this will give me confidence. I would like to work in a museum, especially with old stuff. It's amazing the history behind things. They're like hidden secrets. If not I'd like to get an office job. I can't do physical labor anymore with my bad back and leg.

[*Reggie,* 11, is relatively short, slightly chubby, Indian looking, not as swarthy as Randy. He is very verbal and articulate and was a straight A student in the mentally gifted program at his school until the family became homeless. At the time of the interviews, he was in the fifth grade, a grade behind, due to excessive absences. His conversation veered between the childlike and the adult. He had so much to say, talking about his life, that the discussion was long.]

Being poor is terrible. It's particularly embarrassing when my father tells everyone about it. I don't like being seen by other people going into the shelters. I don't like moving around. Yet the [program], all the people and the moving is like an adventure.

I have an adult mentor outside the program through the Big Brothers. My mentor's a journalist. He often takes me to museums and talks to me. We do other things together. My mentor also gave me gifts and, sometimes, money. My dad is jealous of my mentor. I don't know why. My dad sometimes accused me of stealing the money and took it away.

I love science, especially astronomy. I want to be an astronaut to go up among the stars although astronauts can't really go too far away from earth, yet. [He talked a lot about the universe, the black hole and a white hole.] I love to look at the stars. It was interesting to see, at the museum, that constellations actually are not on the same plane, as they are seen by human eyes. For example, Orion, when seen from the side in the museum, is composed of stars at various distances from us, not together at all. It just looks that way from here. I also like to read, particularly adventure stories. I'm saving money to buy a real telescope so I can see what's beyond the world. It is the funnest thing to see that.

My mother is a person who has to spend money. She used to steal our money and spend it all. Because of that we couldn't pay the rent and so got evicted. She is a crazy person. It is very embarrassing. She said all kinds of things and didn't care. She threw things at my father, like a pot of hot coffee, and used to hit him. She didn't pack until the day before we had to leave and so we left a lot of things behind. I had to leave most of my toys and had only a few little things with which to play. Most of our things were put in a storage room. It's so crowded we put the washing machine on top of two dressers. It looks like everything will fall out when you open the door. We left a couch and some chairs at the house.

Things have changed since we've been in the program. Aside from Mom having to go away Dad has become stricter. He saw that from the other parents in the program and copied that from them. I get blamed for too much. Melanie often tells him lies about me, blames me for things. Then he hits me and talks to me but I'm not guilty. Dad believes her. It's like Dad thinks I steal money when I got it from my mentor. I don't understand why I got so much responsibility of taking care of the other children and helping my parents in other ways and yet I'm always yelled at and punished.

A long time ago my mom and I were in a shelter. That wasn't a good time. They should not have taken Diamond away. She is so innocent. . . .

Diamond wasn't neglected! We can take care of her. I miss her and want her to be with the family again.

I want Bonita to be able to spend time with us. I wish we had gotten custody. I see my grandmother sometimes, although my dad doesn't know about it. Despite everything I wish we could have a home again and be a real family with my mother. I also wish we weren't so poor.

This program is good. It's a good idea. It helps families pick themselves up.

[Some months after the interviews, Reggie was sent to a boarding school in the same state but several counties away. He had gone from being a straight A student in the mentally gifted program to a C student in the regular school program. The boarding school program was for gifted children with problems that prevent them from achieving their potential. He did very well at the school and came home periodically to visit the family.]

[Randy was asked how he felt about Reggie being sent away.] I'm used to having my children taken away and not being with me. What can I do? They took away Diamond, didn't let me have Bonita and now Reggie. [He said this without emotion. Then, asked what he felt, he said] Maybe it's the best thing that could have happened to Reggie. [After 11 months in the program Randy got a house and a federal rent subsidy and the family moved. Reggie was doing well at the school.]

[*Melanie,* 6, is a fair-haired, intelligent, pretty girl, very Anglo looking. She veered between being very pleasant and congenial with the other children and being aggressive and regressive. She seemed to need lots of attention, liking to have a volunteer spend time especially with her, reading, talking, and playing. At times she played peacefully with the other children, and at other times she cried, took things, and seemed distressed. She appeared to be bright.]

[*Linus* appears to be a normal 2-year-old. He looked like a mixture of Indian and Anglo, with medium brown hair. He played well with the other children and seemed to be generally well adjusted. After having been in the program for several months, he had apparently accepted the situation and caused relatively few problems. He ate relatively well, had normal motor skills, and talked normally. He often took care of his twin.]

[*Freya* was named, by Randy, after the goddess. Randy said, "If Mary knew that the name is a pagan goddess she would be upset." Freya was cross-eyed and seemed developmentally delayed. She was rather sloppy in her eating, making a terrible mess. She mixed everything together and took much more than she ate. She didn't interact much with the other children, except her brother Linus. She didn't talk very much or understandably.]

* * *

The next family is from a middle-class background but very low social status; the mother's stepfather had porno shops. The mother had a very bad relationship with her stepfather, both her biological parents having died. She was involved in drugs and a common-law marriage. She resisted the program and eventually left it and returned her children to their father so that she could have a relationship with another man.

MIRIAM, DAISY, AND CHRISTOPHER

[Miriam, 32, Caucasian, of Eastern European, Jewish background, is a petite, fair-skinned woman with long, straight, black hair. Her two fair-haired children, Daisy, 8, and Chris, 9, are from her 14-year common-law relationship with Chris Sr., a Caucasian of Catholic background.] Chris and I met at a carnival when I was 18 and he was 17. He was a friend of an acquaintance and offered me a ride home. He took my phone number, called me the next day, and we have been together since. A week ago I left him and came to the program.

When we met he was into drugs and took everything. After two years I also got into heroin and amphetamines. When the children were born we both became clean. Things were going terrific. After a few years we bought a house. Some friend brought stuff to celebrate. We got hooked again. Because of that we lost the house and had to move back to live with Chris's parents. We've been there since. I left him at his parents'.

I don't know very much about my parents and their families. My grandparents and father died when I was very young. I don't know what my father did for a living or anything about his education but don't think he was an immigrant. My mother, also probably not an immigrant, died when I was 11. But two years before, she remarried another Jewish man. I remained with my stepfather until I was 17, when he threw me out. I haven't seen him since. I never got along with him. He was nothing much. After I left him I lived with two different men, then I moved in with Chris.

My stepfather owns five porno stores and is rich. He gets along good with my brother but not with my sister or me. I'm not sure what kind of relationship he has with his own son of his first marriage.

My brother is four years older than me. He owns a shop on jewelers' row and is well-to-do. He went to college and is married to a Jewish woman. They have two children. My sister, two years older, isn't married.

She also went to college and is a professional. They all live near here. I haven't seen my brother and his family in a long time and my sister for eight months since she moved. My family never approved of my relationship with Chris. I don't know my stepbrother. He never lived with us.

Chris has a good relationship with his parents. Their house is in [a middle-class area]. He is the youngest of eight. One of four sisters is a nun in South America, the other three are married and working middle class. One brother who has a wife and children manages a large supermarket. The other three didn't do so good. A second brother died of an overdose and the third is also a dopey. I think the family members get along good with each other.

We both graduated from high school. He worked as a laborer in construction until the last few years. I haven't worked too much. For a few months I worked for a fast-food chain. One night after work my car was hijacked. I couldn't let them get my car without a fight. But it was against company policy to resist and because of that I was fired. On top of that the automobile crashed during the incident and I was injured. Me and the children have been receiving public assistance since then.

When Chris and I first got together we lived a few months with his parents. Then we got our own apartment. When we decided to have a child, we both went to a drug program and got clean. We stayed clean through the birth of both kids and while we were saving to buy a house.

We bought a house in [a working-class area]. The gift of stuff started us both on down into use again. In late 1989 I got disgusted and decided to stop. I went back to the drug program and since then I've been involved with it and clean. Chris first went with me and remained clean for two years. One and a half years ago Chris got involved with drugs again. He never abused me or the children but there were other problems all along. I decided I didn't want to live like that anymore and didn't want that life for the children. I tried to get him off drugs. A week before the interview I gave him an ultimatum: Get off drugs, get back to work and get your life together or we leave. He refused to go back into treatment.

[A counselor at the drug program connected her with the program.] I didn't tell Chris and his parents until we were about to leave. Chris at first didn't want us to leave. We had a big argument. Finally he agreed to let me and Daisy go but he wanted Chris Jr. to stay with him. He took the boy upstairs and put him to bed. Chris Jr. got up, came downstairs and said he wanted to go with me. This was repeated for about an hour and finally Chris let us all go. We haven't been in touch and I don't think Chris knows where we are.

I'm not sure what the future holds for me. I'm not very connected with Jewish tradition but me and Daisy we're Jews. Chris Jr. was baptized Catholic and I'm not sure what he will be. I want to get a job to support myself. Since we've been in the program I've gotten a very good connection with all the children. I'm better with other people's kids than my own. One of the counselors found me a job in a day care, prekindergarten program, which starts in a month. I'm looking forward to starting a new life. I want to get our own place to live. I'm not sure if working with kids is my future. I feel good about the future. I'm finally moving on my own and taking charge of my life. I want my kids to have a normal childhood, go to school and make something of themselves. If you think positive things will work out.

[*Chris Jr.*, a slender, fair, 9-year-old, was generally quiet. He played well with the other children. He seemed to have a pleasant relationship with his mother and sister Daisy. His development seemed on observation to be normal in all ways—speech, motor abilities. He did not seem unduly attached to his mother, but listened to what she said and did what he was asked, usually. He generally ate what was served. There did not seem to be any time during observation that he needed or received any reprimand. It became impossible to interview either child so I don't know how they perceived the situation.]

[*Daisy*, a slender, fair-haired, 8-year-old, seemed more aggressive than her brother and to have a mildly abrasive relationship with her mother. She was reprimanded, several times, by Miriam. Her development was seemingly normal, as were her speech, interaction with other children, and motor abilities.] She's a picky eater like I am [said Miriam. Occasionally she was whiny but that might have been due more to the evening hours than anything else. In general she seemed normal.]

[Epilogue: Miriam got involved with a man, maybe several, and started staying out of the program, often. She never took the job and sent her children to live with their father and grandparents. Eventually, she was asked to leave the program.]

DISCUSSION

Above are the stories of five families—five women and one man, and 12 of their children—who were homeless. Five other children were separated from their parent and siblings.

Although of various ethnic, religious, and "racial" backgrounds, there are striking similarities between them. All of the parents were accepted by a highly selective program, being deemed most likely to reach the goals of steady income and a stable residence.

All of the parents have had serious problems with their own parents, even though, of interest, at the beginning several said they came from good families. Most seemed to have caring and pleasant relationships with their children. All indicated a strong commitment to family and caring for their children. Most were cut adrift while in their adolescence or earlier. All had problematic relationships with mates. Several had histories of drug or alcohol use but were reported to be not using when in the program, and for some time prior had been drug free.

Two of the five parents were dismissed from their program as uncooperative. The one male parent and another female stayed in their programs for substantially longer than the "maximum" allotted time before graduating. It would seem that the standard midterm amount of time was not sufficient for these highly select families.

None of the parents directly reported poverty and insufficient low-income housing as a precipitating cause of their homelessness. They either had serious relationship problems and/or some specific other causal factor, such as injudicious spending.

The children interviewed seemed rather bright. They didn't seem to be terribly distressed about their situations as long as they were with their parent. Some of them were exceptional in their intellectual responses. All wanted to have a more stable family and home situation.

Often people experience broad societal developments as personal defeats or triumphs. It is particularly hard to fit yourself into the statistics of the day. For example, the social factors that are causing divorce are not seen by most divorcing couples as what made them divorce. The social factors behind one- and two-child families or many-child families are not seen as the motivating forces behind a family's decision to have or not to have children. And yet the social factors are there and surely operate as causal agents. The same is true for most homeless families. In many ways, these families are much like many families who never actually become homeless. However, they can be seen to have many interconnected problems.

The children seem able to stand almost anything as long as they are with a parent. They all yearn for getting all their siblings together with the parent in their own home. They have the same dreams other children have.

Chapter 7

BABIES

Homeless babies! Who can accept the idea of homeless babies? This chapter will attempt to clarify some of the issues related to homelessness among babies. Babies homeless with their parent(s) and alone, sick and healthy, will be discussed.

Homeless and abandoned babies are not new phenomena. Babies have been neglected and/or abandoned in all eras (Whitlow, 1993). During times of war, severe poverty, and hardship, babies often were major victims, either through loss of parents or the inability of parents to provide adequate sustenance and care. The abandonment and homelessness of babies are ancient and common.

In modern America, babies are highly and sentimentally regarded. Homeless babies are assumed not to exist. However, there are homeless babies. Most are children of homeless women. Others become homeless because of various factors. There have been reports of an upsurge of abandonment and babies left in hospitals. This chapter will examine the parameters of the issue.

DEVELOPMENTAL ISSUES

Infancy, when the child is most helpless and vulnerable, is a most crucial time in human development. Survival and/or development is impossible without consistent contact with and care from adults. The developmental needs of babies have been exhaustively documented and discussed in numerous books and articles.

Homelessness and the attendant unstable care almost certainly interfere in the responses that children and particularly babies need for adequate if not optimum development. FTT (failure to thrive) syndrome is identified with many of the factors present in homelessness. Having the parental connection disrupted as a neonate or infant thus has probable lifelong negative effects. "Babies born to homeless women are at high risk of developing serious medical and developmental problems. . . . Homeless mothers must overcome . . . barriers to caring for . . . [them] in very compromised settings . . . often without meaningful and effective supports" (Weinreb et al., 1995, p. 493).

HOMELESS WOMEN WITH BABIES

Information, other than intuitional and anecdotal, about babies who are homeless because their mothers (some of them children) are homeless, is virtually nonexistent. It is, however, not difficult to put facts together to uncover a large problem.

Weinreb et al. (1995) suggest that being pregnant or having a child younger than 1 year old is highly associated with homelessness. Studies they cited found AFDC recipients who are pregnant or with newborns to be nine times more likely to be homeless than other AFDC recipients. They also cite findings of up to a 35% pregnancy rate among homeless women. Many programs for homeless families report a high percentage of the children to be under 3 with many less than a year old.

Another index of the probability of homeless babies is the increasing incidence of babies born to unmarried young women. Unmarried mothers have a high risk of being homeless. Each year in the United States many babies are born to unmarried teenagers. Many more are born to or find themselves in single-mother families. In 1989, of all babies born in the United States, 19% of Caucasian and 64.5% of black babies were born out of wedlock. The Caucasian rate has increased four times and the black rate has doubled since 1970 (Liebman, 1993, p. 40).

Among teenage young women in shelter programs, a number are usually pregnant. Many terminate the pregnancies. However, a large number of homeless women either give birth or already have babies. In a Philadelphia program for homeless women, 12 out of 16 of the unaccompanied minor women in the program had at least one baby. Other statistics point to an incidence of around 10% of homeless girls with babies (Shane, 1989).

Many researchers have found homeless mothers to be beset with stress:

> Babies born to homeless women are at high risk of developing serious medical
> and developmental problems. . . . Homeless mothers must overcome the
> continuing barriers to caring for and mothering their newborns in very
> compromised settings and often without meaningful and effective supports.
> (Weinreb et al., 1995, p. 493)

This is a serious aspect of the situation of homeless youth and children. It
needs to be addressed. There is a need for research to ascertain the extent
of the situation and the responses available for this particularly vulnerable
population. Special programs might need to be developed to prevent the
particular damage such a situation can cause.

Teenage homeless mothers and their babies are particularly vulnerable.
Young women, still emotionally immature, are beset with the problems of
homelessness and caring for a baby. How can the homeless teenage mother
adequately provide for and nurture her child(ren) while living an unstable
life, moving from one place to another, under stress, without emotional or
other support, often without any regular source of income? All this at the
very moment in developmental time when both mother and child need the
most consistency and care.

In addition, young mothers are among the least served homeless people.
Many shelters for unaccompanied teens do not accept babies into residence. Many programs for women with children do not accept women
under 21 and even more reject those under 18. There are no solid data about
or special programs or resources for babies of homeless teenage or other
women in the United States at the time of writing. Weinreb et al. (1995)
report on a prenatal program specific to homeless women.

ABANDONED BABIES

In the United States in the late 1980s and early 1990s, there were news
reports of a general increase in abandonment of babies of all ethnicities. In
cities around the United States, abandoned babies were reported as being
found on doorsteps and cars in numbers "not seen recently." There were
"no available statistics on the number of children left in hospitals, churches
or on street corners in cities around the country" (Whitlow, 1993).

Professional organizations became concerned. CWLA (the Child Welfare League of America) conducted a survey of 36 child welfare agencies

in the country to ascertain the extent of the problem of abandoned babies. The agencies reported almost 3,800 abandoned babies or young children during the 12 months of 1991-1992 (CWLA, 1992, p. 7). This was the only verification that such a problem indeed was widespread. Other studies indicate a problem of babies remaining in inner-city hospitals but very little abandonment. Part of the problem may be mixing data of children kept in hospitals after their mothers' discharge (boarder babies) with those of abandonment.

BABIES IN HOSPITALS

Data show that a large number of babies remain in hospitals, in specific locations, longer than necessary. In general, infants kept or left for a period of time in hospitals are of two types: those in need of medical care, and "boarder babies," those not in need of such care. Studies of this problem have been published by CWLA and the New Jersey Hospital Association (NJHA). Data in New Jersey (NJHA, 1991, 1993), Pennsylvania, New York, and in the major metropolitan hospitals surveyed by CWLA (1991) show that many babies are kept or left in hospitals in these areas.

Sources of Data

A CWLA (1991) survey of babies left in hospitals was based on 72 hospitals in 12 cities. (There are, however, problems with generalization of the data. Not having been collected under the same conditions, they cannot be universalized. The data from New York City were from a city-organized survey including 43 hospitals in the city. The figures for Washington, D.C., similarly collected, included 10 hospitals. Other cities had one or two hospitals surveyed directly by CWLA.) Another caveat needed to help understand the data is that different child protective agencies and state laws mandate different diagnoses and dispositions of various cases.

The NJHA did studies of babies and children in New Jersey hospitals in the first quarters of 1991 and 1993. In 1991 and 1993, 75 hospitals were sent questionnaires. In 1991, 57 responded, and 34 reported having boarder babies and children. In 1993, 42 hospitals responded, and 27 reported having boarder babies (NJHA, 1991, 1993). Several different reasons for babies being left in hospitals were found.

Medical Fragility

Some infants were kept in hospitals, often at the direction of the child protective system, because they needed medical care or observation. This is the group of babies considered *medically fragile,*

> a term used by the child protective agency to mean [infants and children who are]: HIV+, drug-exposed, with serious medical conditions requiring strict medical follow-up and/or frequent hospitalizations, Failure-to-Thrive, (FTT) [those] between one and three years who are significantly developmentally delayed or require extraordinary care, over age three and not able to provide adequate personal care to themselves and those requiring specialized medical treatment at home. (NJHA, 1991, p. 11)

In both NJHA surveys, 12% of the boarding children were in hospitals because of medical fragility. CWLA, however, did not report on this condition.

HIV+ babies. Of the medically fragile babies, those who are HIV+ or with AIDS present a special picture. Because they were infected by their HIV+ or AIDS mothers, they are in particularly vulnerable situations. NJHA found in both years that 6% of babies kept in reporting hospitals were HIV+ (NJHA 1991, p. 15; 1993, p. 19). CWLA, in a similar survey, found 2%, or 146, of a sample of 7,284 babies tested HIV+ (although not all were tested) (CWLA, 1992, p. 3). Obviously, the problem has become more serious in areas of the country with the highest incidence of HIV+ women. Thus, in the early 1990s, there were reports of a crisis of HIV+ babies in New York City, Newark, New Jersey, Washington, D.C., Los Angeles, and other cities with high female HIV+ rates.

Addicted babies. Another large group of medically fragile children are born to drug- or alcohol-abusing women. Some are born with addictions or special problems. Addictions are most common with drug-using mothers. Developmental damage is most common with alcoholic and crack-using mothers. Many "crack babies" have been found to be hyperactive and have been diagnosed with attention deficient syndrome. They are hard to place if the mother or family is unable or unwilling to care for them.

CWLA found that 85% of reported babies boarding in hospitals had been exposed to drugs and/or alcohol (CWLA, 1992, p. 3). The New Jersey study does not specify whether the babies were born with drug or alcohol complications. We can assume that, among the babies considered medically fragile, some if not all were suffering from these complications. Of 311 boarder babies in the 1991 New Jersey study, 117, or 37%, had mothers who had used crack, alcohol, or a combination of drugs and/or alcohol. Of these babies, 37 were boarding because they were medically fragile and needed special care not yet available at home; among this group, 5 were awaiting special placement. This is in addition to the 20 HIV+ babies whose mothers also may have used drugs or alcohol and who also may have had some alcohol- or drug-related complications.

Although medically fragile, drug- or alcohol-affected and HIV+ babies do present a difficult scenario in terms of aftercare, but they do not fit into the homeless baby category. However, often as a condition for taking the child home, the mother must enter rehabilitation programs, some of which do not allow babies. Thus babies with extra needs are most likely to have the most complicated and least satisfactory care possibilities.

Boarder babies/children. Most children staying in hospitals longer than necessary are "boarder babies." Boarder babies are the group most often put in the abandoned baby category. Let's see if this is a reasonable assumption.

The Association for Children of New Jersey (ACNJ) reported on the problem of boarder babies in New Jersey in the early 1990s (Patterson, 1993). Boarder babies are "infant[s] who, though medically cleared for discharge cannot go home because there is neither a biological home nor an alternative placement immediately available" (CWLA, 1991, p. 1). A sample description that I received from a major hospital in Newark, New Jersey (University Hospital), for November 1992 through June 1993 shows a total of 71 "boarder babies." All were referred to DYFS, the state child welfare agency.

Three New Jersey counties with the most distressed urban centers and populations—Essex (including Newark), Hudson, and Camden Counties—contained the majority of the problem. In them the numbers were the same or higher in 1993 than in 1991. In three other counties with distressed urban areas, the numbers of children involved were moderate. In most other counties, there were few boarder children.

During the 1991 quarter, the NJHA survey reported 311 boarder babies/children in 34 New Jersey hospitals, and in 1993, 226 boarder babies/children in 27 hospitals. In both years, the overwhelming majority of the children were neonates and infants under a year: 89% in 1991 and 85% in 1993. Children between 1 and 5 years old constituted 8% in 1991 and 7% in 1993. Children between 5 and 18 years old constituted 4% in 1991 and 8% in 1993. The CWLA survey found over 80% of the babies to be under 1 month old and only 5% to be over 1 year old.

Although reports of long stays are common, boarder babies usually spend a relatively short time in hospitals. During the New Jersey study periods, 46% and 48% (for the respective years) were boarders for less than a week, 18% and 19% for two to three weeks, 16% for one to two months, and 1% and 2% for over six months. Thus two thirds spent under three weeks in the hospital.

The primary immediate cause of children becoming boarder babies in the hospitals studied was drug use by the mother; other factors were inadequate housing or inability to properly care for the child.

In New Jersey, DYFS encourages drug testing of delivering mothers and their babies. Positive results must be reported to DYFS. Regulations mandate a drug-positive result be followed by an investigation. DYFS must certify that leaving the hospital is in the baby's best interests.

In Pennsylvania, the situation was quite different. Although drug tests were legal, the child protective system by regulation could not use this information to initiate a family study. In late 1993, there was initiation of legislative action to change this.

Many boarder babies were in hospitals because of bureaucratic misfunction. In 1991, 45%, and in 1993, 55% of the children were in hospitals because the state child protective agency was assessing their situations.

These surveys belie the claims of large numbers of babies abandoned in hospitals. Of the boarder and medically fragile babies in the NJHA survey, *only one was abandoned by its mother.* Approximately half the babies went home to their mothers and another 12.5% went to relatives. From University Hospital, 36 babies went home to their mothers, most within a month. Nine went home to relatives, within the same time period, including the babies of two mothers who were incarcerated. Seven, or 10%, were put in foster care, and two were adopted. Two were sent to another hospital with facilities for more intensively affected babies, one of whom was eventually placed with relatives. For 18 of the children, the outcome is not noted. The survey of New York City hospitals showed that 55% of the boarder babies were eventually discharged to parents or relatives. The rest went into foster care.

However, the sample outside New York City, New Jersey, and Philadelphia had different results. About two thirds were reported not to go to family or relatives. Including the New York data, from all the hospitals surveyed by CWLA only 20+% of the babies were "expected" eventually to leave the hospital with their birth parent(s) and another 15% with relatives. Just under 65% were waiting for alternative care arrangements. Almost 60% of the babies were expected to be placed in one of the following: foster care (accounting for about 50%), group homes, or other residential facilities; 5% were awaiting adoption (CWLA, 1992). Thus, outside of New York, Newark, and Philadelphia, the expected discharge rate to families seems to have been minuscule.

A confusing element of this is the count of *expected* discharge. In New York and the other cities, *actual* discharges are counted. There is no way to determine whether *expected* and *actual* are the same. In addition, there is no indication that the babies were abandoned. It may well have been a result of differential child protective standards in areas outside of the mid-Atlantic metropolitan area.

Longer-term stays. For the cases with hospital stays of over a month (a third of the sample), there were two primary causes. One was that the child protective process was slow. Restricted child protective agency budgets, overloaded workers, and a generally high turnover in staff due to burnout, poor pay, and poor working conditions slow down the process. The other is the lack of alternatives when placement away from the family is necessary. The NJHA (1991) explains this as follows: "Perhaps because of the negative images associated with orphanages, there are very few group homes or shelters for young children in New Jersey." Available foster care placements are insufficient to the demand.

Hospital Issues

The hospitals are unhappy with the situation. The NJHA (1991) describes hospitals as being "the parents of last resort for some of New Jersey's children." They illustrate how "hospitals make good surrogate foster parents." Hospitals function around the clock and every day of the year. The staff "is highly trained. Children have their own beds, food is regular and healthy. The facilities are warm, safe and clean."

The association also stated the problem for the hospitals: They are extremely expensive places for people to "live" in, especially babies and small children. Needs other than basic physical ones cannot be met adequately. The consistent nurturing, stimulating, and loving environment that children need is not available. "Busy nursing personnel do not have time to cuddle babies. Social workers cannot spend their workdays parenting. . . . This frustrates hospital staff who see infants and children in need of affection and a stable home environment." For babies, living in this emotionally barren environment is not good for personal development. Developmental necessities of space for playing and stimulation are also absent. Finally, being in an environment in which illness is the norm puts healthy babies at risk of illness (NJHA, 1991, p. 1).

For hospitals and governmental authorities, the financial burden is of most concern. Both studies and interviews highlight the expense of boarder babies for hospitals and reimbursing governments. In 1992, in each city costs were high. The New York City Department of Human Resources estimated it cost the city $22,683,000 for under 4,300 babies. In Washington, D.C., the estimated cost was $875,000 for about 450 babies. In Los Angeles, the estimate was $7.34 million for under 1,000 babies.

In New Jersey, according to NJHA (1991), after 12 days hospitals are faced with supporting the children without any reimbursement. New Jersey Medicaid pays for 12 days of "social necessity" hospital stays at skilled nursing rates of $80 per day. After that, there is no reimbursement. "Hospitals lose thousands of dollars caring for boarder babies" because many of the babies come from indigent families and are not covered by insurance for nonacute, residential care.

There are other impacts upon hospital and staff. The babies and children use bed space that is needed for other children, which produces "a negative impact on other hospital services." Staff problems develop as well. Staff assume increased work because workloads are not organized around the special needs of these children. They also develop emotional ties to the children (NJHA, 1991).

Hospital responses. Some Philadelphia hospitals have initiated a proactive approach. The social service departments begin work on family discussions and placement options before the child protective system becomes involved. Upon entering boarder baby status, the social work staff are ready to present a package including possible foster placement, when appropriate, to the city child protective authorities with whom they have a close working relationship. Hahnemann, one of the big Philadelphia hospitals, developed a foster care recruitment and training program among hospital staff under a special Abandoned Infants Assistance Grant. These efforts have shortened the length of time children stay in hospitals beyond medical necessity (CWLA, 1992, p. 9).

After-hospital care is a major problem for children whose parents are considered inadequate, particularly those with addictions. The supply of foster homes, already inadequate, is restricted for these children. But kinship care, grandparents, and other relatives taking care of children have become significant resources in many areas.

In some places, concern about medically fragile babies and their needs for homes and loving care has led to the development of institutional responses. The Hale House in Harlem, New York City, grew from a small private initiative into an institution to care for HIV+ and drug-addicted babies during the 1980s and early 1990s. Hale House now conducts large fund-raising campaigns (Hale, 1991). In other cities, there may have been similar developments not well known, widely publicized, or well documented, at least outside their own communities.

SUMMARY

Many babies are homeless at some point in their young lives. Babies separated from parent(s), institutionalized, or with homeless mothers are at high risk. The risk of failure to thrive syndrome is highest when the baby is subject to care from many different caretakers.

The suspected parameters of the problem of abandoned babies in the United States have been examined. The problem has been, probably, highly exaggerated. On the other hand, the growing number of boarder babies left in hospitals for various lengths of time do present unique problems. Many are there because of indications that they would not receive adequate care if discharged. The predominant cause of babies being in hospitals in New Jersey, New York, and Pennsylvania is that the state child protective, investigative, and placement agencies often need added time to resolve the question of what is best for the child(ren).

The large problem is that of babies of homeless women. This issue needs research and discussion. It may warrant special programs.

CONCLUSIONS

The situation of homeless babies is, for me, an emotionally and intellectually horrifying idea. A baby in so untenable a position is anti-life. Unfortunately, there are many of them, most homeless with their parent(s). Among them are babies of homeless unaccompanied girls. Remedies and preventive actions must be instituted without regard to cost or difficulty immediately to deal with these, the most vulnerable of all children.

The next chapter will relate stories of people who survived homelessness as children.

Chapter 8

SURVIVORS

Many ex-homeless and runaway youth, if they are still alive, will be found among the ranks of the adult homeless, alcoholics, drug abusing, or mentally ill. Homelessness is a destructive experience for all children. The probability is that many do not become well-functioning, productive, and happy adults.

Some people who have been homeless children overcome the destructive forces with which they have been beset and build productive and constructive lives. Seita (1996) discusses his survival of abuse and homelessness. "Today I am a professional reflecting on a journey that is becoming increasingly common for many children. [There] are factors that shaped and strengthened my resiliency and allowed me to be here today." We need to learn what factors helped those who were resilient and then use this knowledge to help others survive.

In this chapter are edited stories of five people from varied ethnic and socioeconomic backgrounds: two women and two men in their forties and a young man of 17 who survived. Two came from families with affluent backgrounds, one from poverty, and two from middle-class families. Two came from white Anglo-Saxon Protestant families, two from African American families, and one from a Jewish family. They all had many difficulties on their way to the present. These stories are of hope, of resiliency. The five are "doing well" in spite of what they experienced. Their lives show that even after very destructive life situations during "the formative years" people can recuperate and go forward. These five are not representative of adults who have been runaway and homeless youth, youth from abusive and destructive families. Neither are they unique.

One is often astounded at the ability of people to survive any number of horrors and manage to build seemingly normal and happy lives. As a teacher I am often surprised to learn, from students' papers, of the extreme experiences through which some have lived, and their resilience. A mature evening student, married, with two children and a full-time job, wrote of being an alcoholic and drug abuser by age 6, in jail in his teens, neglected and abused by his parents.

Women and men write and speak of their struggles with teenage alcoholism. Many write of having alcoholic parents, of being abused, abandoned. They are young and middle-aged, from every ethnic, religious, and racial group, working to build productive and satisfying lives. Their survival and strength is a paean to human fortitude, creativity, resourcefulness, resilience, and the ability to change, grow, and overcome adversity.

Let's meet these five people and share some of their experiences. Maybe we can learn where their resiliency came from. The first person we'll meet is "Mona." She's from an upper-middle-class, Jewish family of "old" American stock.

I'M ALL ALONE IN THE WORLD
WITH MY KIDS: MONA

I was born in 1947 on the West Coast. My brother is four years older and my half brother is twelve years younger. Neither experienced what I did nor will even admit they knew about it.

My grandparents were descendants of mid-nineteenth century settlers. All were Jewish, my mother's family of Russian origin and my father's German, which didn't seem to mean much to them. They were all well-to-do pillars of the major Reform and oldest synagogue in the city.

My parents met in high school and got married after finishing college. About six months after I was born my mother read a society page announcement about my father's engagement to another woman, made him leave and never saw him again. They were divorced. We stayed with our mother and also never saw him again. I believe he tried to see us but our mother wouldn't let him.

We grew up living in my maternal grandparents' gardener's house. I spent a lot of time with my grandparents until I was 7, when my mother remarried and we moved. My grandmother was the Temple organist and loved music, reading and other intellectual things. It's from her that I developed my love of these things. It's also from her that I got a sense of being worthwhile and my pride in being Jewish.

My grandparents didn't like or approve of my stepfather. He wasn't Jewish and was a traveling salesman. They thought him somewhat shady. Because of this we hardly ever saw them again. Unfortunately for me, they were right.

My mother insisted that I call him "Dad." I refused so she beat me. I somehow couldn't think of him as my father. I started hating them both. When I was 8 we began moving around until I left them. We moved from one state to another and one city to another. We were often having money problems. I think they moved to avoid paying the rent. I went to many elementary schools and six high schools.

The real problems started for me shortly after we left my hometown. My mother and stepfather had a major argument. She went back to my grandparents with my brother and left me with her husband. The night she left he came and made me have sex. He continued after my mother and brother came back. It was awful. When she came back she started beating me and insulting me. I felt so trapped I wanted to kill myself. He would tell my mother he was going out of town to work then come back after she left for work and have sex with me, sometimes several times. But otherwise he was kind and gave me things. It made me very confused. He was good to me and then took advantage of me. She was never good to me after she returned. She was always nasty and hostile.

When I was 12 and my half brother was born, I started thinking of running away. My stepfather sexually abusing me and giving me gifts. My being dependent on him. My mother beating and being nasty to me. I couldn't stand it. But somehow, I couldn't do it. I withdrew from it all through studying and music. I read, did school work, loved science and listened to music. I always was a very good student.

When I was 15 I told a girlfriend about the situation. She told her mother, who reported it to the school counselor. The counselor discussed it with my mother and then all hell broke loose. My mother accused me of lying and sent me to live with her sister and brother-in-law. They had no children and lived on a ranch in a nearby state. They were alcoholics but at least didn't abuse me. After a few months my stepfather came to visit. He asked me to go to a motel with him and I freaked out. I started screaming and hitting him until he went away. My aunt, after finding out what it was all about, started court action to keep him away from me. I couldn't stay there anymore and went back to _. I thought of it as home because we had lived there most of the time and I had managed to make some friends there. I lived sometimes alone and sometimes with a friend, never with a family member again. I went to court to be declared an emancipated minor. I got in touch with my real father and he came to visit. But he made a remark I felt was sexually suggestive and I freaked out. I never saw him again. At that time I changed my family name. It has nothing to do with anyone in my family, but it is very Jewish.

I was very upset. I had tried suicide a number of times from about age 10 or 12. After I started living as an adult it was a crazy life, drinking, partying, sleeping with guys, using drugs. Depressed and suicidal I was sent to a state hospital, where I spent a year. It probably saved my life being in a place where I was being taken care of. A time-out so to speak. It wasn't so much the therapy that helped as a place to get away from self-destruction and to be protected. I never felt protected from the time I left my grandparents until I was in that hospital.

The social worker betrayed me though. She had told me that if I worked and did well she would get me college and medical school scholarships. She helped me get a job as a medical technician. I really enjoyed it and did well. But, when the six months were over and I asked her for the scholarships, she told me that I didn't need them since I already had a job and a skill. It still makes me furious. I wanted to go to college and medical school so badly. She really betrayed me. I haven't trusted or liked social workers since. It took me a long time to realize my dream of an education.

After I left the hospital I moved to [the] San Francisco, Haight-Ashbury district, and joined the hippie scene. I did all kinds of work, as a go-go dancer, Kelly Girl, waitress. I was raped once. I didn't prostitute myself though I slept with a lot of guys, but never for money. I took all kinds of drugs but never had a bad trip. The only type of help I used was the Free Medical Clinic for toothaches and other minor things. It was some life, exciting, but also depressing and with no future.

I met George during that time. He was a student at a nearby college. He often came into the city with friends. He asked me to go with him when he moved away, and I went. We lived in the Midwest for a year or so in separate apartments. One day he came, packed me up and we came to this area.

We got married and worked with VISTA [Volunteers in Service to America, a War on Poverty program of the late 1960s and early 1970s]. Jonathan and Noah, my two older boys, were born then. After a while, George said he wanted another child. Just after Saul, my youngest son, was born we went into marriage therapy. I thought it was working but one day after what was to have been our last session George told me that he was leaving. Believe me, that was some blow. Two little kids and a baby, alone without a profession. He was terrible about it. Broke off and never gave us anything. He seemed to divorce the children also, hardly ever seeing the boys. But we had to go on so I started working again, as a secretary.

I did very well. The secretarial job, at a large medical college, turned into an administrative job and eventually I've become director of the division. Of course, they don't pay me what they would pay someone with a doctorate. But they paid for me to go to school. I started at a local college and then switched to a B.A.-Ph.D. special program at the most prestigious local university. The Ph.D. part didn't work out yet but I'm on my way.

It took so long but I love being involved in medical education in a significant way. I run an innovative program that has gained respect all over the country. I've been invited to give papers all over the country. Many institutions call for advice on developing similar programs. And I don't even have a B.A., yet. I just don't get the pay and prestige, at my institution, I would if I had an M.D. or Ph.D. I love my work even with all the petty bureaucratic garbage that goes along with it. It gives me a chance to be creative. I love school and getting A's in courses. I've written some terrific papers. Writing is my strong point. The problem is it will take forever for me to finish my studies. I wish I could have done this a long time ago.

My two older sons went to college and the younger has done well at a good specialized academic public high school. It's not that they haven't suffered from their father's neglect. They dropped his name first, then I did. We all use the family name I picked when I became emancipated. I have a very good family. I love the boys and they seem to love me. I'm unhappy that my oldest has chosen to live on the other side of the country but he calls often and we talk a lot. I'm proud of my boys and how well they get along.

I've had no contact with my mother or brothers for many years. They never would deal with the past truthfully and I couldn't stand lying anymore. I guess I won't even know when my mother dies. It's not good being so alone in the world. I still get depressed and it seems that things often go wrong for me.

I've been in therapy, periodically, and it's helped. I'd love to meet someone, have a relationship and maybe get married again, but there seem to be only kooks out there. In general, though, my life with all its problems is good. I think that the love and attention I received from my grandparents, particularly my grandmother, helped me survive everything and come out well on the other side.

* * *

Mona, after years of familial abuse and then self-destructive behavior used her memory of her grandparents' love and her cultural identity to make a life for herself and her children. The next woman, Veronica, was born into a family that had been poor and struggling for several generations. Her maternal grandmother had been a "pioneer." The family probably also had been afflicted with alcoholism for generations.

ALL THE KIDS RAN AWAY: VERONICA

I was born in 1947 in the West. My parents had six children and I am the youngest. The oldest, my only brother, is 15 years older than I am. All of us ran away from home during our early or mid-teens. Our parents were violent alcoholics and life was a mixture of poverty and constant fighting. We were moving constantly, although we didn't go very far, just around the same city. I think they moved to get away from the rent collector. We lived in really dilapidated houses, often with outhouses, and there were mostly Mexicans. We were often one of a few Anglo families in the neighborhood.

I left home during the first week of 10th grade. I didn't want to do what my sisters had done, go on the streets. Two of them even prostituted themselves. I was afraid of that and trouble with the law. I think my biggest fear was getting in trouble with the law and being put in a detention house. It happened to two of my sisters and was awful.

I don't know anything about my family except for my mother and her mother. My grandmother came from Pennsylvania. The family were probably German and English Protestants. She met and married my grandfather in the Midwest. He was probably an alcoholic. She moved to the Rocky Mountains when he abandoned her and the two children. She went because some of her sisters lived there.

She bought an acre of land, built her own house, grew her own food and worked as a maid in a hotel. She was a survivor and strong. I stayed with her when things got too bad at home. I often wonder if the strength to do the things I've achieved came from the love and support I got from her.

My mother, born in 1913, and her brother were the only ones to survive to adulthood. I think my mother graduated from high school. Her brother, a career officer in the [armed forces], had little contact with any of us. My mother worked full time as a waitress and a maid. She always had a job. She also was always angry and yelled and hit us a lot.

My father, born in 1906, was a lineman for the railroad. He may have graduated from high school. He lost his job when I was 5 or 6 years old, probably because his drinking affected his work. That's when the hard times and the moving around really began. Before that we lived in railroad houses. He took care of us and was "nice" when he wasn't sexually abusing one of us. For all I know he even sexually abused my brother. My parents fought and yelled a lot, especially when they were drunk, which was most of the time. It terrified me. Grandma was always there to pick up the pieces. [A physically disabled sister] even lived with her. My parents finally got divorced, after 30 years of marriage. I never heard from or of my father again. They both died in their seventies, which was amazing considering the way they abused their bodies and souls. They must have had strong constitutions.

I was put in foster care for protection for a year when I was a baby. Our family were regular clients of the [child protective agency] because of truancy, neglect and abuse of us kids. I never understood why they returned me to my parents. I certainly needed protection. I sometimes think that the foster care also may have made the difference between me and my sisters in our later lives.

My brother ran away when I was born. He was married and in his own house by the time I was 2. He has four children and repeated the alcoholism and poverty of my parents but somehow managed to have a better family. At least his kids haven't run away.

When I was 11 or 12 I went to California for the summer to visit an older sister. My mother left me there for two and a half years. That sister lived with an artist, real bohemians. They drank, smoked pot and used other mild drugs. Her daughter is the only family member I wanted a relationship with. The rest of them remind me too much of the horrible times of my childhood.

About a year later, at 15, I left home for the first time on my own. Two friends and I were looking for a job in the help wanted ads in the newspaper. We saw an ad for a job with opportunities for travel and money. It sounded good. This was the chance to escape.

It turned out to be with magazine-selling crews that traveled around the West. My friends and I lied and said we were 18. There were several crews. We received room, board, clothes and $5 a day. Each crew had a leader who traveled with us, organizing the itinerary and work. The leaders made lots of money and we, the crew members, were promised lots of things. Actually, it was virtual peonage. We worked house to house from 9 a.m. to 6 or 7 p.m., every day but Sunday and even sometimes on Sunday. Most of the people were decent but I had some harrowing experiences. I was really good at it and sold lots of magazines. The leader was really decent to me, never tried to take advantage of me physically.

I stayed with this crew for about seven months. The friend I signed up with went back home. A month later it really became lonely and I got homesick. I told the leader that I was only 15. He sent me home immediately. Without my knowing it, he also sent a letter to my mother asking for legal guardianship. My mother signed it without discussing it with me and then showed it to me when she sent it back to him. It really hurt me how she was ready to give me up to a stranger. I found out later that she had been sitting in the car and watching as we left on the buses for the crew in the first place. This hurt me terribly also. She really didn't want me. It's still hard to accept.

I never did get back with that crew leader and he never took guardianship. After I had been back with my parents for a few weeks I realized that they both had continued deteriorating. It was really awful being there so I got in touch with the leader. He made arrangements for me to join another crew, which was to connect me to him and his crew when we got to California. But the new leader lied when we got there. He told me the original crew weren't coming to keep me in his crew. I brought in a lot of subscriptions. I didn't like the new crew and especially the leader so after a few weeks I found a third crew and joined it. They traveled through the Southwest. After a few months a friend and I left and went to her hometown. There, I spent the summer working as a waitress and drinking. I had found my profession, being a waitress, and my escape, drinking.

At the end of the summer I returned to my hometown and spent a year with my brother and his family. They lived in a small house. With four kids and drinking it was too much. I decided to finish high school and needed a place with some quiet and privacy so I could study. I moved in with a sister to finish my sophomore year. I'd always enjoyed school and did well, with all the chaos and problems. I also didn't want to get in trouble so I behaved in school to keep the authorities away. My idea was that they either locked you up or threw you out.

I didn't fit in with the white middle-class kids. I didn't fit in well with the black or Mexican kids due to cultural differences. I eventually became part of a largely Mexican group. We were rather wild outside of school with lots of drinking and running around.

I never had any contact with any program or agency, never saw the school counselor. I knew that there was no one interested in or available to help kids like me. The school never questioned me when I was out and let me sign up for classes and attend as if nothing had ever happened when I came back. I guess the school with its long history of trouble with my brother and sisters just gave up on us. If you made trouble in school you got suspended. Otherwise they ignored you.

The juvenile probation department worker who had been working with some of my sisters tried to have me locked up as a precaution once during a hearing for one of my sisters. Two of my sisters had been locked up, one in a reformatory and one in a convent for over two years. They both told me and I saw when I visited them that the places were horrible. The attempt to have me locked up made me terrified of any contact with authorities. So I actively avoided any place that might end up locking me up. If I knew of a shelter or any other place for kids like me I would never get involved with them just to keep from getting locked up.

Believe me, I was depressed by what my life was like. You can imagine how depressed I got when I finally realized my mother didn't want me. Two of my sisters attempted suicide and one eventually succeeded, the one in California. I thought of suicide as a way out. One thing is for sure, if I had kept up the way I was as a teenager I would have become an alcoholic and probably a drug addict.

I met my first husband during that year when I had gone back to school. He was five years older than I, in the service, stationed nearby. We weren't in love but it seemed convenient to get married. I was 17 and it was an escape for me. I'm not sure what it was for him. I tried to continue in school but married or pregnant women or mothers weren't permitted at the school. The marriage never was good though we had a daughter. It was better, at least for the time being, than the alternatives I had seen up to then.

After a year we moved to the South near his parents. I developed a good and active relationship with them. I still have a good relationship with them. I feel like they're my only family. They have always been good to me and my daughter. We lived there a year and a half. My husband had gotten into heavy drinking and then smoking pot and even more. Our marriage didn't last long after we moved away from his parents. I also drank a lot and smoked some pot. I stopped then because it didn't work for me. My daughter was a motivating factor but probably more important was that I didn't want to be like my parents.

At 20, I went into therapy to try and change my life. I didn't want to live the rest of my life as I had been. I didn't want to be like my mother and I didn't want to do to my daughter what had been done to me. For a number of years therapy was my way of finding myself. I have repressed memories of a lot of my childhood. I can hardly remember my father at all, nor much of what I lived through. I worked on remembering until I decided that I may have repressed it all for a good reason.

Once when I was part of a group workshop about family I felt like an orphan. I never had the sense of having a family or people who cared about me nor of leaving them. I think I lived in terror most of my youth. I've often wondered why I changed my lifestyle and my brother and sisters didn't. Though, none of their children ran away so they don't seem to have abused them actively. Maybe it was my grandmother, maybe partially the foster care experience that helped me develop some positive self-identity and psychological strength.

After my divorce I continued waitressing and then opened my own restaurant, which we recently sold. It was quite successful. I periodically did some school thing, getting a high school equivalency and some trade schooling. After about 10 years I married my current husband. I find my marriage good, successful and emotionally satisfying. My daughter is married and it seems to be good. She just had a baby and I spend as much time as possible with him. I take care of him three days a week and I love it. I shortchanged my daughter and I don't want to do the same thing with her son.

I had lots of trouble returning to academic studies. There were many starts and stops. Somehow the library was the most frightening part. I finally completed work at the community college and got an associate degree. From then on it's been smooth sailing. I continued at [a major university] and got a bachelor's in social work. I did very well. Generally, I've been an A student. Now I'm studying for a master's in social work at [another major university, in a nearby state].

I've maintained just a minimum of contact with my brother and sisters. It's painful dealing with them, they haven't gotten out of the poverty and self-destruction. I see history repeating itself. They're all alcoholics though they don't seem to be really abusive to their children but they've not nurtured them too well either. They seem to expect me to help them financially and resent that I'm different from them. I've only kept real contact with one older sister. Her daughter spent several summers with me; it was very hard. I'm not sure if it helped her at all, either.

[What would have helped you and might help others?]

I had no place to go. It would have helped if the counselors at school had been interested in what happened to someone like me. If I hadn't been afraid of being locked up or thrown out. Everybody and every agency seemed to have given up on people like me. I needed and wanted some choices besides uncaring and destructive relatives. I would even have been willing to go to reform school if there had seemed to be some positive in it. People need to remember that young people who make trouble are really in trouble and need help and compassion.

* * *

The next person is a young man who found school to be a refuge from the turmoil in his life.

COLLEGE BOUND: DEREK

I'm 17 and a senior in high school. I am the third child in my family. I have two older and two younger sisters and one younger brother. We're six kids altogether.

I don't know much about my family. Both my parents are black mixed up with everything. We have American Indians, English and other Europeans in our background. My parents were born, raised and married in Rehovoth, where me and my brothers and sisters were born. We all live here. Until I was 8 my Dad was a really good dad. He left us then and I haven't seen him much since. My folks aren't divorced though.

My mom was 30 when I was born. She graduated from high school, worked and went to community college on and off before they got married. Mom is very intelligent and reads a lot. She never finished the community college. She hasn't worked either in over 10 years. I guess they got married before my oldest sister was born.

Mom's family was real messed up. Her mother never got married and had six children, all with different fathers. My mom and her brothers and sisters were raised by their mom's mother, my great-grandmother. Actually, my great-grandmother is practically the only relative I know. I still see her and we even lived with her for a while. That was about the best time in my childhood.

Mom's mother was a little crazy, they say. I think she was either schizophrenic or manic-depressive. She tried to kill my mom several times. She died when my mom was a teenager. My mom never even knew who her dad was. When I was 16 my mom was diagnosed as both schizophrenic and manic-depressive. They started giving her treatment then. Before Dad left she drank a lot, used drugs and smoked.

My dad is about a year younger than Mom. He graduated from high school and went to some technical schools, I'm not sure for what. He then spent four to six years in the Marines and finally went to Bible college. I don't know if he graduated but he acted like a minister and was very involved in a large church, Baptist, I think.

He always worked but for some reason stopped giving us money even before he left us. Then we went on public assistance. After Dad left our family really got bad. I don't know why he left us when he left Mom.

After he left us he started moving around. Sometimes he lived with his mother. She is about 60. He kept his things at her house. When I was about 12 he got in a fight, killed the man and went to jail for a few years. The man was a druggy who lived with his mom and abused her. One day my dad told the guy to stop bothering his mother and the guy attacked him and stabbed him with a knife. Dad took the knife and stabbed the guy to death. Dad was real close to his mother. He called her every day from jail. She visited him twice a month and paid for his lawyer.

I know my grandmother. She lives here in Rehovoth and I've seen her sometimes. I never knew his father or anything about him except that he was part Indian. I met Dad's brother twice but don't know if he is dead or alive. I don't even know if my dad had any other brothers or sisters. I don't know where his folks come from or what they did or anything.

I visited Dad in jail several times. The last time I went was on my 16th birthday. I'd rather not have much to do with him anymore. But I really loved him when I was little.

About my sisters and brother, both older sisters ran away when they were in the fifth grade, after Dad left. They moved around, sometimes they lived with Dad and sometimes with friends, sometimes together and sometimes alone. Once one of them lived right across the street from us and Mom didn't do anything. The older one is involved with an Italian guy and has two kids. She's on public assistance. The other one, just older than me, is really intelligent. She graduated from community college and went to the university. She hasn't married nor had any children but is interested in business and making money.

I'm closest to my little brother. I call him and go to see him. He's in [an institution for troubled children waiting placement]. He was in two foster homes but made trouble and is now waiting for a third one. My two sisters have been in foster care and seem to be doing OK. The four of us have been together more.

After Dad left us we lost our apartment and moved in with my mom's grandmother. We were there for a year but one day the door was locked when we came home and we had to go to a shelter. We stayed in the shelter for about a year and then moved to the project [widely known for being full of problems, drugs, crime, and so on]. After we moved in with my great-grandmother, when I was 10, I started staying away from home overnight and then a few nights and sometimes even a week at a time. I stayed mostly at friends'. Other times I just stayed out until 3 or 4 in the morning. When we moved to the project I kept it up and started staying at friends' for longer periods. The family situation was just crazy. There often wasn't any food and the place was never clean.

Through it all I continued to do very well in school. I got straight A's in my first year in high school. I also had done very well in junior high. I always did very well in math and science so I went to Science High. During my sophomore year the situation started really getting to me and my grades went down. The school counselor called me in and we talked about everything. He got me connected with my older sister's child protective worker. She then started working with me and the younger kids. This got me to thinking about finding a more permanent solution to the crazy way of living. I didn't want anything to interfere with my schoolwork. I talked to a friend and his family agreed to take me in for foster care. I got the place approved and stayed there a year. I started feeling that they weren't doing what they should have for me other than giving me a room and food. I wasn't being treated like a member of the family.

I had gotten back in touch with my junior high science teacher. He had been really good and we got along very well. I hadn't known he was homosexual but that didn't matter. We arranged for me to live with him and his companion. They had a nice big, well-kept house. I made the arrangements with the agency and moved in with them as a foster child. I've lived with them since and although I sometimes get annoyed that they make too many rules and watch me too closely I'll be going back there when I come home on college breaks. They're probably the closest thing I have to a family, aside from my girlfriend.

I always loved school and studying. I'm the president of my class and I have lots of friends. I'm going to be valedictorian at graduation. But I never confide in anyone, I never let them in. I'm going to become an engineer so I can make good money. But what I love the most is being involved in the arts. I'm going to save a lot of money and then open up an art gallery. I dance with a ballet company, take music lessons and I've studied art at [famous art school]. I work in the art school library. That's what I really love, all the arts, music, dance and fine arts.

[What about the system?]

The child protective system didn't do anything until I went to them. They knew all about my family from working with my older sisters and they left us alone until I talked to the school counselor. Even after they got involved they didn't take an active role. They didn't adequately supervise my first foster home to make sure I got what I needed. They just sent checks. I don't even know who my new worker is now. The school counselors were very helpful. They came to me and asked if I needed help. They made me feel that they were interested in me and in helping me.

I can't stand the attitude that a lot of people seem to have, "Pity the poor black kid, we've got to do him a favor." I don't want any favors. I'm not looking for pity, just help. I know what I want and who I am. I don't need anyone's approval. I do a lot of self-examination and I am my own strongest critic. I never lie to myself.

Kids like me should have someone to talk with. People who are supposed to help us should be interested in us and look for us, not wait for us to come to them.

[The future?]

Someday I'd like to have a family, but not like mine. I love my mom very much but right now I can't do anything to help her. I don't want anything from my dad. I hope that someday Mom will get the help she needs and then we'll be able to have a good loving relationship and be a whole family again. Until then I only have myself to depend upon and to make my life what I want. My dad wrote from jail that, "Your only limits are your imagination and your degree of dedication." That's become my motto. Next year I'm going to college and then on from there.

* * *

Derek made his own places of refuge. His memory of his great-grand-mother's care and the positive responses he got at school seemed to have protected him from the immediate destruction of his situation. The next person is David, from a middle-class black family. He had the longest stretch of destructive and self-destructive experiences of any of the five. He escaped from the cycle three years prior to the interviews at the age of 42. Amazingly, after the years of abuse and self-abuse, he was one of the most articulate of people.

YOU CAN BE HOMELESS AT HOME: DAVID

I'm 45 and although I started leaving home when I was 8 until three years ago I've always been homeless. If home isn't safe and loving you're homeless even if you're there. My mother never loved or wanted me and used to attack me, so I never felt safe when I was a child. When I was 8 I ran away to escape from one of her attacks. Actually I went and sat on a neighbor's steps. They sent me back home. Then I found a place to hide in the basement. I learned not to stay in the neighborhood when I went away. From then on I avoided going home whenever I could, even though I loved my dad. Whenever it looked like things were about to get dangerous I left home. She hit me with the heels of her high heel shoes, whatever she could get her hands on.

My parents met and got married shortly after the Second World War. My dad had just returned from the army. They met here in Rehovoth and we always lived here. My brother and I were born here and we all still live here, except my dad died. My dad was born in 1920 on a farm in the next state. My mother was born in 1926 on a farm in a state in the South.

Our family looked normal and stable to everyone. To me it was anything but. Our house was always well taken care of. I did most of the work. My parents didn't fight. We were always clean and fed.

My dad died in 1992. His parents were sharecroppers who ended up owning a big farm. Dad graduated from high school and went into the army at the beginning of the war. He was in for six years and received several medals. It was a very important time in his life. He always told us about it and tried to organize our family on army principles.

When he came to Rehovoth after the war he had some trouble getting work, because of being black. Since he was married, he worked at whatever he could. At first he drove a cab and then got a job in a steel mill. He started at the bottom doing unskilled work. He rose to be a heavy equipment operator. He always did well and we always lived well. We owned our own house. The family was in the hands of my mother. She was the power in the house. I loved Daddy dearly, worshipped him.

Daddy had 11 sisters and one brother. Most of them have good families and most of my cousins are college graduates and live nicely. They all own pieces of the land that grandfather owned. My grandparents stayed and worked together all their lives. They made a family tradition which put an emphasis on the importance of education.

My mother was also from a farming family. She had one sister and three brothers. Her mother died when they were children. Granddaddy kept the boys but sent my mother and her sister to live with relatives. The boys were expected to take care of themselves and help Granddaddy. I remember him as a very strong, tall slender man. I remember him putting me on a horse.

My mother was a very intelligent woman who read a lot. She took courses at college and read mostly nonfiction, particularly psychology. I often read her books when I was young. She said she worked but I only remember her being at home except for short periods when she got dressed up and went out somewhere. She was also very hostile.

My relationship with her was always troubled. I don't remember ever being held, cuddled, kissed or hugged by her. I never could understand why she seemed to be jealous of me and partial to my older brother. Often when Dad said he was taking both of us out my mother would make sure I couldn't go. Usually one of my shoes would suddenly be missing. I couldn't go without it so I had to stay home while Dad and my brother went out. I cried when that happened, often. Only recently in therapy did I figure out that she hid'the shoe.

I loved and admired my older brother. He always was the extrovert and was good at many things. He was very popular in school and around the neighborhood. He was big and strong. He wasn't interested in school but loved dancing and social life.

He always found the easy way to get by. This led him into trouble very early. My mother always protected him. He never graduated from high school but got mixed up in illegal things. His life was very unstable, up and down, although he never was homeless, like I was. He mostly dealt in drugs and other illegal things. Once he and a white friend held up a series of gas stations. They finally got caught and sent to prison. After that he avoided that kind of thing but kept doing illegal things.

He got married but left her and was always involved with different women. Not long ago I found out that he had a son who died of AIDS at age 17. I feel terrible that I never knew my nephew. I feel very deprived and angry at my brother for never telling me about his son. My brother moved in with our mother after Dad died. He's having a lot of trouble with her.

I always loved school and did well, but only finished 11th grade. School was always a happy place where people liked and appreciated me. It was a place of refuge, a place to get away from the fear and hostility at home.

My mother used me as a servant, a Cinderella. I became the housekeeper. I cleaned, scrubbed, waxed floors, did laundry, did the bathrooms and the kitchen. Our house was three stories with hardwood floors. When people came to visit they would often compliment my mother on how well kept it was, how nice the floors were and how hard it must have been to keep it that way. I always felt so strange knowing that she didn't do anything, I did it all. She would say, "I try my best." I thought how ironic that was since her best was my best. But anything positive I ever tried to do on my own she sabotaged.

When I was 8 and ran away I just went around the corner and sat on a neighbor's stoop. The neighbor called my parents and my dad came to get me. I soon learned that I couldn't run away in the neighborhood so I ran to other parts of the city. As I got older I stayed away for longer and longer. I felt better anyplace away from home. Whenever I was home and saw my mother getting angry I took off. I knew I'd get the worst of it. Sometimes I found men who would keep me and I'd stay with them for short periods. I thought it normal to sleep with them in exchange for their help and care. That's when I started drinking and smoking marijuana.

When I was 13, one morning while I was eating breakfast, my mother came up behind me and stabbed me in the head with an old fashioned can opener. I got up, walked out of the house with blood running down my face. My dad was outside and asked what was wrong. I answered, "I'm out of here." He didn't say anything.

I went to live with a man I met and stayed there a year. Then I met a mailman who was very good to me. I stayed with him for five years. He tried to train me to be someone and gave me everything. He became almost like a father to me. I still consider him my best friend and have contact with him. He has helped me and I've worked for him over the years. I could always depend on him no matter how bad my life was. When I became an adult our friendship became platonic. He mostly wanted relationships with teenagers who he could control and mold.

While I was living with him I got shot and almost died. A friend was attacked by a robber and I went to help him. I woke up in the hospital. A blond doctor was holding my foot as if to hold on to my life. At first I thought he was an angel. Obviously I survived.

When I was 19 I decided I wanted to live my own life. I met someone who when he heard me sing suggested I go to Detroit to break into the music business. The guy also was interested in me for sex but we never got into that. I left my mailman friend and moved to Detroit. I got my own apartment and fixed it up. It was great, living on my own, making contacts, going to parties with people in the business. I met famous people and it looked like I might really do something with my life.

One day my mother called. She told me it was an emergency, Dad was sick and I had to come right home. I sold everything, left it all and returned to Rehovoth. As I walked up to the house Dad was on a ladder painting the house. I scolded him for doing this when he was so sick. Dad said there was nothing wrong with him. I asked why my mother had called and told me he was sick. Dad just shrugged. When I asked my mother why, she said they just wanted me to come home. Somehow this took everything out of me. Leaving everything for a lie. I just couldn't go back, somehow. I got very depressed and discouraged. I'd never be able to escape.

I tried living on my own here. I got a job as a security man at a big department store. I was really good at it. But I also got back into drugs and became addicted to heroin. They fired me and I got into shoplifting. I started with small things, becoming more confident, I got bigger. Eventually, I was taking VCRs and large boomboxes. I always was careful how I looked, well dressed and well groomed. After five years I got off heroin but continued with my newfound profession. I also got into other drugs, acid and amphetamines. I finally got caught after another five years, ten years altogether. I said to the guard, "It's about time, what took you so long?" I was glad to get caught, the stress had become almost unbearable. Although I was sentenced to seven to fifteen years I got let out with a cleared record after fifteen days, I never knew why.

I was determined to change my life and enlisted in the army. I was going to make it a career. My dad was very proud. I liked it and I did very well in basic training. But, after three months during a routine X-ray they found a bullet in my back. I didn't even know it was there. It must have been left from when I had been shot and nearly died. They discharged me for fraudulent enlistment. I had answered "no" to the question about having had a serious medical or surgical experience. I fought for two months, successfully, to avoid a dishonorable discharge. But the discharge and failure totally discouraged me.

I came back to Rehovoth, got a small room and worked at odd jobs. I often worked for my mailman friend. I started going downhill, using speed, snorting, then smoking, cocaine. I was going nowhere, floundering. There was no stability in my life. I got various jobs, dishwashing, janitor, painting, and did them all well. I didn't want to steal anymore and began picking up aluminum cans in the street. I developed a system of working at night and early in the morning, when everyone was asleep. I could make $50 to $80 a day that way. But I got deeper into drugs and used it all for that. Finally, I lost my room and gave up everything for drugs. I lived on the streets, slept all day and scavenged at night. I became just skin and bones, working for 13 hours and spending it all in 10 minutes.

My dad saw me once on the streets and that was the only time I ever saw tears in his eyes. This made me feel even worse and I went further into despair and downward. I was contemplating suicide and was totally miserable.

On the last day I was behind a dumpster, on my knees and crying. I prayed for help. Suddenly, like a miracle, a hand came around the dumpster and a voice asked, "Do you want help?" Did I ever.

When I took the hand extended to me, the man became my brother. He gave me my life back. I've been free of drugs since that minute. He worked for this program [outreach to homeless people].

First they took me to a shelter. I immediately started working, cleaning the place including the bathrooms, like I did at home. Within eight days they offered me a job at the shelter. Shortly later the outreach program offered me a job.

I've been working here ever since. I've been in group and individual therapy also. I've learned a lot about myself and people. I've found people with even worse situations than mine. I always believed in God, through it all. I think that helped save me.

I saw my father again, after I had become clean and healthy. He died shortly after that. I'm so grateful that my dad saw me like this before he died. I'm still angry that my mother didn't give me the kind of emotional care I needed to achieve my capabilities. I wasted so much of my life because of that. I couldn't make a home and family of my own. But I'm on a different road now.

I would like to go to college and get a degree in either social work or administration. I want to advance in this agency and get into the administration of the agency. I don't want to take on any responsibility for which I'm not prepared and I still need to learn a lot. I'd really like to find a life companion, a wife, maybe even have a family. Maybe I'm too old for that now. I think I'm finally living and contributing. I feel really good about myself and my life, finally.

I'd like to tell people they should never give up on themselves even though important people in their lives have. You can only find happiness and satisfaction from within yourself. It can't come from goods and possessions; it only comes from emotional satisfaction and a feeling of achievement. Everyone is capable of that. Most important, family and people need to listen to children. No one would listen to me. What saved me finally was someone listening. Only it took too many years. I want to devote the rest of my life to listening and helping.

[David picked himself up almost immediately after being offered a helping hand. In turn he has dedicated his life to providing that helping hand to others. His recovery is truly an amazing tribute to the resiliency of human beings. It also tells us that no one should be discarded and consigned to the rubbish heap.]

* * *

The next and last person comes from an old, established, wealthy family. He recovered earlier than David but also has used his experience to help those having similar lives.

JOSEPH ROGERS

I want to tell my story under my own name, I don't want to hide. I was on the Oprah show and told about my life experiences there. I use this as a way to educate people about the homeless.

I'm 42 years old, born in the early '50s, and live in Philadelphia. I am the Deputy Executive Director of the Mental Health Association of Southeastern Pennsylvania, in charge of programs for homeless people.

I was born and raised in a small town north of Orlando, Florida. My parents were from New Jersey, and moved to Florida when they married. They lived in one of my father's parents' winter homes. Both his parents were rich, birthright Quakers from South Jersey. My father's mother was a daughter of the founder of Abbott's Dairies, still one of the largest dairy companies in the Middle Atlantic region.

My father was a World War II vet. He was born in 1919 and died in 1968. His only brother was killed in the Battle of the Bulge. Both had high school diplomas. My father, a moderate alcoholic, managed a local fuel and appliance business.

My mother, who was born in 1925, was badly alcoholic. She was one of two daughters of immigrant Catholics. Her father, a plumber, was from Germany. Her mother, a state worker and Democratic party worker, was Irish. As my mother got older her alcoholism grew worse and she was often almost comatose. I think her father also was a drinker.

My two brothers and sister live in Florida. My sister is six years older and one brother is three years older than I am. The other brother is a year and a half younger than me. My sister has a master's degree in education. She never got married and works with the homeless. Both my brothers are electricians. They both have children, were divorced and are remarried. All of us have serious emotional problems stemming from our childhood.

At 12 I started staying away from home when the family situation got bad. My mother was drunk often and my father was often away. Summers I worked as a migrant farmhand. I would hook up with a family and stay with them. The crews were almost all black. At 15 I was asked to be a crew boss by the crew, since I could read and write. By then I was almost completely on my own. I started drinking and smoking grass when I was 13.

From time to time I went back to try and live with my mother or my father's mother. I couldn't stay with my mother because it was total chaos. I couldn't stay with my grandmother because I was too used to being on my own. I didn't want adult rules and direction. I also felt that I was a nuisance and a burden. I thought I was an adult and wanted to do my own thing. I loved to read but drifted away from school and sort of finished eighth or ninth grade. I got depressed very often and began drifting around, trying to stay away from the cops. I did not want to go to detention. So I often camped in the woods. I could hide out in the woods for long periods of time. Most of the time I spent reading, everything.

Because I was big I passed for older. I never told anyone my age. I let them guess. When I was 15, I rented a shack for $60 a month, with four 20-year-old guys I knew. It was on the edge of the black part of town. We weren't very welcome. We were boisterous and they considered us white trash.

When I was 17 I had a manic-depressive psychotic break. That's when I began a new career of going in and out of hospitals. By 19 I graduated to the state psychiatric hospital. After two months I was released to a halfway house in a deinstitutionalization program. After six months I left the place and headed north.

First I came to Philadelphia and then went to New York. By 20 I was a hard-core street person. I generally slept in Washington Square Park in Greenwich Village. I was usually blitzed out on cheap booze. Toward winter I moved to the East Village and broke into a basement. It was a warm place to live though it got flooded periodically. Once I hid in a hole in the wall when some people came down to attend to the furnace. I ate out of dumpsters with an international flavor: Chinatown, Little Italy, Jewish delicatessen, everywhere. This lasted for about a year. I had lots of company. There were a lot of young people in circumstances like mine. There were also a lot of drugs which I couldn't afford. I stuck to cheap wine. When I wasn't blitzed I would go to the library and read. I spent hours and days there getting my education.

I was afraid of being rehospitalized so I stayed away from social services. I was suspicious of everyone and everything. But after a while I started going to a soup kitchen run by VISTA [Volunteers in Service to America, a War on Poverty program]. The volunteers were sensitive to my fears and approached me slowly. They eventually helped me find alternatives. I went to East Orange, New Jersey, got food stamps, a place to stay, and antipsychosis medicine for my manic-depression. I slowly started to rebuild my life, but scrounged until I was 25. That's when I met my wife. She helped me stabilize myself. I got involved in all kinds of social causes, demonstrating, organizing, etc. I found this a good outlet for my anger.

After we got married I passed my high school equivalency and began college. I was interested in mental health. I got an A.A. from Essex County [New Jersey] Community College and took courses at several four-year colleges, including Rutgers University at Newark. I had an internship at a mental health center and proposed some programs for people who had been deinstitutionalized. Most traditional mental health workers, social workers and psychologists, were afraid of working with these people. I wrote a grant to develop peer programs for this group and began working full-time at the center. This ended my college career.

In 1981, I was working on some proposals and other projects with professionals from Philadelphia. They invited me to Southeast Pennsylvania to develop similar programs. I had no problem moving. Since then I've worked in Philadelphia with the Mental Health Association of Southeastern Pennsylvania in consumer-run services, peer and self-help programs. Now [1993] I'm Deputy Executive Director of the association in charge of outreach and related programs for homeless and other mentally ill people in the city.

I don't think the situation for homeless children is much different now than it was 20 years ago. Services don't generally address children's needs. They are still seen as property of their parents. For many this means being abused and neglected. Children who are seriously troubled need specialized programs; they have a right to services. It is actually cost-effective for the society to provide help. It is cheaper and easier to help them become productive than wait until they are seriously damaged and in jail, mental hospital or on the streets.

* * *

Here's a man who used his experiences as a building block to help others with similar experiences. He created programs in two places that provided help to adult homeless who were often mentally ill.

EPILOGUE

All five survivors made a very strong impression on me. They all seemed creative and had begun realizing their incredible potentialities. It was inspiring to have been entrusted with their stories. Although damaged childhoods do not usually produce healthy adults, and all five have paid dearly for their childhood experiences, there may be others like these survivors. Most important, with our knowledge and experience, we could ensure that there are many more.

The women and older men have found their rocky roads to satisfying, productive lives. They have also spent many years and much effort to get there. The young man navigated through the shoals in his life, managing to maintain himself, although we can't yet know at what psychic and future costs.

All five came from dysfunctional families. Four of the five came from families with alcoholism and/or mental illness. All had been neglected and abused. Both women were sexually abused. Their families seemed bent on their destruction.

Four of the five experienced emotional dysfunction. Mona was hospitalized several times for depression and attempted suicide. Veronica thought of suicide, although having a child helped stop her from acting on the thought. David almost killed himself through neglect and drug abuse. Joe was hospitalized for mental illness.

Their roads have included many calls for help, some of which were successfully answered. Yet many more went unanswered by unheeding adults. There were the high school counselors who only thought of them as nuisances rather than as youth crying for help. There were the juvenile probation officers who wanted to incarcerate Veronica; the social worker who motivated Mona and then abandoned her; there was David's father, who took such a passive role in the family; and Joe avoided anyone who might lock him up. All five, today, are working, studying, and living decent lives.

DISCUSSION

From these five people we learn that children and youth are crying for help and being ignored. We further learn that these are people with enormous potential. David teaches us that even after many years of abuse and self-abuse, people can be reached and develop positive, productive ways of life. Their contributions are of value. One wonders about others whose contributions are never realized, who are never helped out of despair and destruction.

All five have had very stressful lives. Their families, although from varied socioeconomic levels and ethnic groups, had similar destructive and pathological elements. For those with alcoholism and mental illness, the problems stretch back into past generations. Their childhood experiences are not what is commonly portrayed in Norman Rockwell pictures. For them, youth was hell. They were all abused, rejected, neglected, and left to find their own way. Yet they survived.

Their health was affected. But they all had a common factor in their lives that may have helped them survive. From their stories, they all had someone in their youth who cared about them and who they cared about. Often it was a grandmother. In David's case, it was his father. Veronica thought that foster care when she was a baby might have helped her. Although these influences couldn't prevent what happened, they may have provided the inner strength for picking up afterward.

Listening for and hearing the cries for help from youth and positively answering them needs to become a goal of the society and the helping elements within it. We need to learn how to build into families, schools, community centers, and communities those elements that promote resiliency in children (Bernard, 1996). Some ideas for doing this will be discussed in Chapter 12.

Chapter 9

THROUGH THE CAMERA'S LENS

The camera gives people the ability to see what exists and happens to others in other places. Television has made it particularly powerful. Earthquakes in India, volcanoes in the Philippines, starvation in Somalia, economic, political, social unrest in any corner of the world and in our community are edited and transmitted in moving color into our lives instantaneously.

The lens of the camera has become a participant in the development of social policy. What is seen, how it's presented, and for how long shapes our concepts of the extent and parameters of problems. The camera has thus shaped a vision of homeless and runaway youth. The production and distribution of films about homeless children and families is an important step in public recognition and definition of this phenomenon. It provides a public forum for the children and their families.

In this chapter, some films and/or videos about homeless children produced during the late 1980s and early 1990s will be used for an analysis of what the camera has told us. They were variously short advertisements (spots) and educational, documentary, and commercial films. In general, the aim of the producers of the documentaries and programs has been positive, to acquaint the general public with homeless and runaway youth as a national problem. The intentions and desires of the writers, directors, and producers clearly were to help people.

Spots and educational films provide specific information about a subject. Documentaries primarily acquaint the public with a situation, probably to solicit concern. Commercial films are for making money, are sometimes for expressing the author's concerns and feelings, and are works of art.

SPOTS AND EDUCATION

The National Association of Social Workers (NASW) produced a half-minute TV segment about runaway children in English and Spanish. The "spot" received the highest award in the public service category at the 1992 Houston, Texas, international film and video festival, Annual Worldfest. Its stated purpose was to "dispel traditional myths about why young people run away from home and to alert parents, youth and others to sources of help" (Hiratsuka, 1992). Unfortunately, this was an overstatement of the possibility.

A spot has major built-in liabilities. Being extremely short, it is able only to give very basic information, mainly that there is a problem and how help can be accessed. This spot affirms that runaway or throwaway children come from difficult family situations and are not intrinsically bad. It provides the national runaway and missing youth hot line phone number for general information and for those who may need it.

A short spot, able only to provide basic information, leaves one with many questions. Depicting a few very unhappy, dirty faces can neither dispel stereotypes nor provide enlightenment about causality. It gives youth needing help and people wanting further information a method of finding it. The spot, however, can leave a viewer with a sense of dismay, unease, and dissatisfaction. That may have been an intention of the makers, a way of motivating people to reach out for information.

On the Run (1989) is an educational video produced by the Missing Person's Bureau of the New Jersey State Police in cooperation with the New Jersey Network (the state's public television network). Focusing on the law enforcement aspects of running away, it gives information on places that offer help to runaway youth. To discourage or prevent youth from leaving home, life on the streets is painted in its unpleasantness and difficulty. An ex-runaway says that home, no matter how bad, is better than being on the street.

The police role in helping prevent and resolve runaway youth situations is highlighted. Police personnel are shown as involved and concerned with youth. A policeman meets and talks to young people in various settings. He discusses with them the benefit of staying home and putting their lives in order. Depicted as a streetwise and caring human being, he crusades for the lives of children.

The "scared straight" movement, which brings youth in trouble into prisons, is also depicted. Convicts talk about how terrible prison is to frighten youth. From this, one gets the impression that criminality and going to prison occur as a result of running away.

Positives are that the film does highlight the ethnic and economic diversity of homeless youth. Information is provided on how to recognize warnings of incipient runaway behavior. The counseling process for youth and families with problems is synopsized.

Negatives are that the video ignores homeless youth who are not runaways. No attention is given to family problems too serious to be resolved through will and hanging in. Some family situations *are* worse than anything. Stereotypes are perpetuated, i.e. that every child has a caring family, that leaving home is voluntary, and that counseling will resolve the problem.

These educational films simplify a complicated issue. They provide simplistic information, leave out important aspects of the situation, and perpetuate stereotypes.

DOCUMENTARIES

Documentaries attempt to portray a particular aspect of real life. Some of the problems of the medium will be discussed later.

A public television documentary (*Children of the Night,* 1989) attempted to acquaint the public with the situation of homeless youth. The sympathetic narrator points out the pathos and tragedy of the youths', as well as their families', lives. She takes the audience through the vicissitudes of life on the streets.

Children of the Night focuses on a specific runaway young man. The producers had been following him for more than a year until his suicide at age 18. There are also vignettes of other homeless youth and some of the programs, institutions, and people he and other youth encountered during life on the streets of Los Angeles and San Francisco.

Unfortunately, the program betrays its own goals. It begins with a clear statement that stereotypes of homeless and runaway youth, as prostitutes, alcohol and drug users, thieves, and so on, are generally untrue. And then the program proceeds to reinforce the stereotypes.

The video starts with dark pictures of youth on the streets, panning to a young man leaning against a street lamp and smoking. The narrator then asks, "Why did Iain run, why did he die?" It then proceeds to tell the story.

A baby born to an unmarried woman immediately adopted by a white middle-class couple who had been unable to have children, becomes Iain Brown. A short while later, a second son is adopted. The wife then gets pregnant, producing a third son. The family is materially comfortable and seemingly emotionally stable.

Tragically, in Latin America, when Iain is 11, the second son had a fatal accident while the two were playing together. The family soon after moved to Boston when the youngest became seriously ill. Iain helped care for him. After he recovered, the family moved to an upper-middle-class San Francisco suburb where Iain attended high school.

During the first year in high school, Iain's infractions were relatively minor—truancy, theft, school problems, misbehavior of various sorts with slight response. Iain and a friend then stole a sailboat, wrecking it. His parents paid the damages. The two went to Los Angeles and were initiated into the world of the street. After several weeks, he returned home.

More problems at school and he ran away to San Francisco. He got into minor drug and alcohol use and "voluntary" prostitution. He returned home, then back to the streets. He became the "father" of a multiethnic, heterosexual "family." He had a girlfriend. The young men supported the group primarily by homosexual prostitution to prevent the women from prostituting themselves.

The life conditions of the "family" were complicated and difficult. The film shows the resistance of the world to let them help themselves or to help them. They became increasingly alienated from the adult world.

Finally, at age 18, Iain returned home, got a part-time job, and went back to high school, where he was ostracized and victimized by the younger youth. Shortly thereafter, he committed suicide.

Along the way, there are interviews of street workers, other street youth, Iain's mother, a neighbor, and several other people involved in his life. They indicated strong desires to help him but they couldn't understand him or figure out what to do. How could this happen to such a good family? It must be the work of the fates, a modern Greek tragedy.

The superficiality of analysis is coupled with portrayal of the helping people as unsophisticated and untrained. Those interviewed could not indicate any insight into the development of the situation and its tragic denouement.

However, it is well known that there are crises in people's lives during which they are vulnerable and at risk. Among these are death, family breakup, illness, passage from one life cycle to another, moving, migration, and changing schools or jobs. Iain suffered almost all over a relatively short time period, during one of the most vulnerable life transitions, from childhood to adolescence. In addition to the traumatic death, the family proceeds to have a serious illness, move to a new place and culture, move again, which requires changing schools again, and so on. Neither the parents nor anyone else seems to have helped Iain cope with his accretion of losses, guilt, and fears.

Iain's slow escalation of behavior is portrayed as a series of isolated, inexplicable activities. It can be understood as accelerating screams of pain, which beg for help, reassurance, and consolation—"acting out." No one—not school personnel, street workers, neighbor, filmmakers—no one involved tunes into his feelings of abandonment.

The primary failures of the film are threefold, from my perspective. Most egregious, to me, is the total lack of psychological and social analysis. Many people with professional training and experience could have analyzed the problems. The situation was not inevitable. The clear and consistent causes and signs of the deterioration of this young man should have led to intervention. This troubled young life was cut short largely because his increasingly loud screams for help went unnoticed and unanswered. In addition, if proper analysis had been provided, some other families might have been helped to listen and seek help when a child cries for help and thus forestall another such tragedy. It would also have given the message that people can gain some control over the events of their lives.

Life happenings are not mysterious. Any social scientist or helping professional can confirm that there are always reasons for what happens to people, including children, even though life may often look and feel like a Greek tragedy, all a matter of fate and the gods' caprices.

Social science and professional experience tell us that it *is* possible to change life directions and avoid personal disasters. Positive, helpful intervention and changes are not only possible, they occur all the time. The audience is owed information to help them understand this. The producers' emotional passivity in this situation, with the relatively immense resources behind them, became outrageous to me.

Another failing of the film was that, although verbally denying the stereotypes of runaway youth as prostitutes and drug users in the introduction, in its portrayals it reinforced that very image. Prostitution was, apparently, the primary source of income for most of the "actors" and many were seen as drug and alcohol users, if not abusers. As documented elsewhere in this book, the vast majority of homeless youth do not resort to prostitution to support themselves, nor do they become drug addicts or alcoholics. They may indulge in sexual activity and use alcohol and/or drugs recreationally, much like their nonhomeless peers.

The third difficulty is voyeurism. It is difficult to reconcile journalistic objectivity and noninterference in a probably preventable tragedy. There is something horrifying about the fact that the producers apparently followed this youth for some time without ever trying to help him save his life. The announcement that he committed suicide shortly after the last scene climaxes the tragedy.

Does the objective nature of journalism permit and indeed encourage such voyeurism? Although presented with the best intentions, one might accuse the producers of passive—though unintended—murder, or at least accessory to murder.

Streetwise (1984)

Another documentary, *Streetwise* is a slice-of-life approach to the world of street kids in Seattle, Washington. I found some of the same shortcomings that I found in *Children of the Night.* It also ends with a tragic suicide. It also does not provide any analysis although it was made by people who were trying to help and understand the youth. The lack of analysis is similarly a very negative aspect of the film. Life is pictured again as like a Greek tragedy.

The film opens with a rather poetic photograph of a 14-year-old boy and continues to portray the lives of several street youth in Seattle, Washington. They feed themselves by rummaging in dumpsters behind restaurants and fast-food places. There is a lot of loitering around, fighting, begging, soliciting, and hostile encounters. The movie records a rather grimy, undifferentiated, boring, day-to-day struggle to exist.

There is a large ethnically, socioeconomically, and racially mixed cast of characters. Some have "marital" relationships; others, buddieships. Most seem to be alone. Many of the characters maintain some sort of relationship with their parents. One young woman has arguments with her mother over the phone. Others are seen to maintain less negative contact. A family visits their son in detention and expresses love for him but can't help. This may be a true depiction of street life, but is it enough?

A 12- or 13-year-old woman, in a sense the costar of the film, sporadically sees her mother. She is and looks like a child. She plays dress up to support herself through prostitution. She goes periodically to the luncheonette in which her mother works to talk and eat. She visits her mother and dog in the rather dilapidated house in which the mother lives. She asks her mother to buy her cosmetics. They talk about the mother's "husband," who apparently is abusive. She gives the mother advice. The connection seems "sisterly." The mother's life seems to be overwhelming, with intimations of alcohol problems.

The boy in the beginning frames is her friend. The relationship between the two is, at least on the surface, essentially emotionless—as is almost everything else in the film. His mother is dead and his father, whom he visits several times, is in prison. The boy shares an abandoned hotel with an older "buddy." They are rather resourceful and clean—taking showers and cleaning their clothes.

There are several scenes of the boy and girl talking about their lives and hopes for the future. Maybe they'll get married. Both exhibit an expectation that things will not work out.

At the end, he seems to be planning a trip to visit one of their old buddies in another city. He invites the girl to join him. She isn't sure. Before she can decide, he leaves. The movie ends with a memorial service for him after his suicide.

A wider range of activities is portrayed than in *Children of the Night.* The stereotypes are more diverse. Possibly the greatest failing of the film is the objective, unemotional approach. Society is apart from the events of the film. Also missing is analysis of any of the situations that have led to the homelessness of the children. The filmmakers probably wanted to portray the humanity of the young people and develop our sympathy for them.

However, I got a message that nothing can be done about the hopelessness, self-destruction, and despair. There is no clue how to channel the verve and resistance to dehumanization that the children show. The prime message is the truism that life on the streets isn't easy or pleasant. Existential hopelessness is portrayed. Life is tough, and death is the way out.

Innocence Lost (1987)

Innocence Lost is a Geraldo Rivera TV program about the crisis of disintegration and destruction of life of youth in the United States in the late 1980s. It partially deals with homeless and runaway youth.

The section dealing with street youth makes the point that they come from all ethnic and economic segments of the population and from all types of communities. The situation is portrayed primarily as a problem of abusive and neglectful families, although sometimes it is shown primarily as a problem of poor communication. Contrary to *On the Run,* many of the youth indicate that, however bad and difficult it is on the streets, it was worse at home.

The program was filmed partially out of the studio and partially in front of a studio audience. It has the same dismal portrayal as the other videos of life for young people on the streets. There are episodes from Ft. Lauderdale, Florida, Hollywood, and New York City. A number of teens living on the streets are interviewed. One hears the familiar story of abuse and hostility at home. Many are pictured as throwaways, with the stepfather often the one insisting on the child leaving. Many do not have families that want them or can make a place for them. Drugs, prostitution, and theft are shown as the major means of making a living by the street youth, both male and female.

The overall portrayal is not as dismal as the previous two films. Alternative scenarios are given of minors who have made an independent life for themselves through low-paying jobs and struggle. They have a more positive outlook and a more positive future orientation.

In one episode, the problem of youth fleeing or being ousted from the foster care or child protective system is discussed. The problem of many youth in foster care going through multiple foster families is broached but not discussed in any depth. Problems of group homes and children leaving them are also touched on. It is clearly stated that part of the problem is the "law, government, and bureaucracy."

There are teary scenes when some runaways are reunited with their parents. One of the parents says she realizes that they all need help in reconstituting their family but they all need to work at it. The implication is that they will go for family counseling.

There is a conscious effort to blame neither the parents nor the children for their situations. There is also a strong pitch for young people not to leave home, but to go for help. Where to get help is rather vague, except for the hot line number given several times and mention of the 500+ youth shelters around the country.

Helpful police are depicted trying to deflect runaways from hitting the streets in the first place. An obvious aim is to discourage young people from leaving home, although the program clearly says that many have no choice about the matter. Again, no analysis of what can be done about the problem is offered, nor is there an analysis of why there is such a problem. However, the producer clearly wanted to provide a rounded view of the problems of youth including how some have managed to overcome and develop a more positive life for themselves.

COMMERCIAL MOVIES

King of the Hill (1993)

King of the Hill is a commercial movie, released in September 1993, with a primarily artistic vision. Based on a memoir, it tells of Aaron, a teenage boy. His family's vicissitudes during the Depression of the 1930s led to his being abandoned and homeless for a short time.

The film graphically shows the plight of the homeless not only through Aaron but through scenes of a shack community formed by families evicted for nonpayment of rent. The attempts of all the down-and-out characters to maintain dignity are assaulted on all sides. Contrasts with the world and intolerance of the affluent and the authorities form the background to the family's story.

The action centers on Aaron, an eighth-grade boy. He and his younger brother, with whom he is very close, live with their unemployed, somewhat ineffectual father and consumptive mother in a hotel room, a single-room occupancy (SRO). All the other residents of the hotel are in similarly severe economic straits.

The family starts to unravel, which leaves Aaron alone. The younger brother is sent away to a relative in another city. The mother is hospitalized in a closed sanitorium. The father leaves the city for work. The hotel management know nothing of all this. The police attack and destroy a squatter settlement as Aaron watches. Aaron's teacher is shown as the only sympathetic and caring person outside of the group of dispossessed in the hotel.

The arrangements made to feed and take care of the boy fall apart. He is reduced to eating stale rolls and paper cutouts of food. Within a short time, he is notified of eviction. Aaron, totally alone, becomes desperate and locks himself in the room. He is starving, hallucinating, and about to lose the roof over his head and all his family's belongings. He goes through a state of panic and delirium from starvation, on the verge of total disaster. He is enraged with his father. It is clear that catastrophe is to follow.

Miraculously, the situation is resolved positively, at the last minute. The father returns to a job with the WPA (a federal jobs program) and the family is reunited in a decent apartment. However, the potential of another less kind ending is clearly there and very emotionally draining.

The film is extremely effective and well done. It engaged me, and my partner, emotionally and seemed to similarly hold the rest of the audience. It engendered caring and concern for the youth and all the characters whose lives are being destroyed through the failure of the economic system. The lack of sympathy exhibited by most of the other characters—police, wealthy classmates, and their families—was quite disturbing. The salvation of the family through social welfare programs had powerful modern reverberations.

The emotional content of the film, the engagement of the audience with the youth and his travails, was excellent. The horror of the child's situation became real. His desperation and inability to comprehend it was palpable. His helplessness was graphically portrayed. One cared about him and his life in one's guts and felt as helpless as he did.

This film provided a hint of social causality in both the family situation and the social situation. The setting indicated the social conditions of poverty and lack of jobs, which produced family homelessness. A resolution to the problem of poor and homeless families was given through the fulfilled hope placed on the WPA jobs program.

Through the prism of art, *King of the Hill* showed the multidimensional external and internal elements of the homeless youth story. It dug beneath the surface of reportage that made the other films seem shallow and superficial to me.

The Grapes of Wrath (1984)

The final film is *The Grapes of Wrath*, based on the John Steinbeck novel about the Depression years. Poor, uneducated farm families were dispossessed from their land by changing social conditions. They became homeless, exploited, buffeted, migrant farmworkers in California during the 1930s. The plight of the children is clear.

The responsibility of social forces for the family's condition also are obvious. The social message is clear. It might be called New Deal or liberal propaganda by some and portrays the government as a munificent, protective, if somewhat impotent helper to beaten people.

The forces destroying the lives of the family and others like them are part of the story. Homelessness is portrayed as a social pattern rather than an idiosyncratic event. It points to what could be done both by homeless people and by society to deal with the problem. For the end of the century, it may be regarded as old-fashioned and simplistic, but the same conditions are recognizable and reported on regularly today.

DISCUSSION

The differences between the documentaries and educational films and the art films are of major consequence in forming a response to the problems of the medium. They may be crucial. Artistic work is essentially analysis from within. Documentaries and educational films extrinsically focus on facts that are potentially powerful, but the results often seem superficial.

There are several similar threads that run through the documentary and educational films about homeless and runaway youth. They deal almost exclusively with youth on the streets. This in many ways is the most dramatic aspect of the lives of some homeless children. They rightfully picture a difficult, futureless, unpleasant, and often fatal life. They often present stories that are tragic and in themselves wrenching.

For me, most of these types of films did not contain the emotional element necessary to engage viewers and make viewing a personal experience. It may be that they try to tell too many stories, too objectively, too passively, too much as a slice of life. The main problem seemed to be that they do not analyze causality and go deeper than idiosyncratic breakdown of family and attendant abuse and neglect of children; this makes them diffuse.

Without the sense that something can be done, the viewer is left with impotence and fatalism. If it is all predetermined, then what can be done except to provide bandages or sandwiches, or turn your head?

There is, in addition, a somewhat simplistic element to all of the documentary and educational films, except *Innocence Lost.* It alone showed a possibility of building a mature, independent life as well as the difficulty of short-term responses. The others posit returning or remaining home, with perhaps the help of an emergency shelter or counseling as the only positive alternative for these youth.

Two of the six films end in a youth's suicide or death. Their desperation while alive and suffering is muted in part by the documentary medium. Homeless families with children are ignored as are young women with babies.

It is the depth of *King of the Hill* and *The Grapes of Wrath* that gives them power. The artistic interpretation colors everything and provides the emotional and implicit analytic element missing in the documentaries and educational films.

Documentaries seem to be an essentially problematic medium. They have to be dramatic to gain and maintain attention. They have to simplify and pick examples. They need to satisfy limited theatrical and artistic demands, fit within a rather short time frame to be practical, and at the same time provide information. But they are denied the power of the art film and analysis.

Often the documentary merely titillates or provides sketchy or truncated information. With the best intentions, film documentaries remain voyeuristic. They put people's lives on view. When showing people in pain, they cannot interfere with the subjects' lives because they would then lose their documentary status of dispassionate reporting. So one is reduced to peeping at and being "entertained" by other people's suffering.

And yet, paradoxically, they change the situation simply by being there. In addition, reporting leads to choosing and editing complicated life situations to fit into a specific time, philosophical, and artistic frame. This often causes inadequate or skewed coverage and analysis.

The role of society both as causing homelessness and helping solve the problem could be pictured. The passion against societal failure that fuels *The Grapes of Wrath* needs to be focused on the modern tragedy of homeless children. More and better films are needed to help us understand what causes and what can change this destructive situation. The camera's lens need not be half closed.

Part III

RESPONSES

The Found Boy (continued)

"Oh!" she said, "How terrible to be so cold!

Let me mend you."

"Yes," the little boy said.

So she took out her sewing basket and began to mend

him. (From "The Found Boy" in *Somebody Else's Nut Tree* by Ruth Krauss)

The account of homeless children and families lies also in the individuals and agencies trying to help the children and their families. In this section are descriptions of the attempts to mend what is already broken. The efforts resemble the Dutch legend of the boy with his finger in the dike; however, *this* dike constantly springs more leaks. The attempt to plug the leaks and repair the damage done is honorable work but it is never over—being only reparative. The basic necessity is to prevent the circumstances that produce the leaks.

The society, through governmental and private means, has also been involved in responding to the damage. The second chapter in this section is a discussion of America's efforts to deal with the situation of homeless children and families.

Many of the people working with homeless children and families are dedicated, poorly paid, and fighting a battle against great odds. Knowledge about these attempts and the resources and training currently being invested is needed to be able to see how the "helping" system functions. It is also needed to determine if the system can be fixed or expanded, or needs reconstruction.

Programs in southeast Pennsylvania are described to present a specific picture of how a major metropolitan area in the United States addresses the homelessness of children and families. Many communities in the country have developed similar institutions and yet slightly different systems for responding to the challenge of homelessness. There are shelters and other programs for homeless adults, families, independent children, and youth, primarily under private, nonprofit auspices. Churches and synagogues and members of their congregations have become involved in various ways. Public agencies provide money and supervision as well as some services.

Some programs only provide emergency help, others long-range help, and still others a combination. Some only work with throwaway and runaway youth, others with families, others only with women and children, others only with babies, and there are various subsets and mixtures of these.

THE AREA

The southeast Pennsylvania region is part of the Philadelphia metropolitan area, the fifth largest in the nation. It is also a region for both state and federal departments for statistical and program purposes. It consists of Philadelphia city/county, like an axle of half a wheel, and spokes, the four counties to the north, west, and south of it—Bucks, Montgomery, Chester, and Delaware. The wheel is cut by the Delaware River, its eastern boundary. (The federal metropolitan area contains a few counties and the city of Camden, New Jersey, directly across the Delaware River.)

The regional population has been relatively stable, although shifting within the region. Suburbanization and exurbanization are proceeding as in other areas of the country. In 1990, the five counties had a population of about 3,730,000, an increase over the previous decade of 1.3%. The redistribution of the population that began after World War II continued in the decade of the 1980s. Philadelphia, with a 1990 population of about 1,585,000, lost 6%; Delaware County, with a population of about 542,000, lost 1.3%; Montgomery County, with about 678,000, gained 5.5%; Bucks County, with about 541,000, gained 12.9%; and Chester County, with about 376,000, gained 19%. The urban areas, parts of Delaware County and Philadelphia, lost population, and the suburban areas gained significant population—over 10%.

Southeast Pennsylvania contains several sites of importance from the Revolutionary War, most notably Valley Forge in Chester County and Independence Hall in Philadelphia. The region has the largest concentration of higher education and medical education institutions in the country.

The region and city, 100 miles southwest of New York City and 140 miles northeast of Washington, D.C., is central to the northeastern megalopolis. The metropolitan region overlaps with both New York City to the northeast and Wilmington, Delaware, to the south. Bucks County has some areas that are suburbs of Trenton, New Jersey, and exurbs of New York City. Delaware County also is a suburban area of Wilmington, Delaware.

The four outer counties contain very high-income, middle-income, and working-class suburbs as well as college towns and old, small cities. They also contain high-growth industries and businesses often situated in "industrial parks." The further reaches of Bucks, Montgomery, and Chester Counties remain largely rural.

The suburban and exurban areas are experiencing high development and an economic boom while the cities, including Philadelphia, suffer the fate of most older cities in the country: high poverty, large populations of minority residents, soaring social costs, near bankruptcy, and deindustrialization. Chester City in Delaware County is one of the most distressed small cities in the country.

The region was the site of much of the early industry in the country, including steel mills and production of machinery, railroad equipment, and cars, until the national growth of suburbanization and decline in industry began in the 1960s. The period since has seen a steady decline in the industrial base and growth in service industries throughout the region. The region was also a major agricultural center, which is rapidly being converted to suburban developments. It is an area of rolling hills, fields, forests, lakes, and streams.

This region, as is true for many American metropolitan areas, is a place of burgeoning suburbs and white and middle-class flight from the cities. The industrial base of the economy is being replaced by a high-technology and service-centered economy, suburban business parks, a relatively well-paid white-collar class and generally low-paid blue-collar, service class. The problems of the cities have infiltrated the older suburbs.

THE CITY

Philadelphia, the fifth-largest city in the United States, was a major port and industrial center until recently. It remains a large business center. It was the largest city in North America at the time of the Revolution. The city contains many places of major and minor significance to American, particularly colonial and revolutionary, history in Center City, in Independence National Park, and elsewhere in the city confines. At the turn of the twentieth century, it was one of the major wealthy, industrial cities in the world.

Center City, which comprises most of the original city, is unusual in the country in being both a business and a residential center. It contains many large office buildings. It is at the same time a densely populated, heterogeneous, primarily middle-class residential area. There are major universities in the city and many smaller institutions of higher education in and around the city. In Center City, there are major arts institutions, theaters, musical organizations, museums, and schools, including the University of the Arts and Curtis Institute, a world renowned-musical conservatory.

Through the city run a small river and a number of streams around which have developed the largest municipal park in the world, Fairmount Park. Although designed primarily to protect the water supply, the park has become a major recreational, environmental, and aesthetic resource. The eastern boundary of the city, the Delaware River, is a major port system.

There are some sections of Philadelphia of old mansions, extensive areas of solid middle-class and working-class neighborhoods, and large areas of devastation and poverty. The population in 1990 was about 40% black, 10% Hispanic, 2%-3% Asian, and the rest a mixture of various European ethnicities.

The social problems of poverty, despair, drugs, alcohol, undereducation, and underemployment among inner-city populations—Caucasian, black, Hispanic, and Asian—are increasing as the city's financial base and support from both state and federal governments have diminished. Philadelphia is simultaneously a beautiful city of culture, great presence, affluence, potentiality, and promise, and an ugly, partially destroyed urban environment of severe deprivation and suffering.

What has been developed there to respond to homeless children and families?

Chapter 10

PROGRAMS FOR UNACCOMPANIED YOUTH AND FAMILIES

This chapter presents short histories of programs for unaccompanied youth and homeless families, and their range in southeast Pennsylvania.

HISTORY OF SERVICES TO UNACCOMPANIED YOUTH

Throughout history, children have been left homeless. Parents died or became unable to care for them due to poverty, war, and natural catastrophes, hardship, illness, injury, incarceration, or other reasons. In the United States, immigration produced special historical conditions leading to orphaning and abandonment. Particularly because of the variety of ethnic and religious backgrounds, responses in the United States varied.

In the older sections of the country, the early seventeenth-century "Poor Laws" created public orphanages in most counties. Due to the nondenominational Protestant nature of public institutions, large numbers of private, ethnoreligious children's institutions and orphanages were founded in most urban areas.

Programs were sponsored by the Roman Catholic Church (often ethnic in origin, that is, German, Italian, Polish), by the Jewish, black, and Hispanic communities, and by various Protestant denominations including Baptist, Protestant Episcopal, and Lutheran. Nonethnic and secular, private institutions also arose, primarily during the latter half of the twentieth century. In newer areas of the country, the emphasis was on nonsectarian institutions.

Since World War II, the concept of large institutions has become discredited and obsolete. Foster care, substitute families, relatives, and small group homes and institutions have taken their place, in general becoming part of the child protective system. Reconstituting institutional care of dependent children was suggested in the mid-1990s, primarily because of cost factors. Through 1996, however, it had not led to major changes.

Development of Services

With the passage of the national Runaway Youth Act in 1971 (amended in 1977 as the Runaway and Homeless Youth Act [RHYA]), an uneven proliferation of shelters and other emergency programs for unaccompanied youth occurred throughout the United States. Emergency shelters exist in all areas of the country. They vary in size and services. Most shelters and/or host home programs serve a relatively small number at any one time. Covenant House serves hundreds at each site. With experience, many programs have added counseling, educational, and other services.

The distribution of services is neither uniform nor directly related to need. Some areas have a multiplicity, others have virtually none. Sponsorship varies: public and private, sectarian and secular, large and small. Some are independent organizations focused specifically, others are part of larger organizations.

Networking

Most of the RHYA programs are members of the National Network of Runaway and Youth Services (discussed in the next chapter). Local or regional networks or coalitions also exist: in New Jersey, the Garden State Coalition of Youth and Family Services; in New York, the Empire State Coalition; and in Pennsylvania, Delaware, Maryland, Washington, D.C., Virginia, and West Virginia, a regional group, the Mid-Atlantic Network of Runaway and Youth Services. Similar groups exist in other states and regions.

As with the programs themselves, the coalitions or networks vary in cohesiveness, strength, mission, and activity not only from place to place but from time to time. Their activity often depends upon a few involved individuals.

A major function of the networks is to help members deal with federal and state agencies that provide funds and regulate services. They also serve as informational and organizational exchanges that help each other and the clients. They have consulted with state legislatures for legislation benefiting the youth and the service providers.

In Philadelphia, a multiagency coalition, the Youth Collaborative, which is not affiliated with the National Network, was initiated in 1991. Meeting monthly, it focuses on coordination of efforts and self-education for youth-serving professionals and involves 25 agencies including those serving unaccompanied homeless youth as well as family court, the school district, the police, the Department of Human Services, and others. The commitment of agencies varies.

Agencies

Agencies working with unaccompanied children are usually refitted old orphanages or are relatively new, having been established in the 1970s or later. Older agencies, with relatively large facilities, are generally affiliated with the sectarian philanthropic organizations. The newer, nonsectarian agencies also working with the child protective system generally operate on small budgets, have small staffs, and serve relatively small numbers of clients for short periods of time.

The average homeless/runaway youth program has from 6 to 15 residential places, time limits of two weeks to a month, a staff of 1 or 2 to 15 plus volunteers, and a yearly budget of tens of thousands to a few hundred thousand dollars. They may provide a wide range of services, often non-residentially and on various grants.

Covenant House is a notable exception, with several operations of over a hundred short-term beds in a number of areas of the country and internationally. They had, in 1992, a budget of $67 million, mostly from private contributions, and a reported clientele of almost 14,000 youth (Covenant House, 1993).

Agency staff. People working in youth shelters and services come from a variety of backgrounds. Educational backgrounds vary widely from high school to those who have graduate degrees in social work or other related fields. Staff is overwhelmingly female and, in general, educational standards and pay and benefits are rather low for professional work, with high staff turnover, except for directors and top staff. Many line staff salaries are under $20,000 per year with directors making up to the high $40,000 range.

The southeast Pennsylvania situation is described briefly.

Philadelphia and Southeast Pennsylvania

Slowly during the twentieth century, Philadelphia and Pennsylvania, under federal mandates, took more responsibility for the welfare of dependent and neglected children, among other vulnerable and needy population groups. The development of services historically varied from one political area to another. But services have slowly become similar under federal and state direction although specific services and agencies remain local.

Unlike New Jersey and New York, where there are scattered RHYA shelters and programs, the southeast Pennsylvania region has only three small RHYA programs.

In general, children without family support or adequate parental care and supervision are legally defined as neglected dependent children. They then are the responsibility of the child protective agencies. In Pennsylvania, these are the Philadelphia Department of Human Services (DHS) and/or the Pennsylvania Department of Health and Human Services, Division of Children and Youth (C&Y), through county agencies.

Private residential and treatment programs have become part of the "emergency service" system. The child protective offices often use "emergency services" as an entry into the foster care system or for "time-out" for the families with which they are working. In Philadelphia, many of these services have developed over 200 years. All, since shortly after World War II, have, by law and government policy, served multiethnic and multireligious populations without discrimination.

The services usually serve particular youth populations, such as 2- to 12-year-olds, teenage boys or girls, babies, and/or youth with court-ordered placements. Youth in the emergency shelter system are under county supervision and funding.

It is possible that there exists an underground of hidden homeless youth outside of institutional connections, as in Canada and other highly institutionalized systems. "Anarchist" squatter houses are an example of this phenomenon.

In changing and economically deteriorating areas, agencies have become overwhelmed. This reflects the relationship of homelessness and family breakdown to social conditions. In southeast Pennsylvania, such areas are overwhelmingly urban.

People administering or working in programs for children in economically disadvantaged communities, Philadelphia and Chester particularly, cited the crack cocaine epidemic, a symptom of social disintegration and hopelessness, as having had a devastating effect on the welfare and well-being of children and families. Agency inadequacy also reflects reductions in societal response to social problems since the political opponents of such involvement have gained ascendancy. Problems are compounded by lack of coordination and lack of planning. More affluent suburban areas in Bucks, Montgomery, Delaware, and Chester Counties were less overwhelmed.

In Philadelphia, the DHS contracts for services with the transformed private programs, often through their respective communal social service organizations: the Greater Philadelphia Federation of Jewish Agencies, Lutheran Social Services, Catholic Social Services, and so on. An example of these facilities is St. Vincent's, which serves as a DHS comprehensive emergency shelter for 2- to 12-year-old dependent children. Other Catholic-sponsored institutions include St. Gabriel's for court-committed boys; Catholic Home for Girls, using scattered group homes; St. Joseph's and St. Francis's for dependent boys over 12; and St. Mary's, with a very therapeutic environment.

Other programs have direct contracts. Among the latter, in Philadelphia, are two private nonsectarian agencies that have RHYA emergency shelters: Voyage House, with a "host home" and drop-in program, and Youth Emergency Services (YES) with the Runaway Youth Program (RYP) emergency shelter. In Bucks County, the only other locally accessible RHYA program is part of a larger youth-serving agency. Unfortunately, even with the plethora of services and agencies available, needs are met unevenly. This necessitates the placement of some children out of the area, even in distant states.

Squatters

"Anarchist" squatter houses (illegally occupied empty houses), part of the counterculture community, comprise an informal housing system. These resemble the countercultural communes of the 1960s, young informants said, and at times they are refuges for homeless minors. There are also specific youth squatter houses with predominantly teenage inhabitants. In Philadelphia, one has been in the University City area, near the University of Pennsylvania, and another in Mt. Airy, a large, socially, ethnically, and economically mixed community with liberal tendencies. However, it proved impossible for me to gain access to these houses.

A reported, informal national network of squatter houses maintains loose ties between them. They often are found in cities with college and university populations. Often they are near university communities with other anarchist institutions such as bookstores, coffee houses, and so forth. The number of youth in these squatter houses is probably relatively small.

They resemble "krakker" (squatter) houses in the Netherlands and other European countries, in which some runaway youths live.

Discussion

The similarities as well as the problems are striking. Staff and programs have demonstrated a commitment to at-risk and homeless children. They have been involved in serving this population through improvisation and dedication. All provide some form of basic care at least on a short-term basis. Most agencies survive by piecing together funds from a variety of government and private sources. All except Covenant Houses operate at a bare-bones level. All plead for sufficient and consistent funding.

Staff are overwhelmingly female. Most jobs in these child service agencies pay low salaries, particularly those with direct client contact and responsibility. Staff are of varying levels of education, primarily nonprofessional with some college. Many agencies have trouble with staff turnover, particularly on the direct care level.

In the next section, programs for homeless families will be discussed.

HISTORY OF PROGRAMS FOR FAMILIES

Americans are possibly the most mobile people in the world. The openness of the North American continent and its seemingly endless riches have led to a notion of boundless opportunity and an attitude that one can move on if things don't go well. In the late twentieth century, approximately one fifth of the population moves every year.

Historically, living conditions for the poor were often grossly inadequate. Jacob Riis (1889) exposed the living conditions for many of the poor, of all ethnic backgrounds, in late nineteenth-century New York City. Housing in coal bins, attics, outhouses, and hand-built shacks with extreme crowding and dilapidated conditions was common.

For most of American history, government has played a minimal role in helping families in distress. To avoid almshouses, for many the answer to hard times was to move on, try somewhere else. Many of the pioneers were such families. This is true also of most immigrants who came as families. Only slowly did an idea of societal responsibility for the welfare of families develop. At first it was in the provision of land to encourage settlement, or homesteading.

National governmental responsibility for family welfare was only institutionalized in American society during the New Deal era in response to the

Depression of the 1930s. It was a time of dislocation of large parts of the population; evictions and dispossessions were widespread. Many programs were developed to help people in emergency situations, such as Aid to Dependent Children (ADC) (now Aid to Families With Dependent Children, or AFDC), and the development of government-sponsored and built low-income housing, housing subsidies, and emergency housing camps (such as in *The Grapes of Wrath*).

Since the 1980s, these concepts of governmental responsibility and the programs themselves have been subject to severe attack and reduction. At the same time, the economic and social situation within the country (see Chapter 4) has increased family instability and decreased the supply of low-income housing. With a return to local responsibility, grassroots, private attempts to help the growing number of homeless families and individuals have resulted.

By the 1990s, many programs had developed throughout the United States with individualized, curative approaches. Sponsored by local governments and/or the nonprofit voluntary sector, most provide, at the least, basic temporary shelter. Others also provide other help such as food, clothing, counseling, job training, and programs for children. The overwhelmingly female staffs of most programs are partially professionalized and often underpaid. Many, particularly private programs, depend on volunteers. Sporadic and inadequate funding is universal. Congregational programs with very low budgets, almost no paid staff, and large volunteer efforts have also developed throughout the country.

PROGRAMS

The rest of this chapter will outline programs and facilities available to homeless families in southeast Pennsylvania. Every area of the country is somewhat different in the organization and distribution of programs responding to homelessness in general and to homelessness of children and families in particular. There are differences within neighboring communities in an integrated, social, and economic region. Yet, in general, the approaches and the fragmentation, insufficiency, and lack of direction are similar throughout the country.

Philadelphia

In Philadelphia, as the problem of homelessness became more and more obvious and prevalent in the 1970s, the Office of Services to Homeless

Adults (OSHA) of the City of Philadelphia was set up to deal specifically with the problems of homeless adults. It then was made responsible for homeless families. Programs for adult, homeless mentally ill are under the supervision of the Department of Health, Office of Mental Health and Retardation (OMH). Privately organized and run shelters were supervised and largely funded with public money and through subcontract with the city.

In 1989, the numbers of homeless people in families, primarily headed by single women, started growing dramatically. In 1991, it became evident that there was a need for special programming and services for families. By 1992, there were 450 families in emergency shelters under OSHA subcontract, with 900 to 950 children up to 16 years of age. The average number of children per family was two.

By law, all school-age children in the shelters must attend school either at the school proximal to the shelter or at the school the children attended prior to moving to the shelter. The Philadelphia School District, under state mandate, in late 1991 and early 1992 developed special programs for these children.

The School of Social Administration at Temple University developed a comprehensive social services program for homeless children in cooperation with both the school district and OSHA. Master's level students were placed in schools to provide social work services as well as tutorial help.

The Four Counties

The four counties do not have official agencies dealing with homeless adults, although each one developed a Comprehensive Housing (CHAS) plan for the U.S. Department of Housing and Urban Development (HUD), mandated by federal regulations for counties to receive federal housing money. By 1996, the plans had not yet had much visible effect upon the situation of homeless families in these counties. County C&Y offices often had to help homeless families with dependent children.

Scattered throughout the four counties are privately organized shelters and programs for homeless families. Some of the shelters or emergency housing for families are only open at night or in cold weather. A few are barracks-like with relatively large areas shared by several families. In other shelters, each family has a room. In a number of cases, county C&Y programs have contracts with residential family programs outside of the county and even outside the metropolitan area to provide residential and special (usually addiction) services to needy families. There are also special residential programs for women and children fleeing abusive situations.

Bucks. Bucks County alone of the suburban counties has a number of programs developed cooperatively by county and private sources. People working in human services began noticing homeless families in the 1970s. Increases since then have produced programs providing help to those already without homes or to prevent families from becoming homeless. Family shelters are only part of the system.

The county C&Y office served 1,600 to 1,700 children a month, in 1993—about 10,000 a year. Some were long-term cases, some were new, most were short term. Due to special efforts to keep children with their families, only 200 children per year were in foster placement. The average number of children per homeless family had dropped to a low of 2.4 in 1992.

Bucks County is an example of creative use of various funding sources, that is, federal, state, county, local, and private resources. A semipublic joint Red Cross-C&Y shelter is unique to the county. There are also several other shelters in urbanized areas. The former C&Y director reminisced that in warm weather homeless families were put in tents in camping areas in local state and county parks.

In the 1970s, a program unique to Bucks County was developed cooperatively by public and private agencies, the Bucks County Housing Group Inc. Its programs, for county residents only, include three shelters, transitional housing for 20-25 families, permanent housing designed to remove families from homelessness, and mortgage programs to prevent loss of homes through mortgage foreclosure. One goal is to rehabilitate housing for low-income people. Several small apartment houses have been rehabilitated, some for transitional living, some for more permanent rental. Funding for these programs comes from combinations of state, federal, local, and some private sources (Gordon, 1993).

The Red Cross shelter, the largest in the county, is a specially constructed building on county land near the northern border of Philadelphia. Constructed primarily to provide inexpensive, cold weather shelter for families, it is the only shelter in Bucks County that admits single people if space is available. Privacy and other amenities were neglected in the planning and construction. Sleeping accommodations are a dormitory room with 75 cots and several cribs. With restricted funding until the early 1990s, the shelter was open for five winter months. Funding was found to open the shelter for nine months in 1992-1993. In 1993-1994, there were plans to open for it ten months, September through June, so children could attend a full school year. However, available funding only permitted it to be open through March 1994.

Funding sources for 1993-1994 indicate the variety of sources used. They included one-year grants of $200,000 from the Pennsylvania Department of Community Affairs, $75,000 from a federal HUD Community Development Block Grant, $50,000 from the local United Way, and a hoped-for grant of $37,500 from the township. The director had applied for the $300,000 additional funding from other sources to keep the program going through the end of the school year. There were uncertain hopes for funding for full-year operation in 1994 and thereafter (Boccella, 1993).

Other shelters in Bucks County for families only are much smaller. One is operated by a local committee in three neighboring townships in upper Bucks. A Salvation Army shelter in lower Bucks is near the Red Cross shelter, and the Bucks County Housing Group runs three shelters across the county. Other groups periodically discuss new shelters but the plans often don't materialize.

Because low-income housing is insufficient for needs in Bucks County, in 1986 a transitional housing program was developed in the C&Y office to help find apartments for homeless families. Rent is subsidized for up to one year while social services, budgeting help, and job training are provided. Self-sufficiency is the goal. The family then can remain in the apartment. As units are taken, new ones are developed for new families. The director and staff of the C&Y office would like to see it become a two-year program.

Transportation is a major problem in Bucks County because of poor public transportation. Programs often have to help families get cars as part of their services toward independence and self-sufficiency.

The Human Services director and staff would like to see a more rational, sequential program that could be tailored to a family's needs. A short-term component for adjustment time and assessment of the family's situation and needs would feed a middle-term component for families to work out their problems. A transitional program then would lead to independent "normal" living. The aim would be to avoid placement of children. The staff found that, after they are removed, it is hard to put children back into their family setting. (Shealy, 1995, gives a comprehensive discussion of the psychosocial issues.) In the early 1980s, a number of children were placed due to family homelessness. That was rare in the 1990s.

Families in Bucks County, the C&Y staff reported, were living in cars, the woods, shacks, abandoned buildings, and abandoned tractor trailers. A family in 1992 was living in a tractor trailer without water, electricity, or modern cooking facilities. The father was outraged that the authorities thought it an unfit place for children.

The other three counties rely mostly on foster care and some emergency shelters for help with homeless families. The C&Y offices usually contract with private organizations to provide shelter for those in need.

Delaware. In Delaware County, there is one emergency shelter, Wesley House. It houses both women with children and men for a maximum of 90 days. The maximum occupancy level is 40 women and children and 30 men. There is often a waiting list. The C&Y office also can place families, in an emergency, for 3 to 5 days in area hotels and motels. The main goal is to prevent foster or institutional placement of children in emergencies.

A transitional housing program subsidizes rent for six months, after which families are expected to assume full payment of rent. The WAWA (Women's Association for Women's Alternatives) facility serves women with young children for three to six months, with shelter, counseling, parent education, career development, and home management skills training. A 30-day emergency shelter, with a maximum occupancy of 25 women and children, serves victims of domestic abuse. In 1991-1992, WAWA served 91 women and 125 children.

Chester. Three family shelters exist in the county as well as a program run through a network of churches. A program for the Spanish-speaking population of the county was being organized in late 1993.

Montgomery. In Montgomery County, there were four general family shelters in 1993. Two are operated by the Salvation Army in different sections of the county; the third, by Mother Teresa's religious order; and the fourth, by a Protestant church. There are also two interfaith hospitality networks, described below. The Norristown Ministries opened a daytime hospitality center for homeless families needing daytime shelter.

Private Programs

A range of privately organized and sponsored programs for homeless people exists in the metropolitan area, in the central city, and in suburban and exurban sectors. Most programs in the city are nonsectarian; almost all outside the city and Bucks County are related to religious organizations. A number of variants have developed, some using church/synagogue facilities and volunteers; others using just volunteers; some shorter term, others longer term.

UNMET AND PRESSING NEEDS

The biggest needs in the area are for decent low-income housing, decent, affordable, and accessible child care, and services that address the needs of the children in these families. Most programs are designed primarily for the parents. Particularly in need of help are teenage children. There are major gaps in services for pregnant women, women aged 18 to 21, and those with learning disabilities, mild retardation, or other reasons they would need more than a year to achieve financial independence.

Discussion

The region presents a fragmented picture of a diversity of programs and approaches to the issues of homeless families. The services available present a mosaic of a relatively small number of effective and creative programs and a large number of fingers in the dike. Most rehabilitative programs tend to be quite selective, often serving only one in ten applicants, and are relatively short term.

Only Bucks county developed a program concept and had a somewhat integrated response to homeless families. In the other suburban counties, resources were limited to private programs and foster care.

In Philadelphia, the needs of homeless families overwhelmed the available resources, and efforts were primarily focused on providing some sort of shelter. The city programs, while extensive and expensive, in addition served primarily one segment of the homeless family population—black, female-headed, single-parent families. It was not possible to find out what happened to other homeless families in the city.

There was little communication between programs, departments, and counties. This contrasts with the concerns and desires of the directors and workers in the field. Most were overwhelmed by the need as well as the insufficiency of responses.

The state provided some direction but usually under federal guidelines. A new state program under federal Title XX had begun to address the child care issue. Each county had an agency under this program working on provision of services.

All programs and public services seemed to look to the federal government for guidance and sustenance. Until the end of 1993, this was forthcoming only in meager measure, contrary to the stated philosophy of the outgoing national administration. In 1993, the incoming administration, though of different philosophical bent, had not yet made homeless families a priority for discussion. With the congressional elections of 1994, the likelihood of governmental preventive and effective curative response faded even further into the future.

The notion of primary prevention is unthought of and certainly unstated on all levels. In fact, a recent issue of a program newsletter says specifically, "[The program's] efforts are not to end homelessness but give people a safe place among caring people while they gather together the things necessary for independent living" ("Book Details," 1994). The closest that any program or thinking comes to prevention is on the secondary and tertiary levels, preventing a particular family from becoming or remaining homeless.

These programs are a compassionate response to a difficult problem. Some are more effectively conceived, some less so; some more selective, some less; all are designed to help people in distress, and some even to help them get out of distress, but none to prevent the distress in the first place.

In the next chapter, a wider range of social responses to the homelessness of children will be discussed. We can see a variety of creative responses. An overview will be given of the organization of programs for homeless children and families in southeast Pennsylvania as well as a more general overview of national developments and some comparative international approaches.

Ideas about what would be effective programs and approaches are set forth. These are based upon differing suppositions about what is to be achieved, that is, prevention, amelioration, or maintenance of the status quo.

Chapter 11

SOCIETAL RESPONSES
TO HOMELESSNESS

The Found Boy (continued)

He was so many rags,
one spool of her thread was not enough.
So when her spool of white thread was gone,
she began to mend in her yellow thread.
And when her yellow thread was gone,
she began to mend in the blue.
And when the blue was gone she began in the pink
and when the pink was gone she began in violet,
and then in red and in orange and in purple and green—
all the colors in her basket she was mending in,
which was practically all the colors in the world.
(From "The Found Boy" in *Somebody Else's Nut Tree* by Ruth Krauss)

In this chapter, social policies and programs related to homeless children
will be examined. They have one of four foci: prevention, punishment,
amelioration of consequences, or not dealing with the phenomenon. Until
the 1970s, American social policy and programs took the last of the three
approaches. Since then, federal and state legislation and regulations have
developed and some semblance of a policy has emerged.

BACKGROUND

American social policy developed from an individualistic, antigovernment social philosophy. Historically, each family was to be responsible for its own well-being. Children belonged to and were the responsibility of the family.

The 1930s Depression brought a change. The national government, under the New Deal, assumed some responsibility to help individuals and families. Through the 1960s and early 1970s, many governmental programs were developed. In general, children continued to be seen as belonging to and the responsibility of their parent(s). The concept of personal responsibility remained strong and, for some, in conflict with the new governmental roles.

During the 1980s and early 1990s, these two social philosophies came into conflict. A major attempt was initiated to return to earlier concepts. Some of the programmatic disarray found in the early 1990s came from the conflict. Budgets were cut. Major disruptions of programs, decreasing financial resources, morale problems, but not general disbanding of such programs, resulted by 1996.

States were pressured to move in similar directions. Punitive legislation was introduced and at times passed, i.e., the Washington State "Becca" law (E2SSB 5439, 1995 and E2SHB 2217, 1996). Billed as "parents' rights" laws (Cameron, 1994) they raised the age of consent and reinstated running away or street activities as status offenses with possible penalties of incarceration or involuntary hospitalization (Final Bill Report, E2SHB 2217, Washington State, 1996). Similar legislation was introduced on the federal level in 1996.

This movement was resisted, the Washington State legislation was partially vetoed and federal legislation was not enacted. In 1996 public programs remainded children of the national government often with major state and local input.

AMERICAN RESPONSES

American policies regarding homelessness assume its existence and focus on amelioration of suffering and some sequelae. Many programs have been organized and much money has been spent to help homeless children and families.

Many activities and programs around the United States to help the homeless are often very effective in what they do. Other programs are essentially holding actions. Public and private shelters, rehabilitative residences, boarding houses, and "flop" houses exist. There are educational, rehabilitative, housing, and job programs, food kitchens, clothing and toy collection agencies, and others.

Organizations of homeless adults provide self-help and try to influence the government and the public. The National Network of Runaway and Youth Services (described later) and local or regional coalitions/networks try to give homeless and runaway youth a political voice, although they are primarily organizations of service and care providers.

The personal, altruistic, and compassionate response of a suburban Philadelphia teen named Trevor is an example of how some programs develop. Seeing people living on the streets of the city, he returned to distribute sandwiches, hot drinks, and blankets regularly. Publicized in the news media, it grew into Trevor's Campaign. Trevor's Place started subsequently as a shelter for homeless people and families. Growing out of one boy's humanitarian impulses, much individual time, energy, and money has been invested and some suffering has been alleviated.

Legislative and programmatic responses have combined public and private resources and services. Often public agencies oversee the work of private services and/or contract with them to provide services. Direct public services also have been developed.

State child protective and welfare agencies are partially funded by, operate under, and are supervised by federal regulations. As federal and state laws have been passed, and to increase local responsibility for vulnerable people, the necessary county and local departments have developed with some variety from one state to another.

Federal Legislation and Programs

Federal legislation and programs have formed the backbone of programs for homeless children. A short summary follows of the legislation and programs that have addressed various aspects related to homelessness: housing, education, health, employment. They also have been aimed at specific groups—adults, older teenagers, young teenagers, children—and/or by status—unaccompanied youth, single people, two-parent families, and single-parent families.

The McKinney Homeless Assistance Act. A wide range of services for homeless families were mandated and developed under this act, including emergency shelter and food, rehabilitation of housing, physical and mental health services, and long-term and follow-up services. Educational programs came from this act, such as the Pennsylvania Homeless Children's Initiative.

The Runaway and Homeless Youth Act (RHYA). RHYA targets unaccompanied homeless youth. Until the early 1970s, the juvenile justice and corrections systems mixed criminal and noncriminal youth. About one third of the youth in these systems were status offenders, that is, out of their homes and/or schools without permission. Many were runaways. The act responded to the idea that status offenses should be decriminalized and deinstitutionalized, treated nonlegalistically and more sympathetically.

The history of the act illuminates relevant developments. The Juvenile Justice and Delinquency Prevention Act (JJDPA), part of which was the Runaway Youth Act, was passed in 1974 by Congress. (Amended in 1977, it became the Runaway and Homeless Youth Act [RHYA].)

Jurisdiction over programs was split. Most of the JJDPA would be administered by the Department of Justice and the RHYA by the Department of Health and Human Services' Family and Youth Services Bureau. In 1988, this became part of the Administration for Children, Youth and Families. In 1988, RHYA was amended, creating the Transitional Living Grant Program for Homeless Youth (TLP) to move older youth to self-sufficient living. Another program to move older youth toward independent adult living is the Independent Living Program for Youth in Foster Care, created in 1986 under Title IV-E of the Social Security Act.

Through the early 1990s, there was consistent growth in funding and program development. In 1975, 120 programs were funded under RHYA to provide emergency shelter and essential services, which increased by 1989 to almost 350 agencies. Some of the agencies had been providing services for youth for over a century; others developed since 1975.

Initially, services under RHYA provided a short-term, safe place to stay and clothing, food, and crisis counseling. Allowable services have since expanded to include dealing with physical and sexual abuse, substance abuse, mental health, pregnancy and parenting, and education including learning disabilities.

There continues to be recognition among community-based youth-serving agencies of the need for a continuum of coordinated services for youth including primary prevention, emergency shelters, and long-term transitional living programs with specific components for sexual abuse, pregnancy and early parenting, education, employment, and alcohol and other drug treatment (National Network, 1991, p. 14).

Health Initiatives

Legislation on health issues focuses primarily on sexuality and substance abuse. Parts of the Omnibus Drug Initiative Act of 1988 set up the Office for Substance Abuse Prevention in the Public Health Service; Title X of the Public Health Service Act, for family planning; and Title XX of the same act to address teenage sexual behavior and pregnancy. The Centers for Disease Control of the National Institute of Health (NIH) set up DASH (Division of Adolescent and School Health) and directed the Center for Prevention Services to develop programs to prevent the spread of HIV+.

Funding

Programs serving homeless youth piece together federal, state, local, and private funding sources. In 1990, the federal government appropriated about $26 million for RHYA Basic Center grants, $10 million for transitional living grants, and $15 million for substance abuse prevention, among others. Federal money, often funneled through state auspices, was provided through the Office of Substance Abuse Prevention, the Mental Health Administration, and the McKinney Act for educational and health services, among others.

By 1995, heavy federal budget cuts had affected all social services. With the lessening of federal support, some states and localities tried to supplement funding for the homeless. Over two thirds of program money in 1995 was estimated to come from state and local sources, and about 22% from federal sources.

Myriad private sources of funds, including private fund-raising, organizations like the United Way, foundations, corporations, individuals, and others, provided about one quarter of the funds for services for runaway and homeless youth. "Juggling a variety of different funding sources has become an art for many community-based agencies. One agency reported 64 different funding sources" (National Network, 1991, p. 15).

In addition, funding is unstable. As the public becomes aware of a problem, funds go for that while older problems may be neglected. Private services pick the populations and problems with which they will deal, that is, children, teens, women and children, families. Some fund or provide services for substance abusers; others forbid substance abuse. Some support emergency programs; others support programs that are short term, long term; and so on. Services often are directed to fit funding specifics. Funding sources discourage pyramiding of monies.

National Youth Policy

To encourage stability in services for children, in the late 1980s there were calls for a national youth policy to ensure young Americans rights and health, educational, and social services on a coordinated continuum. The National Network was a major influence. A beginning attempt was the Young Americans Act of 1990, which was part of the Human Services Reauthorization Act.

The act mandated organization of the Administration of Children, Youth and Families (ACYF) in the U.S. Department of Health and Human Services (DHHS). The law provided congressional approval for modification of this separate administrative entity to prevent future national administrations from executively reorganizing it out of existence. The preamble to the act aimed to change the commitment of the nation to its youth:

> Children and youth are [the nation's] most valuable resource;
>
> Their welfare, protection, healthy development and positive role in society are essential to the Nation;
>
> Children and youth deserve love, respect and guidance as well as good health, shelter, food, education, productive work and preparation for responsible participation in community life;
>
> The family is the primary caregiver and the source of social learning and must be supported and strengthened;
>
> When families, however, are unable to ensure the satisfaction of these needs, it is society's responsibility to assist them. (Able-Peterson & Bucy, 1993, p. 15)

The implementation and success of a national youth policy and the ACYF remain to be seen. The concept of a national policy that guarantees health, education, and security for all American youth may have become politically impossible in 1995.

Organization of Services

Services, usually organized on the basis of local needs and developments, have been uncoordinated. To help readers understand the system, metropolitan Philadelphia-southeast Pennsylvania (see the introduction to Part III) will be examined.

Southeast Pennsylvania exhibits the severe stress and overload under which these services, especially the public ones, suffer, as well as the creative and fragmented provision of ameliorative services to homeless children. It is similar to other metropolitan areas. Agencies and programs helping children and families tend to be overburdened, understaffed, undertrained, underfunded, and undervalued. Each county has slightly different services under varying auspices and funding, public and private, often with no communication or coordination.

General differences between Pennsylvania, New York, and New Jersey are highlighted prior to the description of services in the Pennsylvania region.

NEW YORK AND NEW JERSEY

New York State, New Jersey, and Pennsylvania are each organized on slightly different principles.[1] In Pennsylvania, strongly influenced by the federalist tradition, counties have more power and independence than in the two other states. New Jersey has more central authority, and New York State is somewhat intermediate.

In New Jersey, children's programs are a state responsibility. DYFS (the Division of Youth and Family Services), of the Department of Human Services, provides and supervises all child protective services within the state. It has branch offices throughout the state.

New York state has a Runaway and Homeless Youth (RHY) Act, first passed in 1978. It functions through the New York State Division for Youth. Under it, state funds are allocated to certified programs serving RHY. A directory of these programs by county is compiled yearly. Each county is required to have a RHY coordinator. The programs vary between counties (Dunston, Devane, Preudhomme, & Glick, 1994).

Definitions and regulations vary between states. Definitions of abuse and who can be given involuntary service are somewhat conservative in Pennsylvania. To provide nonvoluntary services to families, exacting proof of abuse and neglect must be offered. Danger of abuse and neglect is not sufficient for provision of involuntary service.

In 1993, legislation was introduced in Pennsylvania to more closely resemble that of New York and New Jersey. There, child protective services can take a more proactive stance in cases in which there is suspicion of neglect or abuse. However, the same problems and complaints of inadequacy and insufficient service are aired about all three state child protective systems.

SOUTHEAST PENNSYLVANIA

Organization and Funding of Programs

Every county in Pennsylvania, under commonwealth (state) law, which was inspired by federal law, has a public agency responsible for providing help and protection to dependent and neglected children, and by extension to homeless children and families, because the commonwealth defines homeless children as "dependent."

Each county office provides services directly or by contract with private agencies. The mix varies with the same two goals. The first is to find immediate shelter for any child without shelter and develop some longer range plan and program. Second, children separated from parents are to be returned to their custody and supervision or as close a relative as possible, as quickly as possible, without endangering the child.

Because of its size and unique position as a class one, home-rule city/county, the situation in Philadelphia differs in kind and in numbers from the surrounding counties. But, in essence, the function of the program is similar.

Dependent children are under the supervision of the Commonwealth of Pennsylvania Department of Public Welfare, Office of Children, Youth and Families. State regulations define the number of families each worker can provide service to, what neglect and abuse are, the minimum amount of time to be spent with "cases," and who is eligible for service on involuntary and voluntary bases.

Pennsylvania child protective workers are limited to working with no more than 30 "cases" or families (60 to 100 children). They supervise foster care and investigate situations of abuse and neglect to determine eligibility for service. Staff are expected to revive and retrieve the severely damaged victims of family and social dysfunction.

In each county, the children and youth programs have a slightly different name and place in the county bureaucracy, that is, the Bureau of C&Y, Office of C&Y, and so on. Programs and services to homeless children in the five counties combine public and private initiatives and receive public money either in grants or as fees for service.

Suburban counties offer fewer services than the city. In the counties, most programs are private. Some agencies are specific to a county; others have programs in two or more counties. However, major similarities between the organization of services become apparent.

People working in it say that the system is both compassionate and deficient. As a person who has spent time examining the system, I believe that most people to whom I spoke and with whom I met are caring, concerned, and compassionate people. Administrators in many agencies affirm that there is a good collaborative spirit.

Here are some of the variations found in southeast Pennsylvania.

Philadelphia

In addition to having much more autonomy, the county/city is expected to pay a higher proportion of the costs of its programs through monies raised from its class one taxing abilities. The social services of the city have very old roots and consume a large and rising proportion of the city's budget. The city's Department of Human Services (DHS) (previously the Department of Public Welfare), Office of Children and Youth is the child protective agency of Philadelphia.

It was formed in 1919 when the federal government passed a County Institution District Act, which gave counties responsibility for supervising their children's institutions. With passage of the national Social Security Act in 1935, the responsibility of county supervision was increased. The new charter of 1953 made the department responsible for all minors, especially those neglected, abused, or endangered, as well as the homeless, aged, prisoners, and criminally insane. In the 1970s, the city council created the current name of the department.

DHS is an example of child protective agencies in urban and other areas with high levels of poverty and social problems. In a common pattern in the urban northeastern states, most services are provided through contract with what were and often remain sectarian and/or ethnic agencies. Social service systems, some quite large and old, are under Roman Catholic, Jewish, Episcopal, Lutheran, Hispanic, black, and nonsectarian private auspices.

Philadelphia has a bureau for homeless families that is outside of the child protective system. The Office of Services to Homeless Adults (OSHA) coordinates, supervises, and helps fund private services to homeless adults and families. It oversees 16 shelters for families (and other adult shelters) as well as other services for homeless families and adults. OSHA had made some arrangements for health care and was developing means of providing social services for children in the shelters in 1993 (Woestendiek, 1993).

Private shelters and programs were supervised and partially funded by OSHA—some also receiving DHS supervision and funding, some more independent, others in some other combination. Each program defined its own mission, goals, service population, and services. One major problem, explained by the director of OSHA, is that much funding specifies the uses of the money and does not permit pyramiding of different funds to make a complete program.

Shelters generally provide spare living conditions for good money. "The city pays $2,205 [per month] minus the families' $112 shelter fees" for each family in a shelter. A typical Philadelphia family shelter has 250 residents at any one time, about 140 of them children.

The families live in single rooms and eat meals provided by the shelter in a common dining room. Used clothing is provided for those who need it. Residents are not supposed to have food (even snacks) in their rooms. Use of alcohol, drugs, or physical conflict is cause for eviction. Life, budgeting, and parenting skills sessions, Narcotics Anonymous (NA) sessions, and minimal health care are provided. "The shelters despite substantial improvements, remain large, loud, dingy, crowded and, by their very nature, unhappy institutions—a tough place to raise a kid. And an even tougher place to be one" (Woestendiek, 1993).

Educational services to school-age children are provided under the McKinney Act (see Chapter 11) and equivalent commonwealth acts. The Philadelphia School District, under contract, provides educational services for homeless children in the shelters. There has been movement toward being flexible and responsive; for example, homeless children can stay in their home schools and receive free transportation, or transfer to schools near shelters in which there may be special programs for them. However, financial crises within the district, uneven commitment, shifts in personnel, overloaded teachers, and problems of morale affect the public school system in the city and, naturally, affect the programs for homeless children.

Services for permanent housing are provided by the city and county housing authorities, U.S. Department of Housing and Urban Development (HUD) programs, and private sources. The Philadelphia Housing Authority (PHA) supervises the city's low-income housing projects and the Section 8 program of subsidizing private housing. In the early 1990s, the PHA had bad publicity due to a number of scandals involving misuse and loss of available funds and administration.

A major factor affecting services in the early 1990s was the serious economic problems of the states and cities and the withdrawal of the federal government from social services. Services provided, although inadequate, are expensive.

> The city spends $167 million a year caring for children. Much of that goes to private agencies, treatment centers and foster families. To cut costs [workers] have been ordered to close an average of one case a month. If cases are not taken off DHS's books, either [workers] would have more than 30 cases—a violation of state regulations—or the city would have to hire more . . . which administration budget officials are reluctant to do. (Woestendiek, 1993)

A woman who had been in a Philadelphia shelter with a young son wrote about her experience in a local paper:

> The system is not designed for individual needs. It's designed to warehouse homeless people, lumping them all into one category and forcing them to fit a pattern. . . . All of the city shelters strive for a clean and sober environment. . . . A tremendous amount of time is devoted to penalizing residents who deviate from rules. . . . In other words the shelter system was not concerned with whether or not its residents are able to resume a normal standard of living or behave as normal adults do. (Whitmore, 1993, p. A23)

The woman, a student at a local university, left the shelter system to live with relatives. Many shelter residents have already exhausted that possibility. They usually enter the shelters when their last relative or friend can no longer help them with housing.

Although regulations and laws vary from one place to another, and one state to another, the complaints about and difficulties of these agencies are similar in many places. A possible explanation is that

> the lives that fall through the cracks . . . fall to the social workers. On the street, . . . at the [DHS, they] face all the symptoms of the city's decline, from crack to homelessness to child abuse. In the office, they face all the symptoms of the decline of the government they work for—shortages of copy paper, cars, telephones and training. (Purdy, 1993, p. 1)

The Counties

Bucks. The C&Y office has helped develop a rather complex system. A multibranched private youth agency, Youth Services of Bucks Co., Inc. (originally a county department, now a private agency working closely with the C&Y office), has expanded its services. It operates several shelters partially funded under RHYA. Bucks County is the only county, other than Philadelphia, with a RHYA shelter for local youth. There are several family shelters, and a group of them are operated by several local governments. Most are under secular auspices.

Montgomery County. Services to families of dependent children are mostly provided directly by workers of the C&Y office. Services to youth are usually contracted out to private agencies. In 1993, religious organizations operated four family shelters. The Salvation Army had two family shelters; Mother Teresa's order, the Sisters of Charity, had a nighttime-only family shelter; and a local Protestant church, a family shelter. The Norristown Ministries aimed to coordinate services for homeless adults and families in that city. They also organized a daytime hospitality center for homeless families and adults in need of a place to go during the day.

Alternatives, Inc., a private agency with several branches, had a RHYA-funded runaway program for youth from out of the area. Its other youth shelter and counseling programs are run, primarily, in cooperation with C&Y and Juvenile Probation. Unaccompanied youth are placed in foster care (about 85%), group homes, or institutions. There were 355 children in placement, under C&Y supervision, in July 1993. Of these, 192 were Caucasian, 157 were black, 5 were Hispanic, and 1 was Asian; 316 were in foster care, 10 in group homes, and 29 in institutions.

A private agency, Tabor Children's Services, has a contract for an Independent Living Training program for 16-year-olds in foster care to learn to live independently.

This county, as the others, has a federally mandated and partially funded Housing Assistance Program (HAP) for families in danger of losing their homes. This provides a maximum of $500 for a family either for help in getting an apartment or to prevent eviction. The major needs in the county to help deal with homelessness, according to child welfare workers, are low-income housing and transportation.

Delaware. The most seriously affected deindustrializing center in the region is Chester City in Delaware County. It has a predominantly low-income, minority population. Formerly a relatively prosperous industrial and port city, it is in physical and psychological ruins. About 50% of child welfare cases in the county come from Chester City, which has about 15% of the total population. The city's problems are of every kind: economic, political, psychological, social, and social psychological.

Much of the system in Delaware County resembles that in the other counties. Many of the services to families in distress are provided through C&Y, which contracts with private agencies when available and appropriate.

Most services are in the county but some are in Philadelphia and surrounding counties. The child protective staff repeats the distress call: They are overwhelmed; they have too few resources and too much need.

Chester County. The C&Y office operates similarly to those in the other counties. In 1993, there was a plan to provide special Spanish-language services, previously unavailable, in the mushroom-growing area. The county has few services of its own and the C&Y office has had little call for service to homeless families or youth.

Other Systems and Services

Corporate social services. The instability of governmental social policies has led to several developments in the organization of private programs. Corporate private social service organizations have developed in response to the fluid, complex funding patterns and concurrent need for a wide range of specific administrative and development specializations.

Central organizations develop management and funding expertise and have numerous, often unrelated, agencies and programs under their aegis. They coordinate, help develop, channel funding for, supervise, and initiate programs, take over floundering programs, and fulfill almost any other varied function in the private, nonprofit health and social services areas throughout the region and beyond, as exemplified by two Philadelphia corporations. A large variety of funding sources, public and private, have been pieced together.

Philadelphia Health Management Corp. (PHMC), founded in 1972, is a health and social services corporation. By 1993, it had grown into a major nonprofit corporation, headquartered in a large office building in Center City, Philadelphia. Health and social services to homeless adults and families are among the many programs they supervise (PHMC, 1993).

Money for social programming funding for their programs in 1992 came from two federal departments, the U.S. DHHS and U.S. DOT (Department of Transportation) including ten different funding sources from within DHHS; five Pennsylvania state departments, and one in Delaware; one municipal department in the District of Columbia; 14 local governmental programs; 23 foundations and private philanthropies; and 38 other private sources including hospitals, unions, universities, businesses, and others.

Resources for Human Development, Inc. (RHD), the other private, primarily nonprofit corporation, evolved in 1970 out of a suburban family counseling agency. It developed a variety of services, at first in Montgomery County. It also took over programs developed by other organizations.

Eventually, Philadelphia programs became the largest element of its programs.

In the mid-1980s, it moved its corporate headquarters to Philadelphia and expanded services and funding. In 1993, it sponsored "over 110 human service programs. Some of them . . . large and funded with government grants (like [their] Head Start sites in Philadelphia). Many small entrepreneurial efforts [were] sponsored" (RHD, 1993).

Family House, a residential treatment program for substance-abusing women, many of whom are homeless, is a constituent agency. The program was taken over by RHD when the initiating agency, a large, regional substance abuse rehabilitation institution, divested.

OTHER DEVELOPMENTS

Other private agencies and services are much more specific. Some deal with the problems of unaccompanied homeless children as contractors for the C&Y programs. In the Philadelphia area, several serve homeless families and women. Services tend to be segregated by those predominantly, although not exclusively, serving Caucasian non-Jewish or Jewish, black, or Hispanic people. Special services to Asian, primarily immigrant, populations are offered through a variety of agencies.

Redefinition of existing programs is one response to new issues. In 1991, New Jersey state government proved its creativity by redirecting an existing program to provide homeless families with the means to permanently house themselves (Enda, 1991). The national program, "Emergency Assistance," which provides temporary, emergency housing had not been previously used in this manner.

Governor Florio's administration suggested that the money being used for temporary, usually inadequate and expensive, shelter be used to subsidize permanent housing for up to a year—for example, a $250-a-month subsidy for an apartment instead of $1,000 to $2,000 for a hotel or motel room.

Unfortunately, with high rental costs, the fear was that the families would become homeless again when they needed to pay full rent. The program could not create low-cost housing, which is severely lacking in the state. It also was threatened by federal cuts that were favored, at the time, by the Bush administration (Enda, 1991) and further by the congressional leadership after 1994.

The needs of pregnant homeless women were addressed by the Better Homes Fund and Ronald McDonald Children's Charity. "Tomorrow's

Child" developed "innovative approaches to [their] special and complex needs" in Baltimore, Maryland; Oakland, California; and Multnomah County, Oregon. They provide "emergency shelter, aggressive outreach and case finding, prenatal services, long-term case management, parenting support and services for special needs" (Weinreb et al., 1995, p. 494).

"First Place," a small nonprofit school in Seattle, Washington, serves children in emergency shelters or temporary/transitional housing. Its educational program (K-6) is supplemented by social service teams. It also provides breakfast, lunch, and snacks, health care, supplies, transportation, tutoring, and on-site psychologist and other services (Cameron, 1994).

"Hope for the Children" set up a foster care community, Hope Meadows. Foster families live rent-free in a newly developed neighborhood on a closed air force base. Parents are paid a yearly salary and provided with support systems. The aim is to develop a stable, nurturing, caring community for foster families to avoid the negative consequences of foster care (Azar, 1995a).

Shelters

Most efforts center on providing temporary, "emergency" shelter and food, particularly in cold weather. They operate under public and private nonprofit, religious and secular auspices. Some municipalities have laws requiring provision of overnight shelter for homeless people under emergency conditions of extreme cold and/or snow. Although the shelters may consist of unused jail cells, they are facilities in which homeless children, families, or adults can, at a minimum, have beds at night and a place to attend to sanitary needs.

Facilities go from large public or quasi-public buildings, such as National Guard armories or office buildings, to those that are like private homes. Some restrict access to nighttime. Others are open 24 hours. Some have dormitory or mass sleeping areas; others provide separate rooms or small areas for a few people or a family. Some provide a bed, bedding, and toilet facilities; others provide services such as education, food, social service, counseling, employment training, help in finding housing or health care.

Outreach

Outreach programs for "street youth" and adults have spread. The U.S. government, through the Department of Health and Human Services, has printed a manual for youth programs that discusses several successful programs in major urban communities and Alaska. "In cities like Boston, San Francisco, Chicago, and New York, with significant, easily observed numbers of homeless youth, streetwork began several years ago" (Able-Peterson & Bucy, 1993, p. 18).

Educational Programs

Head Start, a preschool program, was started during the "War on Poverty" in the 1960s. Considered one of the most successful antipoverty programs, it has spread, with many variations, across the country. A New York City suburb had a pilot Head Start for homeless children expelled from "regular Head Start classes for the homeless." The principle was that children with stress, anger, frustration, "disappointment and madness in their lives" need early intervention to direct and deal with the "blind rage" they feel. The program provided therapy and educational experiences as well as advocacy for the children with their families and others (Winerip, 1993a, p. 25).

Other special programs. Among educational programs with a positive impact are "last resort schools." Chester County Alternative Education Program is "where violent-tempered, unruly high school students go when their behavior is so bad their own schools can't control them." The students come from "broken families, abusive families or families that have abandoned them." The program is based upon understanding and tough demands.

The Martin-Emerick school in New York City is for homosexual youth having severe difficulties in high school. Part of the city public school system but partially funded by a foundation, it is the only school in the United States for homosexual youth.

In Philadelphia, during the 1980s, a special group home was set up for homeless homosexual young men. Due to funding problems and neighbors' resistance, it went out of business.

The Arts

The use of creative, artistic programs for rehabilitation of homeless youth is rare but effective. The life situations of these youth attack their self-esteem and self-concept. The arts and self-expression can help change their lives and self-concept.

In Toronto, a Shakespearian performing group was organized with homeless youth as actors and support staff. "Shakespeare in the wasteland with its bubbling energy and imagination . . . has become both a forum for the youths and a source of money to help them" (Farnsworth, 1993, p. A4).

The sponsoring organization, Kytes (Kensington Youth Theatre and Employment Skills), taught communication, job skills, and self-esteem through involvement in theater. "Troupe members not only create theater, but upgrade themselves academically, find stable housing and confront alcohol or drug use and other problems arising from anger at parents and society." The Canadian government provided some financial backing to the program until 1993. Proceeds of ticket sales then became the major source of funds (Farnsworth, 1993, p. A4).

Another creative program was developed in New York City. It involved writing and the concept of providing a voice for previously voiceless youth. One product of this program was *Foster Care Youth United,* a newspaper written by foster youth. They were involved in all stages of producing the journal. In addition to an opportunity to upgrade academic skills and gain journalistic experience, it provided a forum for expressing their pain and their pride.

Summer Camp

Camp Homeward Bound leases land in Harriman State Park in southeastern New York State. Since 1984, it has served homeless children primarily from New York City. The Coalition, "a service and advocacy organization based in Manhattan," organized the camp (Steinberg, 1993, p. B1). Costs were covered by the DHS of New York City, the U.S. Department of Agriculture, and the Coalition.

Family Preservation/Support

In the 1990s, the American family and society's response to and responsibilities for families became a public policy issue. In the 1992 U.S. presidential election campaign, the issue of "family values" was raised. The deterioration of the position of children in society was attributed to increases in single-parent families, teenage parents, child abuse, children being the largest group of the impoverished, homeless families, and violence and crime among children and youth. All this coincided with professional attempts to address these issues.

"Family preservation services" (Cole & Duva, 1990), or the "family support movement" (Kagan & Weissbord, 1994), were controversial and had opposition (Landers, 1994). Their "origins [were] in the practice of home visiting and in the history of child welfare in America" (Morton, 1993, p. 3). The focus was "high-risk" families and youth (Morton & Grigsby, 1993, p. vii).

The twentieth-century genesis stems from the first White House Conference on Children in 1909. The benefits of keeping children in their own homes and improving the home and family life were brought to public attention there. Eighty years later, policy and practice remain limited (Morton, 1993, p. 7).

Family preservation practice seems to be helpful to individual families and appreciated by many professionals. It also remains little understood, sometimes even by those who are practicing it, which leads to controversy and mistakes (Landers, 1994). Research has shown success (Berry, 1994) or has raised questions of validity or function (Schuerman, Rzepnicki, & Littell, 1994).

Kinship Care

An estimated 60,000-plus Philadelphia children in 1994 were being raised by relatives, often grandparents, other than their parents (Borowski, 1994, p. B1). AARP (the American Association of Retired Persons) estimated in 1992 that 865,000 children, increasing in 1993 to over a million, were being raised by grandparents (Lee, 1994, p. 1). Another national estimate in late 1993 was that almost 4 million children were being raised by grandparents and many more by other relatives (Woodall, 1993, p. B1). The U.S. Census Bureau reported in 1994 that 12% of African American and 3% of "non-Hispanic white children live with grandparents" (Borowski, 1994, p. B2).

Kinship care has many positive elements for children in need of care: "In child advocacy circles, [it] is considered a blessing for the youngsters, for it spares them the dislocation of being placed in foster care [with unrelated and unknown families]. Many experts consider it a vital strategy in family preservation" (Woodall, 1993, p. B1).

Kinship care is not without economic, physical, psychological, and social problems. Financially, many of the children stay outside the child protective system and the caretakers receive little help in providing for them. In fact, often "grandparents become poorer, tapping their Social Security benefits to also support a child" (Borowski, 1994, p. B1).

There are many psychological burdens possible in caring for a child's or sibling's neglected or abandoned child(ren). There is the adjustment to having children, many with major emotional and developmental needs, in the house again. There is need to readjust the organization of one's life. For many it can become a physical burden (Lee, 1994).

A national conference held in Philadelphia in November 1993 dealt with the issues and problems of "kinship care" or "kinship foster care" "to create a nurturing bureaucracy for kinship care." The conference was for child welfare workers to discuss and seek solutions to many of the problems of both the families and the bureaucracy (Woodall, 1993, p. B6).

In some areas, support groups have developed. Kin Can (Kinship Caregivers Assistance Network) was organized in the Philadelphia area in 1993 by 12 independent support groups formed by the relative caregivers (Borowski, 1994; Woodall, 1993, p. B6). AARP developed the Grandparent Information Center, based in Washington, D.C., in 1993 "to offer help and information to grandparents raising grandchildren" (Lee, 1994, p. B3).

Integrated Services

An attempt to overcome the fragmentation of services, programs, and agencies providing help to families is by having a variety of agencies and programs, available and communicating, in one place. In 1990, the Child Welfare League of America (CWLA) convened a colloquium, "Homelessness: The Impact on the Child Welfare System in the 1990s." The need for large-scale, integrated, and coordinated programs was a recurring theme. Development of case management and interagency collaboration was stressed. "Linkage of services across systems" and avoidance of fragmentation were major recommendations. Interagency cooperation in funding for families at risk and for development of family environments was suggested. Integrated community-based practice was a suggested model.

Integration efforts are found in a variety of institutions. Community centers and settlement houses sometimes house a multitude of services and programs. Health care institutions are another venue for integration of services. The most ubiquitous American institution, the neighborhood school, is a logical place.

Community schools. In the early 1990s, the idea of schools as a major community resource was found in many parts of the country under a variety of guises. New York City and Philadelphia, among other cities, developed "school service centers" or "beacon schools," which included a number of supportive programs. The Philadelphia School District began community schools and beacon schools in 1994. It was estimated that there were hundreds of such programs (Winerip, 1993b).

The Children's Aid Society (CAS) and the New York City Board of Education cooperated in a pilot program that opened at 7 a.m. and closed late at night. Social services, health care, and before- and after-school educational and recreational programs for children and adults were run by the CAS. For both the CAS and the school system, the program provided benefits. The CAS didn't pay for facilities, and so used its finances more efficiently; the Board of Education didn't pay for services for the students and their families. A building that had been open half a day, nine months a year, functioned for the benefit of the community practically around the clock and calendar.

Farrell, Pennsylvania, developed an integrated, comprehensive secondary and tertiary preventive system. The "rust-belt" town's severe economic and family problems were seen as disrupting the attempt to educate children. Farrell's public schools and cooperating public and private social agencies developed a system to help children and their families "from womb to tomb" (Santiago, 1993, p. A10). The board of education's motivation was to improve the educational climate and educability of students. They understood that "children who are ill, neglected, hungry or sad, whose families are stressed or broken, cannot be taught."

Under the program, Farrell public schools were opened from 6:30 a.m. to 10:30 p.m. Services included "a child development center [with] Head Start and pre-school classes, teen parenting programs and day care . . . a health clinic [for] immunizations, eye and dental exams and routine medical care." A parent outreach training program sent parent educators into needy homes to "help during the critical early years . . . from checking for developmental delays to driving to doctor's appointments to getting the heat turned back." Outposts in the schools "provide everything from mental health services to drug treatment to help in neglect and abuse cases."

There are other approaches. Cohen and Fish (1993) developed a handbook for school-based help for children and their families. Joy Dryfoos (1994) writes about the "full-service" school, "a piece of real estate we all own, where our most precious future assets are trained to become responsible adults, . . . which could be so vastly enriched by the addition of a whole array of community resources" (p. xvii).

The Yale University Bush Center for Child Development conceived of the "School of the 21st Century." It would include "home visitation [for parenting help] for families with children under 3; all-day child care for 3- to 5-year olds, and before- and after-school care for those up to 12 years" (Winerip, 1993b, p. A10).

Health care. Health care institutions are another possible center for integrated, sequential program developments. Networking in health care aims to "provide services within the framework of existing resources . . . to be a network of support."

Health Care for the Homeless, an RHC affiliate, started a pilot networking program in Philadelphia in 1985. Nurses and social workers work in pairs in shelters and on the streets with homeless people. The aim is to guide those helped to become involved in ongoing care and learn how to find their way to and through the maze of available resources, ultimately becoming independent and taking care of themselves. In 1988, similar programs, using this as a model, were fostered by the federal government in over 100 other cities (Bradley, 1993, p. 39).

Other programs. Large-scale development of after-school programming for youth, in the style of settlement houses and community or neighborhood centers, could provide a youth-friendly and sensitive haven. The development of such programs in school buildings is reasonable but these programs currently exist outside of schools in "Ys," Boys and Girls Clubs, and so on. They could be a front-line corps helping youth deal with the many and varied problems and situations with which they are faced.

Similar programs developed in the late 1800s: Hull House, in Chicago; University Settlement, Henry Street, and the Educational Alliance, in New York; Fuld House, in Newark, New Jersey; and many others. McLaughlin, Irby, and Langman (1994) write about their validity in modern conditions.

NATIONAL NONGOVERNMENTAL ORGANIZATIONS

Many national organizations are concerned with the welfare of children. At the passage of RHYA, it was thought that coordination and integration of services was needed and was supported in the legislation. From this grew the *National Network of Runaway and Youth Services (the National Network)* (1319 F St. NW, Washington, DC 20004), which is a private, nonprofit organization. It represents the interests of runaway and homeless youth and the programs that help them. In 1975, over 50 "alternative youth service agencies" across the United States founded the National Network. By 1992, the National Network had a membership of about 900 community-based agencies and organizations, including most of the 339 RHYA-funded programs.

The goals of the National Network have been to help strengthen the programs of the youth-serving agencies, pool resources and knowledge, extend agencies' impact beyond their immediate communities through national coordination, and be a voice for and of youth. It helped in the production and distribution of the video *Street Kids.* For workers in the field, informational and educational material as well as two periodicals, *Policy Reporter* and *Network News,* are published. A computer network,

Youthnet, was started for sharing ideas, programs, and so on among members.

A major function of the National Network has been to work with the political system both nationally and in some states with local networks, to respond with short-term help and developing long-term policies for the problems of children and youth, particularly those without homes and at risk.

During its annual winter "Symposium" for sharing of information and networking, a day is devoted to meeting with legislators in Washington, D.C. Much national legislation dealing with the problems of youth was developed with the help of, and/or was supported by, the National Network. These include updating the Runaway and Homeless Youth Act (RHYA); the Young Americans Act, an attempt to develop and enact a national youth policy; the Comprehensive Youth Services Act of 1992; the Family Preservation Act; the Freedom of Choice Act; the Child Abuse Prevention and Training Act; and the Job Training Partnership Act.

Others organizations are as follows:

The Child Welfare League of America, Inc. (CWLA) (440 First St., NW, Washington, DC 20001-2085) is the oldest of the nongovernmental, nonprofit organizations. Since 1915, partially inspired by the 1909 White House Conference on Children, it has been primarily a professional organization. Its main focus is the improvement of child welfare and advocacy for children through sponsorship of national meetings of workers in the field of child welfare as well as periodic national conferences. It publishes material relevant to the provision of services to children and families and a professional journal, *Child Welfare.*

The Children's Defense Fund (CDF) (25 E Street, NW, Washington, DC 20001) was formed in 1973 as a nonprofit citizen's advocacy organization. It is dedicated to the improved welfare of America's children. Marian Wright Edelman, its president, has become a major voice in pressing society to make a priority of meeting children's and families' needs. Many of its concerns are related to the homelessness of children. CDF publishes monographs, books, and statistical analyses about children's issues and a yearly book on the current problems and needs of America's children.

The 1993 annual national conference of CDF included a variety of workshops and speakers focusing on children's and families' needs and ways to respond to them constructively. Among them were descriptions of programs that "work," such as "Keeping Families Together and Children Safe: A Look at Family Preservation Programs" and "Every Child Deserves a Home: Successful Strategies to Combat Homelessness." Training for students and organized visits with national legislators were also included in the plans.

Family Service America (FSA) (in Milwaukee, Wisconsin) represents the nonprofit Family Service Associations, family counseling agencies, around the country as well as similar professional service agencies. It has a publishing program for professional and research material related to family issues.

ALTERNATIVE SYSTEMS

Other societies consider homelessness, poverty, and family weakness to be societal rather than personal problems. Brief descriptions of a few of these national programs and policies in other countries follow.

Yugoslavia

The former Socialist Federal Republic of Yugoslavia developed a comprehensive delivery system for social services in response to the devastating effects of World War II, which left many orphans and lost children. Prior to 1991 and the subsequent collapse of the country, a system of neighborhood social work centers (Centar za Socijalni Rad) functioned throughout the country.

Each center was situated in and had specific responsibility for a catchment area, also a public health region, police district, school district, preschool district, and so on. Cooperation was fostered, not always successfully, between the different functions. They were supervised by a city or republic institute, which was also supposed to do research on social and psychological issues.

Two cities had separate systems: Belgrade, with 1.7 million population, had 16 catchment areas. Zagreb, with ¾ million, had 12 catchment areas. The six republics and two autonomous regions were similarly divided.

The centers had interdisciplinary teams of social worker, psychologist, pedagogue (educational specialist) or special educator, and lawyer. In rural areas, the teams were assigned work by subdistricts; in urban areas, by problems; and in some, a combination of the two. The centers were to protect the interests of children and the elderly. A focus on prevention was maintained.

In divorce and predelinquency or delinquency situations, the centers were, by law, part of the process. In certain situations, the centers' decisions were legally binding; in others, they were advisory but with probable acceptance or minor revision. The teams' and centers' functions were strictly service oriented and child protective. Financial assistance was provided through a more centralized bureaucracy.

The centers were mandated to provide several different services to families and children, including mediation for divorces and family breakup. Any family breakup in which children were involved had to include mediation and joint decision making in the center about custody, finances, and other issues to serve the best interests of the children.

In cooperation with the police, the centers served families in which there were predelinquent or delinquent children. Schools and health centers were mandated to report situations involving suspected abuse or neglect of children. The centers were involved in cases of orphans, adoptions, foster care, and guardianship, acting as the society's agent for all social situations in which children were at risk. They provided counseling, supervised family and institutional placements, supervised court-ordered home probation, and developed programs for youth at risk. They saw themselves as the voice of the children and the elderly. The aim was to deal with problems before family breakdown or serious damage occurred.

My observations and knowledge from a year (1989-1990) as a Fulbright Fellow in Yugoslavia found the system uniquely well developed and conceptualized, in spite of the centralization of the society and the risk of political interference.

Other systems. In many European societies, financial and other aid is common for families, and many countries have family allowances. Most Western European societies developed supports for families' welfare and strong programs of public and low-cost housing. In Britain, there has been an extensive system of public housing and social welfare services run by local councils. Germany and Austria have had such programs since the end of World War I.

Communist Eastern Europe had free child care and preschools. Child care facilities were located both in the neighborhood and in many large industrial establishments. Schools were connected with the health system. Health care was free and clinics were centrally located in each community. Subsidies were provided for essentials such as clothing and basic food for children.

Community centers were developed to address health matters in some other countries. In the former Soviet Union, there were regional health, pediatric, and mental health or psychiatric centers. In the United States, in the late 1960s and early 1970s, comprehensive or community mental health and/or mental retardation centers were conceived with catchment areas including all the people. However, caught in changing national priorities, only a remnant exists in the 1990s, quite changed from the original concept.

The Netherlands

In the Netherlands, although the prevalence is relatively low, some minors are on their own (Beke, 1987) and they have a somewhat protected status. In general, in the Netherlands, social rights supersede property rights and social benefits are extended to all in need.

The Netherlands evolved a policy applying to "emancipated" minors. Minors not living with their families or in institutions receive social benefits. Independent-youth shelters developed as self-regulating "safe houses" and are often staffed primarily by university student volunteers. Parents are told the location or able to visit only with the agreement of youth. The police are to protect the identity of youth and the location of the house (Beke, 1987). In some ways, the houses operated like the "youth republic" of Janusz Korczak, a noted Polish Jewish educator and youth worker in the first half of the twentieth century (Lifton, 1988).

Sweden

Sweden is the epitome of the Social Democratic welfare state. Although social problems remain, homelessness is not apparent among adults or children/families. It may be where governmental support for the rights of minors and support of families goes furthest. The system is based on a child-centered model proposed by Gunnar and Alva Myrdal in the 1930s designed to prevent deprivation and avoid class inequalities, particularly for children. Development has continued since then, with many benefits added since the 1970s.

A well-developed system of social welfare provides financial and social support to families. Many of the factors associated with homeless children are minimized under the Swedish system. Single-parent families, of which 90% are female headed, constitute about 20% of all families with children. Less than 10% of these families are "poor." Almost all single mothers work. Women make equal wages for equal work, and single-parent families have average incomes that are almost 90% of the average income for two-parent families.

About 20% of single mothers and 10% of single fathers "are dependent on social assistance," which provides income above the poverty level. Well-developed, inexpensive physical and mental health care is available to all. Relatively high-quality, locally organized day care is widely available. Paid family leave covers all workers. Public housing in which rent is a fixed percentage of income is equal in quality to other housing. Thus many of the economic issues that present stress for single-parent and poor families in the United States are relieved. "Overall it is very clear that Swedish social policy is comparatively interventionist in encouraging parental care of children" (Ginsburg, 1992).

Sweden is not the garden of Eden for all children. Alcoholism remains a serious social problem, and divorce is very common. Thus some of the situations that are related to homelessness among children in the United States—substance abuse and disrupted families—are common also in Sweden, but without homelessness.

SUMMARY

The policies and organization of society have major impacts upon the conditions of life. The approach to homelessness in the United States includes a vast array of services; unfortunately, they are scattered, unintegrated, under varying auspices, and too few and far between.

Private programs developed out of concern and desire to ameliorate suffering are widespread. Many public programs also exist. There are public and private shelters, rehabilitative residences, boarding houses, and flophouses for specific homeless populations. There are educational, housing, and job programs, food kitchens, and clothing and toy collection. There are self-help organizations of homeless adults trying to influence government and the public. In fact, there is every possible mechanism to help homeless children and families.

National and state responses to the problem of homeless children integrate public and private resources and services. Most funds are public. Public agencies often oversee private services. In other cases, direct public services have been developed.

Federal legislation and programs produced the system in the United States. Most state initiatives result from national legislation that focused separately on unaccompanied youth and children homeless with families. As public and private agencies gained experience, the services expanded to include dealing with physical and sexual abuse, substance abuse, mental health, pregnancy and parenting, and education including learning disabilities. Other federal legislation has focused on sexuality and drug and alcohol use.

Funds for programs come from a variety of public and private sources, almost half from state and local governments. Private sources, including private fund-raising, groups like the United Way, foundations, corporations, individuals, and others, provide about one quarter of the funds for services for runaway and homeless youth. Services often are designed to fit funding specifics.

In the late 1980s, there were calls for a national youth policy to ensure young Americans rights and health, educational, and social services on a coordinated continuum. Some legislation has been introduced to achieve this but as of 1996 there was no written policy.

There have been meetings, plans, and other symptoms of thinking beyond the ameliorative on many levels. These have included educational, artistic, camping, and other programs, with some for special populations, that is, preschool, homosexual youth, and older foster children. "Family preservation services," or the "family support movement," have developed to deal with the perceived problems of families in the society.

Integrated services have developed through community centers, health care providers, and neighborhood schools. The use of public schools as community resources is seen as a way of preventing families and children from falling into extremis, including homelessness, with school buildings being used as centers for recreation, child care, nontraditional education, social services, and health care.

There are many national organizations concerned with the welfare of children, often as political advocates, information providers, and coordinators. Among these are the National Network of Runaway and Youth Services, the Children's Defense Fund (CDF), the Child Welfare League of America, Inc. (CWLA), and Family Service America (FSA). With all of this, the problem has gotten larger and has required more answers and a different approach. National programs and policies in the former Yugoslavia, the Netherlands, and Sweden that relate to homelessness and general child welfare were briefly described.

CONCLUSIONS

The picture of American societal responses to homelessness of children is one of great variety. There is no lack of creativity and ideas about helping homeless children. Programs do almost anything one can imagine in any area of need and with any population. With much compassion as well as fragmentation, a wide range of goals and large holes exist in an American system characterized by few resources and funds, dehumanization and institutional bureaucracy, amelioration but not prevention, and a reactive rather than proactive stance. Examining other countries, notably the former Yugoslavia and also Scandinavia, it can be seen that there are comprehensive alternatives.

NOTE

1. Interviews were conducted with directors or appointed staff of C&Y offices of the various counties and other described agencies in winter, spring, and summer of 1993. Information also was obtained from 1992-1993 directories or lists and descriptions of contract agencies of C&Y offices in Bucks, Chester, Delaware, Montgomery, and Philadelphia Counties, Pennsylvania, and in New York State.

Part IV

WHERE TO FROM HERE?

Chapter 12

CONCLUSIONS

The Found Boy (concluded)

And soon the little boy was very very whole again.

And he was warm again too in his coat of many colors.

Everyone could see him now. He was like a rainbow,

When the sun is shining through the rain.

And now there is this little found boy.

      (From "The Found Boy" in *Somebody Else's Nut Tree* by Ruth Krauss)

Poetry and prose encourage dreams about a world with happy endings. A humanistic tenet is that a society that nurtures its members, particularly its children, is humanized. Maurice Sendak (1993) wrote a "children's" book that, while depicting the misery and suffering of homeless children, is an affirmation of family and love. In it, children without families create families and a small, caring society. To realize and maintain this dream in real life, continuous, concerted human action is necessary.

This is the last chapter of the excursion through the world of homeless children, youth, and families. It is a discussion of ideas for acting to stop homelessness of children and families, ways of helping them, and hopes for the future.

Societies have several choices for responding to social problems. They can exacerbate them, ignore them, punish those afflicted with them, provide for amelioration, or prevent them. For most of human, settled history, the first three essentially went together. Society was structured and conceived of serving the needs of the political, economic, and social elite. In the seventeenth and eighteenth centuries, a revolutionary new idea started being discussed, the "Rights of Man." Under that concept, people were seen to have a right to choose their leaders or to have political self-determination and freedom. In the late eighteenth and nineteenth centuries, the idea was further developed to include social and economic protection as well as to include women. Thus the notion that society has a responsibility to either protect or prevent social problems and suffering is a relatively new one.

A similar progression took place in the United States, the first society founded on the concept of the "Rights of Man." It was only during the nineteenth and twentieth centuries that major amelioration of social suffering and prevention were considered options. There is still debate about this in the society. For social workers, there are no options. We cannot accept society's abnegation of responsibility to lessen and remove suffering from its midst. Thus, for us, amelioration and prevention are the only acceptable social policy.

SITUATION

Many children and families in the United States at some time have been without the very bedrock of what is considered necessary for healthy growth and development—a stable, protective home. They need in addition

> at least one caring, invested adult; a family with adequate income and stable secure housing; a safe responsive community with decent education and health care; an environment that fosters play and sociability; and networks of social support for the children and adults. (Azar, 1995a)

Homelessness, particularly for children, youth, and families, provides none of the above and is a social cancer. We must do what is necessary to arrest what produces homelessness and prevent it for all time. If this could happen, then, as Rabbi Hillel said, the rest is commentary. It has become clear, however, that American society has been able neither to agree nor to mobilize itself to this end. In 1994, the voting electorate produced a majority in Congress who made clear their opposition to governmental action on social problems. Regardless, a variety of ways of dealing with the epidemic of homeless children and families will be discussed, including societywide, public and private, local and individual ways.

America's major institutions have not responded preventively or adequately to the assaults on children, which include homelessness. This may stem not only from philosophical disagreement but from several misconceptions. One is the widely sold and held idea that society cannot effectively develop preventive approaches to social problems and/or cannot afford to do so. The neglect of the problem also may come from misconceptions about homeless children. It is believed that homeless children and families are in some way different than the rest of us and that homelessness is their "fault." This is especially convenient in dismissing them as "innately" different or inferior. It relates to the stereotype that most of the homeless are in minority groups. Both ideas are false: The homeless are neither different than us nor predominantly minority.

The ineffectiveness of programs also has been shown not to be true. Whenever the will and wherewithal have allowed it, social programs have successfully helped. Many individual experiences and programs, a number of them described in this book, have shown that, with opportunity and a helping hand, many homeless youth have become integrated into general society. They have been shown to be creative, intelligent, and able to achieve, even after years of destructive lifestyles and experiences. Witness the survivors described in Chapter 8. The success of the Toronto theater group Kytes (Farnsworth, 1993) is a prime example of the potentiality, often never realized, of many homeless youth. Many children have the resilience to develop positively after bad experiences (Bernard, 1996).

Another misconception is that people are homeless due to mental health problems. It is true that many homeless youth and families are mentally and emotionally disturbed. However, it is often difficult to discern which came first, the homelessness or the mental health problem. A large proportion of the housed population also have emotional and mental instability.

For the homeless, in general, and especially for homeless youths, the society's blindness and deafness to them exacerbate their situation. Their suffering and destruction are thus turned back on them.

Although American society, as a whole, has not responded effectively to homeless children, many concerned people have. Workers and volunteers in public and private organizations demonstrate their commitment to helping the children and their families. They are in large public agencies such as the Philadelphia Department of Human Services, the C&Y offices of the surrounding counties, and the Division of Youth and Family Services of New Jersey. They are in the many small private programs, shelters, host homes, and so on.

Concerned people have set up primarily voluntary programs, such as Trevor's Campaign, the Interfaith Hospitality Networks, and many of the shelters and homeless programs. They spend much time and energy volunteering or working for relatively low pay and with few benefits to help adults and children. They work under demoralizing conditions with not enough money or resources to do all that needs to be done. They are generally unappreciated and undervalued by society. Many find they can't continue to do this work due to inadequate resources, stress, and low pay.

LEVELS OF PREVENTION

The public health paradigm of three levels of prevention will be used to organize the discussion. Primary prevention strikes at the roots of a disease to remove its causes and thereby eliminate it. Secondary prevention is aimed at attacking the disease at an early stage to arrest its spread and damage. Tertiary prevention is aimed at healing victims as quickly as possible to prevent further spread of the disease and to allay long-lasting consequences. The three levels of prevention apply on all social planes— micro, mezzo, and macro.

Need for prevention. The Carnegie Task Force on Meeting the Needs of Young Children ("Starting Points," 1995) said,

> A staggering number [of American children] are affected by one or more risk factors that undermine healthy development. . . . [The Task Force] urges a national response. Persuaded that strong families and communities are essential to the healthy development of our youngest children, we call for a broad, integrated approach to ensure that . . . all children have had the opportunity to reach their full potential. (p. 16)

The League of Women Voters ("Children Are," 1995) has charted a course of action for providing a maximal social environment:

> Early intervention and prevention measures are effective in helping children reach their full potential. The League supports policies and programs at all levels of the community and government that promote the well being, encourage the full development and ensure the safety of all children. (p. 4)

Social attention. With a new political administration and era in the United States, in the mid-1990s it was hoped that the issues of children, youth, and families would be given priority in the government agenda. On the last Sunday of 1992, the page 1 article in the *New York Times,* News of the Week in Review, asserted, "The young are still poor, but they have political attention now" (Steinfels, 1992, sec. 4, p. 1). The 1994 elections, however, indicated a major redirection of federal policy away from social problems. As a consequence, there may well be homeless children at least into the late 1990s.

A leader of the "small government" forces proposed residential care for children of problem families. In the ensuing discussion, psychosocial issues relating to removal of children from families highlighted some of the major problems of developing alternatives to family for children (Shealy, 1995, p. 565).

Primary Prevention

Primary prevention of homelessness in general, and especially of children, on the macroplane requires three major societal changes and initiatives: the abolition of poverty; an adequate supply of decent, low-income housing; and family preservation and strengthening.

The first—eradication of poverty among all segments of the population—would mean a major economic and social restructuring of society. Although there is, in the mid-1990s, strong resistance in America to such a movement, in other societies and at other times in American society there has been successful action to reduce and even abolish poverty, or to develop counteracting mechanisms to prevent the damage it does to children.

The second—supplying decent affordable housing sufficient for the need and demand—would be very expensive, but this also has successfully worked in other societies and for a while in America. The third—supporting families—has often seemed the most immediately feasible, but may be the most difficult.

The issue of poverty itself, which demoralizes and destroys people, must be dealt with. Poverty is concurrently a major cause of family breakdown and homelessness, and independently has destructive effects upon children. The need to eradicate the poverty of children is stressed by the National Research Council (1993): "The diverse ways in which poverty harms children and adolescents, inflicts lasting damage and limits their future potential, point to the reduction of poverty as a key step toward improving the condition of many of the nation's youths" (p. 236). The combination of homelessness and poverty is personally and socially destructive.

Halting and reversing the societal factors that produce the continued impoverishment and disenfranchisement of large numbers of people is necessary for improvement in the lives of over a quarter of our children, although it may be unacceptable to powerful elements in society.

Second, as long as there are poor people, the lack of affordable housing is the major cause of homelessness of families. Some private initiatives such as Habitat for Humanity, with which former president Jimmy Carter and his wife Rosalynn are associated, can make small dents in the deficit of low-income housing. Government programs such as urban homesteading (making abandoned housing available for sweat equity and minimal payment to low-income families) work on the micro- and possibly mezzolevels.

Neither can solve the deficit of low-income housing on a macrolevel unless they become comprehensive and greatly expanded. Unfortunately, homesteading and similar programs have been all but abandoned in the 1980s and 1990s. Instead, we see continued erosion of large areas of our cities and many towns. Leaving neighborhoods and houses abandoned while people are homeless seems oxymoronic.

The third primary preventive measure is developing and initiating remedies to prevent and/or cure the disintegration of large numbers of families and the inability of many to nurture and motivate their children. The healthy functioning of families and the social, mental, and physical health of children need to become top priorities for society's attention.

"The negative consequences of homelessness on the health of children will be avoided only when a way is found to prevent children from being homeless in the first place" (Wright, 1989b, p. 96). For the sake of children, families need to be strengthened with the provision of economic, emotional, and social nurturance. This could be done by both public and private sectors at national, state, and local levels.

Secondary Prevention

In the probable event that primary prevention will not soon be undertaken, the society should work on secondary and tertiary prevention. Secondary prevention would avoid the high mortality and morbidity that result from the descent into homelessness as well as the development of chronicity with its attendant problems. This would entail early intervention and the expansion and development of a wide range of services (many of which exist on some level) for both parents and children. Factors that help children be resilient can be supported in the family, school, and community (Bernard, 1996).

A comprehensive, integrated system, with easy, universal access and aggressive outreach for people in need would be most effective. A large variety of supportive and curative help should be interconnected in the system. The system should be flexibly designed so that it could respond to differential needs. Ready access to and availability of the system are necessary.

Data from Philadelphia suggest (Benner et al., 1991) that the first six months of homelessness are the most dangerous. Special health programs and clinics need to be provided for preventive services, early detection and care of illness, and treatment for existing conditions; positive, responsive individuals need to provide emotional support for the children.

To overcome the disabilities of homelessness (and poverty and racism), a wide variety of mechanisms would be needed, both public and private. It is necessary to support and build on the strengths of families, provide high-quality care for children when needed, foster positive parenting skills, and offer a wide range of physical and mental health programs. Easy access to treatment for drug and alcohol abusers is required. The NRC (1993) said that "policies [and concomitant programs] supporting families and neighborhoods and restructuring service institutions are necessary to impart the functional academic, vocational, social, [emotional] and psychological competencies needed by young people" (p. 237).

Ms. Janet Skiba, director of the Bucks County Department of Human Services and former director of the county's Children & Youth Office, said: "The system needs to be integrated and sequential." The sequence she envisions would include short-, mid-, and long-term programs on both large and small scale. In addition, the system should be flexible in its ability to respond to individual children's or family's situations and needs.

Integrated and sequential programs have been developed in a variety of styles scattered across the country (many discussed in Chapter 11). Some are more comprehensive than others. School systems and schools, and health care and social service programs, are being transformed into community service centers. Health care providers are partners in responding to the multiple risks children face in many communities. Community centers have a role to play. Programs that focus on *family preservation or development of stable family substitutes* need to be expanded and developed. Early intervention has repeatedly been shown to be most effective. This could include expansion of the program Health Start (which provides prenatal care to high-risk populations) to include outreach in high-risk communities as well as to cover more populations and communities.

Probably the most widely needed family support is quality, affordable *child day care,* both for preschool and for before and after school. While providing children with the stimulation and developmental help they need, it enables parents to work and/or go to school themselves without worry. It would also provide the possibility of an early warning for needed intervention. Skilled child care workers and teachers can easily see signs of family problems in children's behavior in school.

Other forms of social supports are diverse. Help with *parenting skills* for parents and families at risk, and for relatives, foster parents, adoptive parents, and other caretakers, would also be helpful. Problems of communication, expectations, substance abuse, and so on, which lead to runaway, throwaway, and abandoned children, need to be addressed. Other help to families would include financial support to maintain children in their homes and families, including *in-home support services* and *home care* for those who need them. The family support and preservation movement is discussed in Chapter 11.

For youth who have no family or who cannot return to their families, responses might include development of therapeutic parenting (Shealy, 1995, p. 465), major improvements in foster care, quality medium- and long-term residential programs, independent living programs, emancipated minor programs, drug treatment, counseling and/or therapy, job training and placement. In addition, if the programs are for remediation, *alternative shelter* may need to be provided along with help in preparing for and finding *permanent housing*.

Foster care and alternatives. Where appropriate and necessary, alternatives to in-family care for children, that is, foster care and small group homes, need to be further developed and expanded. On one hand, foster care has the potential for most adequately addressing the needs of many children. In many cases, it is quite effective. Witness the woman who was raised in a foster home and still considers that to be her family (see Chapter 8). On the other hand, some major structural and personal problems are endemic to both foster care and group homes. These issues are discussed at some length in Angenent, Beke, and Shane (1991) and Shealy (1995).

Problems in the foster care and group home systems stem from a potential instability of relationships and an understandable, but dehumanizing, focus on discipline and order. Moving children from one placement to another adds to the destructive effects of removal from parents and family. It further attacks the security and sense of worth of the child. The feeling that "nobody wants me" is not conducive to helping a child develop self-confidence and a positive self-image.

In addition, there is a dearth of families willing to foster children, which often leads to delays in placement as well as to many who provide inadequate foster care. Foster parents and child care workers tend to be less well educated, from lower socioeconomic and minority communities. They may foster for income but also because they may be more accepting.

The New Jersey Hospital Association urges increasing financial supports for foster parenting. In addition, they recommend that the child protective system function more efficiently and quickly when there is need of investigation and/or placements. The approach developed in some Philadelphia hospitals of proactive work on placement either with family or in foster care is a way to shortcut the overwhelmed and regulation-burdened child protective system.

A third drawback to foster care is that it often fails to prepare youth for independent living. These are the "system kids" that June Bucy and others write about (Able-Peterson & Bucy, 1993, p. 4). A major aspect of parenting is preparing children for adulthood. For many, particularly those who experience multiple foster placements, the foster care system fails in this very important aspect. Foster children often need more help in becoming independent than children from intact families. The normal continuing family help that most young adults depend on is often lacking for the "system kids." Models discussed previously that make up for this lack need to be further developed and expanded.

Fostering children is a complicated and multidimensional affair. The children are in great need of reassurance and developmental help. Fostering is often more effective if done by relatives, which is often called "kinship care."

Kinship care is important in providing stable homes and families for children whose parents cannot or will not assume responsibility for raising and caring for them. Kinship care needs to be subsidized and/or in other ways supported by governmental agencies. Many kinship care relatives receive public assistance for the children. Others may need subsidies for day care, special medical care, other special care needs and expenditures, and possibly supplemental help for food costs. There is a need for social support, possibly from self-help groups. In light of some of these and other problems, foster, kinship, and group care need major overhaul, particularly in the major population centers.

Small group homes and *transitional living* programs need to be further developed and expanded as alternative settings for child care. Here also the staff have to be trained as therapeutic parents. Problems of instability of relationships are related to unphased entering and leaving of residents, further exacerbated by rotation of staff. When staff do not live in the home, there are three shifts a day with five-day weeks. Weekends and holidays result in a virtual army of people rotating through a facility and constantly changing authority and nurturing figures. Residences with live-in house parents are in a minority and avoid, in some measure, the rotation problem. But even house parents need vacations and days off.

Expansion of *prenatal care* to ensure its availability to all pregnant women would prevent some of the problems of homeless and poor women bearing at-risk children. Programs like Health Start in New Jersey should be expanded to include outreach in high-risk communities as well as to cover more populations and communities. The simple matter of receiving *immunizations,* which have become procedural for young children, is apt to be almost impossible under conditions of homelessness.

A wide expansion of *substance abuse treatment* programs is needed, with improved access for those who need them. These and other responses need to maximize dignity, self-respect, and potentiality.

Child parents. The increasing incidence of teenage mothers and fathers, particularly those under 16, needs to be addressed. Special services need to be organized to help minimize "children having children." Young women need help in resisting and avoiding predatory adult males. In those cases where the young women do have children, the development of supports for help in child rearing, rather than a simple cash grant, is needed (Woodall, 1993, p. B6). Martin (1993) and others suggest that residential, educational, and therapeutic programs need to be considered and modified.

Many young parents need special educational, developmental, and therapeutic programs. Long-range programs would have to prepare both parents and children for life on their own. Absent fathers need to be helped to actively participate in child care and rearing. Attention to the fathers might do much to avoid abandonment and abuse.

Most important, programs for families must attend to the needs of children. Many current adult and family programs treat children as incidental. Some, for valid therapeutic and logistical reasons, limit the number of children a parent can bring into the program. Others bar all children or those over a certain age. What feelings of abandonment must the left-behind children feel? Some programs have special educational and social psychological services for children.

Programs working with homeless families must respond to the effects upon the children. Addressing the children's educational, emotional, psychological, and social needs must be a priority. These programs must be inclusive, open to every child and family in need.

The value of *artistic and creative* activities and expression in secondary and tertiary prevention for homeless and at-risk children should not be ignored. The Kytes theater program in Toronto (Farnsworth, 1993) and the writing project in New York City prove the value of the arts in helping youth to overcome the negative elements of their lives, and to take responsibility for and change the directions of their lives.

The fundamental principle of the Alaska Youth Initiative (AYI) is valid for all programs:

> *Unconditional care, never giving up no matter what.* It is perceived to be the responsibility of the adults and professionals to develop a treatment that will engage and make change possible for the youth. A failure means that the program must be adjusted, not that the youth is rejected—ever. (Able-Peterson & Bucy, 1993, p. 101)

Tertiary Prevention

Nonintegrated and uncoordinated services of the sort mentioned above can function as a tertiary preventive mode on the micro- and possibly mezzolevels, or as a palliative. To be preventive, they need to be expanded so that they can reach larger portions of the needy population, and their function must be treatment and prevention. The needs of children must be more fully recognized and provided for. The resilience of children must be enhanced, with some help from their friends.

Outreach programs are important. They need to be expanded and introduced wherever there are homeless children or families. David (in Chapter 10) was rescued through an outreach program. A guide for developing outreach programs is contained in Able-Peterson and Bucy (1993).

The above is not an exhaustive list of what is needed if the society is to accept homelessness and try and minimize its deleterious effects upon children and families. It does give some idea of what a total program should include. The primary issues have to be early intervention, accessibility, integration, comprehensiveness, and continuity of care.

RESEARCH DIRECTIONS

An agenda for research into homeless children and families would focus on a few areas. One area is factual and demographic data: who, where, what, when, how long, and so on. Another is means of prevention and ameliorating the consequences of homelessness. A third is examination of the consequences. A fourth is learning what helps some children rebound from bad experiences, and how we can increase such elements in the family, school, and community.

As the NRC report emphasized, attention needs to be paid to risk and protective factors and their interaction at social and individual levels. Longitudinal studies might follow youth over various periods in their lives.

Social factors in youths' lives need as much attention as food, lifestyle, exercise, and the like. Youth at risk need to be studied as well as those already homeless and those who once were homeless youth. Are there models of small institutional settings that are more effective than others for children and youth?

Perhaps the most neglected, least studied homeless children are babies. The effects on babies of homelessness with and without a mother need to be studied. What about emergency foster placement and subsequent interruption of bonds upon re-placement, which is a common practice across the country? Does being a boarder baby have effects? Are there time limits beyond which damage is done, and if so, what are they? How many changes of caretakers and environments can babies and children tolerate? There are innumerable other topics that could be added.

The field of research into the causes, effects, and details of homelessness of children is wide open. Research on the restructuring of social policies, and further research into effects of social policy, also would be helpful. Needed are interest in doing the research and social and financial support.

ACTION NEEDED

Political and social action are urgently needed. They should be focused on changing the direction of the society to more adequately and humanely respond to human needs of all kinds, in particular those of children and families. Action could also focus on development of new approaches and programs to respond to these needs.

SUMMARY

A society that nurtures its members, particularly its children, is humanized. The homelessness of children and families is destructive to individuals, families, and society. This last chapter presented ideas for dealing with the homelessness of children and families—ways of helping them, of humanizing the society, and hopes for the future.

The discussion was organized on the public health paradigm of three levels of prevention—primary, secondary, and tertiary. The levels of prevention apply on all planes—micro, mezzo, and macro.

Primary prevention, attacking the causes of homelessness, seems improbable now. Secondary preventive actions would entail the expansion and development of a wide range of existing and new services for both parents and children. A comprehensive, integrated, flexible system, with easy, universal access and aggressive outreach, interconnected with a large variety of supportive and curative help for people in need, would be most effective.

Such programs should focus on *family preservation or the development of stable family substitutes.* There needs to be early intervention. *Social supports for families* include quality, affordable *child care,* both preschool and ancillary to school, as well as financial support for and development of *in-home support services* and *home care. Parenting skills* must be taught to parents and families at risk as well as other potential caretakers such as relatives, foster parents, and adoptive parents.

For youth without family or those who cannot return to their families, services should include therapeutic parenting, improvements in foster care, medium- and long-term residential programs, independent living programs, emancipated minor programs, drug treatment, counseling and/or therapy, job training and placement. *Alternative shelter,* with help in preparing for and finding *permanent housing,* should be provided. Kinship care, therapeutic parenting, quality foster care, small group homes, and transitional living programs need to be further developed, expanded, and improved.

Prenatal care needs to be available for all. A wide expansion of *substance abuse treatment* programs is needed, including improved access. Services need to be organized to minimize "children having children" and to provide supports for child rearing, rather than just cash grants. *Outreach* programs are needed for the already homeless. *Artistic* and *creative* activities and expression are part of secondary and tertiary prevention for homeless and at-risk children. The main need is early intervention and accessibility, integration, comprehensiveness, and continuity of care.

Research on homeless children and families is needed in two main areas. One area involves factual and demographic data: who, where, what, when, how long, and so on. The other area involves the consequences of homelessness and ways of preventing and ameliorating them.

In addition, political and social action are urgently needed. These should focus on primary prevention and the development of adequate resources and responses to the epidemic of homeless children.

CONCLUDING DISCUSSION

America is faced with a major social and public health dilemma. Homeless and runaway youth are among us, although often hidden and out of our sight.

They are at risk socially, educationally, physically, and mentally. They are at high risk for many physical ailments and for passing these on within the homeless youth population, to the general population, and in the future to any children they might have. Homeless youth are extremely susceptible to mental and emotional problems and illness and to a difficult and possibly bleak and hopeless future—a lifetime of homelessness and dependency.

With determination, America could end and prevent homelessness and the conditions that spawn it. This would mean eliminating poverty and spending large sums of money on decent, affordable housing. It would mean developing economic and social means of supporting and strengthening families. It would mean encouraging creativity and professional and political commitment. America could end the legacy of racism and ethnic discrimination that cripples large segments of the population. It could commit itself to ending poverty and despair through provision of appropriately compensated work and responsive educational systems. All these would substantially end homelessness and much other misery, but they are not probable in the foreseeable future.

Life in the United States often finds families under economic and social strain. It also often finds isolated and stressed family constellations. When these come together and are unstable, either in terms of housing and/or emotional conditions, children suffer. We have taken a long time to come to terms with this and develop responses that are preventive and, in cases of need, curative on a long-term basis. Unfortunately for many youth in America, homeless and at risk, the response is too little, too late.

James and Anne Garbarino (Garbarino, 1992) have written:

> Children always offer an opportunity for making the future better. Our physical resources may diminish, but our human ones will not. The quality of life for the next generation could be better than it was for past ones. To make the human quality of our children's lives better, we must understand children's needs and how to enhance elements in their lives to lead to a richer, more varied, more satisfying growing up both for them and their parents. (p. 303)

A society that loses sight of the future of its children and their families, or of a significant proportion of them, loses sight of its own future.

To reduce and do away with homelessness, our society needs a "pro-life" affirmation of family values by cherishing, enhancing, helping, respecting, and supporting living children and their families. It must be a joint, collaborative effort of government, private agencies, communities, and individuals.

Scientifically, there is a need to produce research that enhances professional and societal abilities to more effectively help people. Politically and socially, there is a need to reaffirm and fulfill a commitment on a large scale to social policies that provide for nourishment and support, dignity and respect, for all families and children.

In the meantime, many groups have responded with compassion and concern, coupled with knowledge and skill. To be more effective, such responses must be more organized, integrated, and sequential, and less at the mercy of fickle funding sources and political fashion, to more consistently and effectively help all in need.

Existing responses already do many things on the secondary and tertiary preventive levels.

We know how to help people repair their lives and move from despair to hope. It is being done every day in many different places and ways. We know how to repair fragile and injured self-images, provide motivation, teach needed skills, and help develop or improve communication. Agencies often work in cooperation and with compassion to repair the ravages of societal and familial dysfunction. The value of these efforts is not to be denigrated while further development, expansion, and integration are called for.

Homeless children and families can be a resource for the nation. Among the homeless are the wide variations found among all people. The nation cannot ignore homeless families, not only because of compassion but for its own good. This is enlightened self-interest. No society can afford to abandon its youth. What was said about Brazil, where the problem of homeless children is catastrophic, applies equally to the United States: "Many more [children] will be lost unless the country sees [them] . . . as the responsibility of a troubled society" (Michaels, 1993, p. 36).

America, the first society in the world to be founded on the concept of constitutionally protected human rights and the dignity of the individual, should extend these concepts to its most valuable and fragile resource, its children and their families. America must act to find and nurture each lost child and prevent others from getting lost. The national game of hide-and-seek should emphasize seeking, not hiding.

In discussing the major economic influence of homelessness of children, the growing income gap, *Business Week* effectively stated the bottom line: "The growing inequality has many sources. The means to reverse the trend are available. But is the will?" ("Attack the Income Gap," 1994, p. 76).

The problems facing our . . . children and their families cannot be solved through piecemeal action. All Americans must work together, in their homes, workplaces and communities, to ensure that children . . . —our most vulnerable citizens—are given the care and protection they need and deserve. If we do, we as a nation can realize our common values: strong families and communities, an informed citizenry, a productive workforce, and a competitive and strong economy. ("Children Are," 1995, p. 19)

REFERENCES

AAP (American Academy of Pediatrics, Committee on Community Health Services). (1988, December). Health needs of homeless children. *Pediatrics, 82*(6), 938-940.

Able-Peterson, T., & Bucy, J. (1993). *The streetwork outreach training manual.* Washington, DC: U.S. DHHS, Public Health Service, Substance Abuse and Mental Health Services Administration, Child and Adolescent Service System Project.

AMA (American Medical Association, Council on Scientific Affairs). (1989). Health care needs of homeless and runaway youths. *Journal of the American Medical Association (JAMA), 262*(10), 1358-1361.

Angenent, H. (1981). Shoplifting: A review. *Criminology and Penology Abstracts, 21*(3), i-ix.

Angenent, H., & Beke, B. (1984). *Runaways.* Nijmegen, the Netherlands: University of Nijmegen Institute for Ortho-pedagogics; Groningen, the Netherlands: Criminological Institute, University of Groningen.

Angenent, H., Beke, B., & Shane, P. (1991). Structural problems in institutional care for youth. *Journal of Health and Social Policy, 2*(4), 83.

Angenent, H., & de Man, A. (1989). Running away: Perspectives on causation. *Journal of Social Behavior and Personality, 4,* 377-388.

Aries, P., & Duby, G. (Eds.). (1987). *A history of private life* (Vol. 1). Cambridge, MA: Belknap Press of Harvard University Press.

Attack the income gap at its source. (1994, August 15). *Business Week,* p. 76.

Azar, B. (1995a, November). Foster children get a taste of stability. *The APA Monitor* (American Psychological Association), p. 8.

Azar, B. (1995b, November). Foster care has bleak history. *The APA Monitor* (American Psychological Association), p. 8.

Back, K. (1992, September). *Field theory, truth and beauty.* Paper presented at the fifth biannual Kurt Lewin conference, SAFT (Society for the Advancement of Field Theory), Philadelphia.

Barlett, D., & Steele, J. (1992). *America: What went wrong?* Kansas City, MO: Andrews and McMeel.

Bassuk, E., Rubin, L., & Lauriat, A. (1986). Characteristics of sheltered homeless families. *American Journal of Public Health, 76*(9), 1100.

Battle, S. (1990). Homeless women and children: The question of poverty. In N. Boxill (Ed.), *Homeless children: The watchers and the waiters* (pp. 111-127). New York: Haworth.

Baum, A., & Burnes, D. (1993). *A nation in denial: The truth about homelessness.* Boulder, CO: Westview.

Becca Bill, E2SHB 2217 (June 6, 1996).

Beke, B. (1987). *Wegglopen minderjarigen uit kinderbeschermingstehuizen.* Nijmegen, the Netherlands: University of Nijmegen.

Benner, L., Benner, M., Okeke, B., & Spencer, R. (1991, June 14-16). *Multiple factors affecting epidemiology of mental illness among Philadelphia's homeless population* (Division of Research and Information Management, Office of Mental Health and Mental Retardation, Department of Public Health, City of Philadelphia). Paper presented to the World Psychiatric Association Section of Epidemiology and Community Psychiatry Symposium, "Psychiatric Epidemiology and Social Science," Oslo, Norway.

Bernard, B. (1996). Fostering resiliency in kids: Protective factors in the family, school and community. *Child Welfare Report, 4*(1-3) (Iola, WI: Jones Publishing, Inc.).

Bernstein, A. (1994, August 15). Inequality: How the gap between rich and poor hurts the economy. *Business Week,* No. 3385, pp. 36-41.

Berry, M. (1994). *Keeping families together.* New York: Garland.

Boccella, K. (1993, September 25). Families offered chance for stability. *Philadelphia Inquirer,* p. B1.

Book details the many facets of the problems of "homelessness." (1994, Spring). *Interfaith Host* (Northwest Philadelphia Interfaith Hospitality Network), p. 3.

Borowski, N. (1994, September 18). When grandparents raise them. *Philadelphia Inquirer,* p. B1.

Bradley, M. (1993, January). Networking for the homeless. *Applause,* p. 39 (Philadelphia).

Burkins, G. (1992, October 13). Hard times take a toll on families. *Philadelphia Inquirer,* p. F1.

Burrell, C. (1993, December 22). Homeless families increase. *Philadelphia Inquirer,* p. A3.

Burt, M. (1995). Critical factors in counting the homeless. *American Journal of Orthopsychiatry, 65*(3).

Burt, M., & Cohen, B. (1989). *America's homeless: Numbers, characteristics, and programs that serve them.* Washington, DC: Urban Institute.

Cameron, M. (1994, December 4). The flaw in Maleng's plan to handle young runaways. *Seattle Times,* p. 10.

CDF (Children's Defense Fund). (1992). *The state of America's children: 1991.* Washington, DC: Author.

Children are focus of new LWVUS positions. (1995, December-January). *The National Voter, 44*(2), 19 (Washington, DC: League of Women Voters).

Cohen, J., & Fish, M. (1993). *Handbook of school-based interventions.* San Francisco: Jossey-Bass.

Cole, E., & Duva, J. (1990). *Family preservation: An orientation for administrators and practitioners.* Washington, DC: Child Welfare League of America.

Commonwealth of Pennsylvania, Department of Education. (1987). *Pennsylvania Homeless Student Plan, 1988-1990.* Harrisburg, PA: Education of Homeless Children and Youth Program.

Commonwealth of Pennsylvania, Department of Education. (1989). *Pennsylvania's Homeless Student Initiative.* Harrisburg, PA: Education of Homeless Children and Youth Program.

Connolly, M. (1990). Adrift in the city: A comparative study of street children in Bogota, Colombia and Guatemala City. In N. Boxill (Ed.), *Homeless children: The watchers and the waiters* (pp. 129-149). New York: Haworth.

Covenant House. (1993). *1992 annual report.* (Available from Covenant House, 346 W. 17th St., New York, NY 10011)

CWLA (Child Welfare League of America). (1991). *Homelessness: The impact on child welfare in the 90's.* Washington, DC: Author.

CWLA (Child Welfare League of America). (1992). *Boarder babies in selected hospitals in the United States: A survey.* Washington, DC: CWLA and National Assoc. of Public Hospitals.

Davis, M. (1995, August 1). "A bunch of rebellious people" celebrate struggle against authority. *Philadelphia Inquirer,* p. B3.

Dryfoos, J. (1994). *Full-service schools.* Jossey-Bass: San Francisco.

Dugger, C. (1995, February 26). Displaced by the welfare wars. *New York Times,* sec. 4, p. 1.

Dunston, L. G., Devane, C. M., Preudhomme, G. R., & Glick, B. (1994). *Runaway and homeless youth program directory.* (Available from the New York State Division for Youth, Rensselaer, NY 12144.)

Edelman, M. (1987). *Families in peril: An agenda for social change.* Cambridge, MA: Harvard University Press.

Enda, J. (1991, September 30). For homeless, new way home. *Philadelphia Inquirer,* p. B1.

Family: Cheaper by the dozen. (1992, September 14). *Newsweek,* p. 52.

Farnsworth, C. (1993, August 17). Youths' dramatic story: Street to stage success. *New York Times,* p. A4.

The far-reaching human toll of the sour economy. (1992, September 6). *Philadelphia Inquirer,* p. F2.

Fischer, P. (1992). Criminal behavior and victimization among homeless people. In R. Jahiel (Ed.), *Homelessness: A prevention-oriented approach.* Baltimore, MD: Johns Hopkins University Press.

Fox, E., & Roth, L. (1989). Homeless children: Philadelphia as a case study. *Annals of the American Academy of Political and Social Science, 506,* 141.

Fuchs, V. (1990). Are Americans underinvesting in children? In D. Blankenhorn et al. (Eds.), *Rebuilding the nest.* Milwaukee, WI: Family Service America.

Garbarino, J., & Garbarino, A. (1992). *Children and families in the social environment.* New York: Aldine de Gruyter.

Garbarino, J., Stott, F., & Faculty of the Erikson Institute. (1992). *What children can tell us.* San Francisco: Jossey-Bass.

Gewirtzman, R., & Fodor, I. (1987). The homeless child at school: From welfare hotel to classroom. *Child Welfare, 66,* 237.

Ginsburg, N. (1992). *Divisions of welfare: A critical introduction to comparative social policy.* London: Sage.

Gordon, D. (1996). *Fat and mean: The corporate squeeze of working Americans and the myth of managerial "downsizing."* Martin Kessler Books/The Free Press, NY.

Gordon, S. (1993, September 10). Helping Bucks County's homeless find homes. *Philadelphia Inquirer,* p. F1.

Hale, L. (1991). *Hale House: Alive with love.* New York: Hale House.

Happy re-birthday. (1993, February 8). *Star Ledger* (Newark, NJ), p. 1.

Hartheimer, J. (1991, July 3). City, state officials praise Queen's Row renovation. *Germantown Courier,* p. 1 (Philadelphia).

The health of the world's children. (1993, September 26). *Philadelphia Inquirer,* p. D3.

Henneberger, M. (1993, February 15). More and more teen-agers crowd shelters in New York. *New York Times,* p. A1.

Hernandez, R. (1992, November 22). Looking for shelter, some families find only an office floor. *New York Times,* p. A43.

Hiratsuka, J. (1992, June). "Runaway youth" TV spot wins award. *NASW News, 37*(6), 1 (National Association of Social Workers, Washington, DC).

Hopper, K. (1995, July). Definitional quandaries and other hazards in counting the homeless. *American Journal of Orthopsychiatry, 65*(3), 340-346.

Howell, R. (1993, September 26). U.S. youth slayings are cited. *Philadelphia Inquirer,* p. A3.

Jahiel, R. (Ed.). (1992). *Homelessness: A prevention-oriented approach.* Baltimore, MD: Johns Hopkins University Press.

Jaynes, G. (1994, September 5). Down and out in Telluride. *Time,* p. 60.

Jennings, L. (1988, September 28). Panel says children fastest-growing portion of homeless. *Education Week,* p. 5.

Jewish Theological Seminary. (1993, September 23). Message for the New Year 5754. *Philadelphia Inquirer,* p. E8.

Jones, M., & Botsko, M. (1987). *Parental lack of supervision: Nature and consequences of a major child neglect problem.* Washington, DC: Child Welfare League of America.

Jones, R. (1995, July). The price of welfare dependency: Children pay. *Social Work, 40*(4), 496-500.

Kagan, S., & Weissbord, B. (Eds.). (1994). *Putting families first.* San Francisco: Jossey-Bass.

Karp, R. (Ed.). (1993). *Malnourished children in the United States: Caught in the cycle of poverty.* New York: Springer.

Knox, A. (1992, August 12). Newark children found among the poorest in US. *Star Ledger,* p. 1 (Newark, NJ).

Krauss, R. (1958). The found boy. In *Somebody else's nut tree and other tales from children* (p. 18). New York: Harper.

Kryder-Coe, J., Salamon, L., & Molnar, J. (Eds.). (1991). *Homeless children and youth.* New Brunswick, NJ: Transaction.

Kurtz, P., Jarvis, S., & Kurtz, G. (1991, July). Problems of homeless youths: Empirical findings and human services issues. *Social Work, 36*(4), 309-314.

Landers, S. (1994, July). Preserving families a balancing act. *NASW News,* p. 3.

Lee, F. (1994, November 21). AIDS toll on elderly: Dying grandchildren. *New York Times,* p. 1.

Lewin, K. (1935). *A dynamic theory of personality: Selected papers.* New York: McGraw-Hill.

Lewin, K. D. (1976). *Field theory in social science: Selected theoretical papers* (D. Cartwright, Ed.). University of Chicago Press: Chicago (Midway Reprint).

Liebman, G. (1993, January). The AFDC conundrum: A new look at an old institution. *Social Work, 38*(1), 36-44.

Lifton, B. (1988). *The king of children: A biography of Janusz Korczak.* New York: Farrar, Straus and Giroux.

Link, B., et al. (1995, July). Lifetime and five-year prevalence of homelessness in the United States: New evidence on an old debate. *American Journal of Orthopsychiatry, 65*(3), 347-354.

Martin, L. (1993, September 8). For children who have children. *New York Times,* p. A23.

Mason, M. (1994). *From fathers' property to children's rights: The history of child custody in the United States.* New York: Columbia University Press.

McChesney, K. (1990). Family homelessness: A systemic problem. *Journal of Social Issues, 46*(4), 191-206.

McGeady, M. (1991). *God's lost children: The shocking story of America's homeless kids.* New York: Covenant House.

McLaughlin, M., Irby, M., & Langman, J. (1994). *Urban sanctuaries.* San Francisco: Jossey-Bass.

Michaels, M. (1993, August 9). Rio's dead end kids. *Time, 142*(6), 36.

Mihaly, L. (1991a). Beyond the numbers: Homeless families with children. In J. Kryder-Coe et al. (Eds.), *Homeless children and youth* (pp. 11-32). New Brunswick, NJ: Transaction.

Mihaly, L. (1991b). *Homeless families: Failed policies and young victims.* Washington, DC: Children's Defense Fund.

Mills, C., & Ota, H. (1989, November). Homeless women with minor children in the Detroit metropolitan area. *Social Work, 34*(6), 485-490.

Morton, E. (1993). The evolution of family preservation. In E. Morton & R. Grigsby (Eds.), *Advancing family preservation practice.* Newbury Park, CA: Sage.

Morton, E., & Grigsby, R. (Eds.). (1993). *Advancing family preservation practice.* Newbury Park, CA: Sage.

Mother leaves baby. (1993, May 23). *New York Times,* p. 34.

National Network (National Network of Runaway and Youth Services, or the Network). (1991). *To whom do they belong: Runaway, homeless and other youth in high-risk situations in the 1990's.* Washington, DC: Author.

New York, Executive Law 532, Article 19, Albany, NY (1978).

The New York Times, (1996). *The downsizing of America.* New York: Times Books/Random House.

NJHA (New Jersey Hospital Association). (1991). Excerpts on boarder babies/boarder children. In *Healthy children: The challenge for New Jersey* (Final report of the New Jersey Hospital Association, Council on Planning, Committee on Children). Princeton, NJ: Author.

NJHA (New Jersey Hospital Association). (1993). *Boarder babies and children: 1993 survey results.* Princeton, NJ: NJHA.

NRC (National Research Council). (1993). *Losing generations: Adolescents in high-risk settings.* Washington, DC: Commission on Behavioral and Social Sciences and Education, Panel on High-Risk Youth/National Academy Press.

Padgett, D., & Struening, E. (1992, October). Victimization and traumatic injuries among the homeless: Associations with alcohol, drug and mental problems. *American Journal of Orthopsychiatry, 62*(4), 512-523.

Patterson, M. (1993, October 27). Report cites social ills as the cause of Jersey's boarder baby problem. *Star Ledger,* p. 23 (Newark, NJ).

PHMC—1993. (1993). (Available from Philadelphia Health Management Corporation, 260 S Broad St., Philadelphia, PA 19102-5085)

Physician Task Force on Hunger in America. (1985). *Hunger in America: The growing epidemic.* Middletown, CT: Wesleyan University Press.

Popenoe, D. (1990). Family decline in America. In D. Blankenhorn et al. (Eds.), *Rebuilding the nest.* Milwaukee, WI: Family Service America.

Purdy, M. (1993, July 4). The corps that tends the victims of a city's shattered families. *Philadelphia Inquirer,* p. 1.

Rafferty, Y. (1991). Developmental and educational consequences of homelessness on children and youth. In J. Kryder-Coe et al. (Eds.), *Homeless children and youth* (pp. 105-142). New Brunswick, NJ: Transaction.

RHD—1993. (1993). (Available from Resources for Human Development, 4101 Kelly Drive, Philadelphia, PA 19129)

Riis, J. (1889). *How the other half lives: Studies among the tenements of New York.* New York: C. Scribner's Sons.

Ritter, B. (1988). *Sometimes God has a kid's face.* New York: Covenant House.

Rivlin, L. (1990). Home and homelessness in the lives of children. In N. Boxill (Ed.), *Homeless children: The watchers and the waiters* (pp. 5-17). New York: Haworth.

Robertson, M. (1992). The prevalence of mental disorder among homeless people. In R. Jahiel (Ed.), *Homelessness: A prevention-oriented approach* (pp. 57-86). Baltimore, MD: Johns Hopkins University Press.

Robinson, E. (1993, September 23). Report says US is no superpower in care for children. *Philadelphia Inquirer,* p. A3.

Rosenberg, A. (1993, September 21). No quick fix for homeless. *Philadelphia Inquirer,* p. B1.

Rotheram-Borus, M., Koopman, C., & Ehrhardt, A. (1991, November). Youths and HIV infection. *American Psychologist, 46*(11), 1188.

Santiago, D. (1993, November 22). Learning shines in an old steel town. *Philadelphia Inquirer,* pp. A1, A10.

Scanlan, C. (1993, October 5). Poverty rate up for third year. *Philadelphia Inquirer,* p. 1.

Schmid, R. (1994, August 10). Census finds household diversity. *Philadelphia Inquirer,* p. A10.

Schmidt, W. E. (1992, January 5). Across Europe, faces of homeless become more visible and vexing. *New York Times,* p. 1.

Schuerman, J., Rzepnicki, T., & Littell, J. (1994). *Putting families first: An experiment in family preservation.* Hawthorne, NY: Aldine de Gruyter.

Seita, J. (1996). Resiliency from the other side of the desk. *Child Welfare Report, 4*(1-3) (Iola, WI: Jones Publishing, Inc.).

Sendak, M. (1993). *We are all in the dumps with Jack and Guy.* New York: Michael di Capua Books/HarperCollins.

Shane, P. (1988, March 30). *Public health issues of homeless/runaway youth.* Paper presented at American Public Health Association annual meeting, San Francisco.

Shane, P. (1989, April). Changing patterns among homeless and runaway youth. *American Journal of Orthopsychiatry, 59*(2), 208-214.

Shane, P. (Ed.). (1991a). Homeless and runaway youth [Special issue]. *Journal of Health and Social Policy, 2*(4).

Shane, P. (1991b). A sample of homeless and runaway youth in New Jersey and their health status. *Journal of Health and Social Policy, 2*(4), 73-82.

Shane, P., & Marjanovic-Shane, A. (1987). *Homeless, runaway and missing youth in selected programs in New Jersey.* Report to the Family and Youth Services Bureau, U.S. DHHS, Washington, DC.

Shealy, C. (1995, August). From *Boys Town* to *Oliver Twist*: Separating fact from fiction in welfare reform and out-of-home placement of children and youth. *American Psychologist, 50*(8), 565-581.

Simons, R., & Whitbeck, L. (1991, June). Running away during adolescence as a precursor to adult homelessness. *Social Service Review, 65*(2), 224-247.

Stafseng, O. (1994). *Autobiography or ethnography in youth theories: Notes from the early history of youth research.* Oslo: Norwegian Research Council.

Starting points: Adapted from the report of the Carnegie Task Force on Meeting the Needs of Young Children. (1995, December-January). *National Voter, 44*(2), 16 (Washington, DC: League of Women Voters).

Steinbeck, J. (1939). *The grapes of wrath.* New York: Viking Press.

Steinberg, J. (1993, August 26). A memorable summer for children in the bargain. *New York Times,* p. B1.

Steinfels, P. (1992, December 27). Seen, heard, even worried about. *New York Times,* sec. 4, p. 1.

Stewart, J. (1992). *Den of thieves.* New York: Touchstone/Simon & Schuster.

Straw, R. (1995, July). Looking behind the numbers in counting the homeless. *American Journal of Orthopsychiatry, 65*(3), 330-333.

Study: For children and teens, the 1980's were a "terrible decade." (1991, February 1). *Philadelphia Inquirer,* p. 4A.

Toro, P., Trickett, E., Wall, D., & Salem, D. (1991). Homelessness in the United States: An ecological perspective. *American Psychologist, 46*(11), 1208-1218.

Weinreb, L., et al. (1995, October). Services for homeless pregnant women: Lessons from the field. *American Journal of Orthopsychiatry, 65*(3), 492-496.

Wheelan, S., Pepitone, E., & Abt, V. (Eds.). (1990). *Advances in field theory.* Newbury Park, CA: Sage.

When a baby is so unaffordable it is abandoned. (1992, September 20). *New York Times,* p. 40.

Whitlow, J. (1993, February 7). Infant dumping is very difficult to rationalize. *Star Ledger,* p. 3 (Newark, NJ).

Whitman, B., et al. (1992). Homeless families and their children: Health, developmental and educational needs. In R. Jahiel (Ed.), *Homelessness: A prevention-oriented approach* (pp. 113-126). Baltimore, MD: Johns Hopkins University Press.

Whitmore, A. (1993, June 2). Struggling college student gladly flunked homelessness 101. *Philadelphia Inquirer,* p. A23.

Winerip, M. (1993a, May 9). Pursuing hope in the trenches at Head Start. *New York Times,* p. 25.

Winerip, M. (1993b, December 8). Public school offers a social-service model. *New York Times,* pp. A1, A10.

Woestendiek, J. (1993, May 9). Shelter's children: Growing up with no place to call home. *Philadelphia Inquirer,* p. 1.

Woodall, M. (1993, November 14). Kinship care: Blessing, burden. *Philadelphia Inquirer,* pp. B1, B6.

Wright, J. (1989a). *Address unknown: The homeless in America.* New York: Aldine de Gruyter.

Wright, J. (1990, Spring). Homelessness is not healthy for children and other living things. *Journal of Child and Youth Services, 14*(1), 65-88.

Wright, J. (1991a). Poverty, homelessness, health, nutrition and children. In J. Kryder-Coe et al. (Eds.), *Homeless children and youth* (pp. 71-104). New Brunswick, NJ: Transaction.

Wright, J. (1991b). Health and the homeless teenager: Evidence from the national health care for the homeless program. *Journal of Health and Social Policy, 2*(4), 15-36.

Wright, J., & Devine, J. (1995, July). Housing dynamics of the homeless: Implications for a count. *American Journal of Orthopsychiatry, 65*(3), 320-329.

Ziesemer, C., & Marcoux, L. (1992, April). Academic and emotional needs of homeless students. *Social Work in Education, 14*(2), 77-85.

ADDITIONAL READINGS

Bassuk, E., & Rubin, L. (1987). Homeless children: A neglected population. *American Journal of Orthopsychiatry, 57*(2), 279-286.

Belluck, P. (1991, October 14). A place to chill their anger. *Philadelphia Inquirer,* p. 1B.

Blankenhorn, D., et al. (Eds.). (1990). *Rebuilding the nest: A new commitment to the American family.* Milwaukee, WI: Family Service America.

Boxill, N. (Ed.). (1990). *Homeless children: The watchers and the waiters.* New York: Haworth.

Daubenmier, J. (1993, March 17). Roving shelters for the homeless. *Philadelphia Inquirer,* p. D34.

Davis, M. (1993, August 1). "A bunch of rebellious people" celebrate struggle against authority. *Philadelphia Inquirer,* p. B3.

Dobie, K. (1993, May 23). In the jungle of cities: The lost children of New York. *San Francisco Examiner, Image,* p. 4.

Fisher, I. (1993, August 18). Small haven for homeless is demolished. *New York Times,* p. B1.

Fox, J. (1995, January 10). Youth as property. *The Stranger,* p. 1 (Seattle, WA).

Garbarino, J., Dubrow, N., Kostelny, K., & Pardo, C. (1992). *Children in danger.* San Francisco: Jossey-Bass.

Grandparents are often denied child-rearing aid. (1994, September 9). *New York Times,* p. A20.

Green, J. (1991, October 13). This school is out. *New York Times Sunday Magazine,* p. 32.

Inter-Faith of Ambler. (1992, Spring). *Network News, 1*(3) (Ambler, PA).

Johnson, C., et al. (1991). *Child poverty in America.* Washington, DC: Children's Defense Fund.

Keene, L. (1994, December 11). First place school gives these kids a fresh start. *Seattle Times,* p. L1.

Knitzer, J. (1982). *Unclaimed children: The failure of public responsibility to children and adolescents in need of mental health services.* Washington, DC: Children's Defense Fund.

Lyall, S. (1993, September 20). Maurice Sendak sheds moonlight on a dark tale. *New York Times,* p. C13.

Maza, P., & Hall, J. (1991). *Homeless children and their families: A preliminary study.* Washington, DC: CWLA.

Molnar, J., Rath, W., & Klein, T. (1990). Constantly compromised: The impact of homelessness on children. *Journal of Social Issues, 46*(4), 109-124.

A moving shelter. (1993, February 8). *News Tribune,* p. 1 (Plainfield, NJ).

National Center for Youth Law. (1991, March-April). *Youth Law News, 12* (San Francisco, CA 94104).

Pecora, P., Whittaker, J., Maluccio, A., Barth, R., & Plotnick, R. (1992). *The child welfare challenge: Policy, practice, and research.* Hawthorne, NY: Aldine de Gruyter.

Sereny, G. (1985). *The invisible children: Child prostitution in America, West Germany and Great Britain.* New York: Knopf.

Shinn, M., & Weitzman, B. (Eds.). (1990). [Special Issue]. Urban homelessness. *Journal of Social Issues, 46*(4).

Subcommittee on the Constitution. (1980). *Homeless youth: The saga of "pushouts" and "throwaways" in America* (Report to the Committee on the Judiciary, U.S. Senate, 92nd Congress, 2nd Session). Washington, DC: Government Printing Office.

U.S. DHHS (Department of Health and Human Services), Office of Human Development Services, Administration for Children, Youth and Families, Family and Youth Services Bureau. (1991). *Annual report to the Congress on the Runaway and Homeless Youth Program, Fiscal year 1990.* Washington, DC: Author.

Wattkes, M. (1993, February 3). Baby found near death in Newark dumpster. *Star Ledger,* p. 1 (Newark, NJ).

Yeich, S. (1994). *The politics of ending homelessness.* Lanham, MD: University Press of America.

FILM AND VIDEO RESOURCES

Children of the night. (1989). *Frontline,* 58 minutes, distributed by PBS video, Alexandria, VA.

Girltalk. (1987). 55 minutes, Kate Davis, producer, A Davis/Denny production, presented on *Point of View,* PBS.

Grapes of wrath, video. (1984). 2 hours, based on John Steinbeck novel of same name, distributed by CBS-Fox, Farmington Hills, MI.

Innocence lost. (1987). Geraldo Rivera Special, 54 minutes, Channel 11, New York, NY.

King of the hill. (1993). 1 hour and 50 minutes, Producer, Albert Berger et al., written and directed by Steven Soderbergh, adapted from memoirs of A. E. Hotchner, photography by Elliot Davis, distributed by Gramercy Pictures.

On the run. (1989). New Jersey Network (NJN), 29 minutes. Produced by the New Jersey State Commission of Missing Persons and NJN, writer Frank Capuzzi, Producer/Director Louis Presti.

Orphan train. (1988). 1 hour and 25 minutes, Production Executive, Paul Cameron, with Glenn Close and Jill Eikenberry, a Roger Gimbel Production for EMI TV Programs, Inc.

Runaway youth. (1991). NASW and USDH and HS, 20- and 30-second spot TV announcements in English or Spanish. Producer Abba Shapiro, Roland House, Arlington, VA.

Streetwise. (1984). Angelika Films, a Bear Creek Production, 90 minutes. Produced and written by Cheryl McCall. Directed by Martin Bell. Photography by Mary Ellen Mark.

INDEX

ABOUT THE AUTHOR

PAUL G. SHANE was born in New York City and attended Music & Art High School. Because of his interest in children and youth, he majored in social psychology at Cornell University and social group work at the New York School of Social Work, Columbia University. After graduation, he was drafted and spent two years in the army. Upon discharge, he went to Chicago, where he worked with youth at the Jewish Community Centers and Hull House. He moved to the Chicago Association for Retarded Citizens and developed community programs and new approaches to diagnosis and habilitation. He received a master's degree in public health and an Sc.D. in the sociology of mental health from the Johns Hopkins University, School of Hygiene and Public Health in Baltimore. His first academic appointment was at Temple University in Philadelphia, where he worked on the development of an innovative approach to mixed residential and nonresidential programming for developmental disabilities while also teaching. Shortly thereafter, he moved to Rutgers University, where he developed the social work department at Newark, New Jersey. He is currently on the faculty of the Social Welfare/Social Work Department at Rutgers—Newark.